First Across the Roof of the World

By the same author

Graeme Dingle: Two Against the Alps
Wall of Shadows
The Seven Year Adventure
The Outdoor World of Graeme Dingle

Peter Hillary: A Sunny Day in the Himalayas

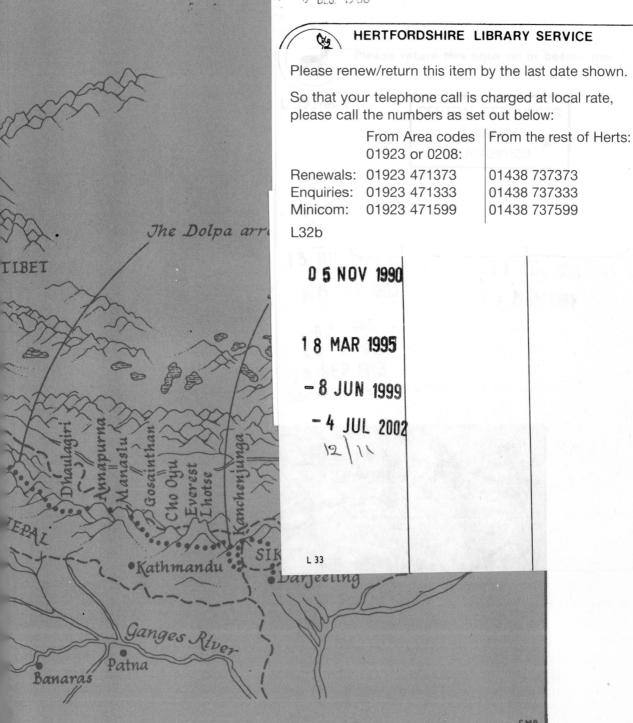

TIBET

The Dolpa arr

Dhaulagiri
Annapurna
Manaslu
Gosainthan
Cho Oyu
Everest
Lhotse
Kanchenjunga

NEPAL

Kathmandu
SIK
Darjeeling

Ganges River
Patna
Banaras

SMP

First Across
the Roof of the World

The First-Ever Traverse of
the Himalayas – 5,000 kilometres from Sikkim to Pakistan

Graeme Dingle & Peter Hillary

HODDER AND STOUGHTON
AUCKLAND LONDON SYDNEY

Book design by Tom Elliott. Maps by Colin Maclaren.

Typeset by Glenfield Graphics Ltd, Auckland.
Printed and bound in Hong Kong for Hodder & Stoughton Ltd, 44-46 View Road,
Glenfield, Auckland, New Zealand.

Contents

Our special thanks to our patron,
Shri Harish Sarin, president of the Indian Mountaineering
Foundation, New Delhi

To Chewang Tashi, instructor at the Himalayan
Mountaineering Institute, and a stalwart friend over the ten
months of our adventure

And to the people of the Himalaya who made our journey
such a fascinating one.

Photographs, except where individually acknowledged,
were taken by Graeme Dingle or Peter Hillary.

Double page photographs:

Prelude

TURNING TO THE west, I could see a snow-white pinnacle protruding from behind a dark and benighted forest. It stood in isolation, glowing in the waxen light. For me it was symbolic as much as it was a good omen. The longest, most all-consuming adventure of our lives awaited us. And as if to celebrate a full moon sailed overhead... a lunar spotlight upon our bid to traverse the world's loftiest range of mountains, the Himalaya. I could feel an excitement pervade my whole being in anticipation of what lay ahead. The optimism inside me had survived, after all.

We climbed slowly out of the snow-covered forest of giant deodars breathing deeply in the cold, morning air. Stepping onto a grassy rise on the ridge, straw gold in its winter plumage, we stood among a congregation of Buddhist prayer flags that flapped lazily in the cool breeze. A constant flow of refrigerated air descended from the huge and imposing bulk that filled the northern sky! Kanchenjunga, the world's third highest mountain, a full 28,000 feet of ice and rock. The lord of the Sikkimese Himalaya and our epic journey's starting point.

In single file we climbed the hillside to Dzongri, feeling a little as if we had crossed the line, the starter gun had been fired. From here on, the relentless trek westward across the Himalayas to Pakistan and Mt K2... our chequered flag.

At the lone yak-herder's hut that comprises Dzongri, we halted. There was the nervous bark of a hairy mastiff, large, black yaks scattered over the hillside, a line of snowy peaks on the horizon and a strongly built Tibetan man standing at the entrance to the stone hut. Tashi whispered that he was related to the King of Sikkim. His proud and noble features certainly supported such a rumour.

'This man's a brute,' Tashi went on. 'He sometimes...,' he gestured with a swing of his fist, 'fighting.' We all looked towards the big Tibetan; his narrow dark eyes, powerful jaw, jet black hair. The unchallenged king of his wild domain.

Tashi asked him about the route ahead, how best to reach Nepal. After some involved deliberation in Tibetan accompanied by a series of complex gesticulations, Tashi turned to us.

'He knows the passes and the high pastures well. He doesn't know where the border is. For him this border business doesn't matter anyway.'

'I'll bet he hasn't got a permit,' I chuckled to myself, remembering the manifold problems we had incurred obtaining the necessary permissions and permits. The only barriers for this man were geographical.

From Dzongri we hiked up the broad, golden-grassed hillside to the Dzongri La pass and descended the far side in gathering cloud and cold, piercing winds. My shoulders were sore from carrying my sixty-pound pack and my head ached with the resonant thud of a high-altitude headache. I was relieved to reach the valley floor at 13,000 feet. We crossed a flimsy two-log bridge that spanned a bubbling stream to a broad pasture where we collected juniper and azalea branches for the evening's campfire. Crawling inside the deserted shepherd's hut where we were to spend the night, I watched Tashi lighting the fire. Graeme and Doug joined us in the dim light with armfuls of firewood. We rolled out our sealed foam mats on the green juniper stems that carpeted the floor and sat there, reaching out our hands towards the licking flames. The dry stone walls of the low-roofed hut had many gaps and crannies which acted like funnels to the icy wind. The Himalayas were still in the grasp of winter.

'Where's S.P.?'

Looking outside, I could see him. Seated in the "lotus" posture on the alpine meadow, his eyes closed with concentration, he performed his evening puja (Hindu religious ceremony). Far above the glaciated mountains of Sikkim were being brushed with sunset pinks and reds. As the light dimmed the Milky Way bridged the expanse between the legions of craggy summits that lined the valley.

Mogul tomb at Agra.

With a cup of hot tea cupped in my hands, I nestled in my sleeping bag feeling warm and comfortable. 'Yes, it will all be worth it,' I assured myself as the thumping in my altitude-plagued cranium momentarily ceased. Leaning against the rock wall I sipped my tea pondering the journey ahead. To traverse the Himalayas had been an ambition of mine for many years. I had developed a love affair with these mountains since I was eleven years of age when with my family I made my first visit to the Mt Everest region. The scale and beauty of the spectacular landscape, the forests of rhododendron and magnolia, the tiny villages, and the toothy grins of the hill people.

8

As I grew older and my interests and expectations changed I found the Himalayas continued to offer a multitude of experiences and rewards. Our family treks in the '60s and '70s developed into mountaineering exploits. My

Walking past Buddhist flags in the Sikkimese foothills at 13,000 ft with Mt Kanchenjunga behind.

H.M.I. basecamp at 15,000 ft on Sikkim-Nepal border. The silver hut was built by Sir Edmund Hillary's 1960 high-altitude physiology expedition.

childhood awe of the many and varied people I met laid the foundations for a rapport with the local people and the development of important friendships. I had been inspired by the Swiss geologist, Toni Hagen and the British explorers, Shipton and Tilman, who travelled Nepal extensively during many expeditions to the kingdom. Their exploits proved to me that such journeys could be executed. My father's many expeditions to Nepal coloured my aspirations (perhaps my own journeying in the East was sociologically inevitable!). Guru Rimpoche, one of the most important figures of Tibetan Lamaistic Buddhism, travelled the Himalayas centuries ago preaching Buddhism to the people of the mountains. So all I had to do was convince myself that, although I wasn't an ancient Tibetan monk, a Swiss geologist or an intrepid British explorer, I could still accomplish a traverse of the Himalayas. I anticipated a great deal of mountaineering and of course, trekking, but never the variety of other experiences. Not for one moment had I expected the psychological and physical stresses that would manifest themselves nor the enormous diversity of interactions with the people of the Himalaya. I had naively imagined the traverse would be a glorious series of high-altitude treks homogenised into one. A clutter of mountaineering escapades. I failed to recognise the difference and make detailed inquiry into the immense test that lay before me; assess its magnitude and its demands. Perhaps it was just as well.

I snuggled in my sleeping bag; a few silent embers in the fireplace. I knew I stood, both boots and all, in a frame of mind combining anticipation and determination. The opportunity to attempt one of my greatest ambitions lay before me. I was delighted.

The sun had not reached the little hut as we made our way over the frost-covered ground, following the meandering track through the juniper and azalea bushes. For two hours we plodded steadily beneath our heavy packs, climbing to nearly 15,000 feet. The track traversed across the vegetated terminal moraine of the Ratong glacier to the permanent basecamp there — a group of stone huts perched on a levelling in the long slope. As we planned to spend three days acclimatising at the camp, we left our packs on the alpine sward beside the huts and the large morainic boulders scattered there. Together we scrambled up the terminus, taking long, deep breaths in the thin air. Wisps of cloud rose from the depths of the valley as we struggled on to the crest. We stood there catching our breath and gazing up the Ratong glacier. Beckoning to us, a remote col lay nestled at the distant head of the glacier, 3000 feet above. Sandwiched by two sheer walled peaks the synclinal groove of the Ratong La stood silhouetted against the sky. Beyond it, according to our maps, was Nepal. I revelled in that knowledge.

Above us soared the inimitable blue of a Himalayan sky. The cold air. The majesty of the mountains paraded all around us and the brilliance of the sun upon their glazed, white flanks. I heard the lonely call of a Himalayan chuff. Looking up I spotted its neat black form... only momentarily. Mysterious boils of turbulence swept the rising cloud across the sky.

We sauntered, chatting as we went, down to the basecamp in a swirling world of white.

1

The Himalayan Traverse

WHO KNOWS WHEN a great idea is born?

In science, sport, exploration and adventure there are usually many people hovering on the brink of a breakthrough, and when success comes, it is often the result of the collective effort that finally pushes one person or team to triumph.

Pete and I weren't the first to consider the almost preposterous idea of traversing the Great Himalayan Range from one end to the other. We were, however, the first silly enough to put our money where our mouths were.

As usual when planning an expedition, the most common question we had to cope with whenever the journey was discussed was: 'Why?' Superman had the best answer with : 'For good and the American way.'

But then he could fly off!

Mallory's 'Because it is there' is catchy but simplistic, and he immortalised that by disappearing on Everest shortly after he said it in 1924. If you say, 'Because I want to,' the question always comes back, 'But, why do you want to?'

Questioners usually understand 'Because it's my job', but this is obviously quite incomplete, so that answer makes me uncomfortable.

Prior to our traverse I wrote: 'I am a mountaineer. The mountains are my vehicle to knowledge and self-fulfilment, so what could be more natural for a mountaineer than to accept an ultimate challenge — a traverse of the greatest mountain range on earth. And the dream was much more than just a bland mountain traverse. The Himalaya conjures up so much romance, not only to the mountaineer, but to anyone with a deep interest in the world's wild places, its people and its animals. Here is the meeting place of cultures, the birthplace of religions and the home of legendary people, animals and myths. Buddhism, Hinduism, Sherpas, Tamangs, Gurkhas, Baltis, snow leopards, red pandas and yetis, to mention a few. Add to this "highest mountains", "deepest gorges", "most spectacular"... God, what a cocktail!'

Not everyone shared our enthusiasm for the idea. When my friend Yvon Chouinard heard about our plans in the United States he wrote these sobering words: 'Your trip through the Himalaya sounds absolutely horrible. I can't imagine anything more painful or dangerous. You must have flipped your lid, ole buddy.'

We wanted to visit the most important areas of the Himalaya in one journey. A journey that would take us past every important mountain and range on earth — from Kanchenjunga to K2.

Clearly it would be impossible (in this age anyway) to traverse over the top of every peak. The compromise was to travel as close as physically and politically acceptable to the main summits. The 5000 kilometres to be covered could take us as long as 300 days, and our major problem was to fit

Back: *Shubash Roy, Corrina, Doug, Ann Louise, Tashi.*
Front: *Graeme, S.P. Chamoli, Peter.*

this in between and around the most severe seasons. We calculated that if we began in the east at the end of the winter we would be able to finish in the west during the beginning of the next winter, and in so doing we hoped to outrun the monsoon which arrives in the eastern and central Himalaya about June. This idea of outrunning nature sounds a bit like farting at thunder, but mountaineers are eternal optimists.

Pete wrote about our proposed journey: 'We wanted to make this incredible high-altitude journey across "the roof of the world" in keeping with our modern alpine-style approach — namely, sleeping rough, eating little, moving fast and thinking big — unencumbered by porters and the barrage of logistics that accompanies them.

'This would enable us to move quickly and stay ahead of the monsoon's advance with its swollen rivers, washed-out bridges, thick grey cloud veiling the mountains and the annual scourge of bloodsucking leeches.'

For 2000 years sages and holy men have wandered those mystic hills spreading the teachings of Buddha — perhaps like them we were in search of ourselves but we weren't "out" to spread anything, except perhaps the suspect ways of our modern world.

Nowadays most expeditions take the shortest crosscountry route to their chosen mountain. After climbing it or failing they go home the same way.

Tashi

Graeme Dingle

Peter Hillary

Only a few hardy individuals, like Younghusband, Tilman, Shipton and Ed Hillary, have done long trans-Himalayan trips, but nothing like the length of journey we were planning had ever been done — even a high-level traverse of Nepal had not been done.

In many ways this kind of journey requires a greater mountaineering skill than the ascent of one difficult peak: you are constantly moving into new and unknown country with all the gear you possess on your back and no camp to retreat to. Life is rough because the gear you can carry is limited. Your tent is smaller than you'd like, you never have enough clothing to keep you warm, you are often hungry and you rarely treat yourself to the luxury of a belay on steep ground — speed is the essence.

One thing that we did have going for us was ultramodern space-age materials — no natural stuff for us. We were walking adverts for petro-chemicals: tents that were waterproof but breathed and weighing less than three pounds, plastic boots, polypropelene tights under our nylon pile suits; nylon packs weighing less than two pounds.

Pete had been brought up in an atmosphere of mountains — his grandfather, Jim Rose, was a president of the New Zealand Alpine Club and of course his father, Ed Hillary, is the most famous mountaineer of all. It was natural for him to want to pit himself against the biggest mountaineering problems. He is a good skier and a strong tenacious climber with a dozen or so top routes in New Zealand's Southern Alps to his credit.

I first got to know him in 1974. Ed Hillary had gathered the "old gang" together to make a film called "The Kaipo Wall". We rollicked around Fiordland climbing and canoeing under his fatherly leadership. The "old gang" was Ed, Mike Gill, Jim Wilson, Murray Jones and me. For this adventure, Peter (then nineteen) had joined us. His enthusiasm and strength impressed us all. One thing particularly stands out in my memory apart from the wild rafting, canoeing, climbing and dripping wet snow caves: Ed kept reminding the tenacious Peter that on the 24th he would have to leave to go to university — the 24th came and went, and Peter remained with the old gang. He was perhaps the only one among us who could effectively resist Ed.

Our next trip together was the memorable "Ocean to Sky" expedition of 1977. On that occasion we clashed violently in the early stages, avoided each other effectively for six weeks, but finished up together on both the summits climbed by the expedition. Again one event stands out which gave me a better insight into this restless man. Ed had collapsed with altitude sickness in our top camp at 18,000 feet and we had taken him down 3000 feet to a helicopter evacuation site.

Once he had been flown out and hospitalised, Murray Jones, Peter and I climbed back up to the top camp to climb Nar Parbat. To minimise cooking we decided to cook one big stew that we could dip into whenever hungry. Everything went into this high-altitude gourmet delight — it filled a two-gallon pot and while it bubbled away on the stove in Pete's tent, Murray and I retreated to our tents to read. While the falling snow pattered on the thin nylon above me I battled through some grotty novel. Suddenly the mountain silence was split by a blasphemous scream followed by a dreadful silence. I

14

pulled on my boots and stumbled across to Pete's tent. Inside was a scene to make the strongest weep. The stove had melted into the snow and had tipped the stew over. The meticulously tidy Peter now lay a speechless island in a sea of squalid grey stew. As I mopped up I tried surreptitiously to scoop some of the stew back into the billy while Pete, finding his voice, protested from his sleeping bag that we would catch some terrible disease from it.

My own plans for traversing the great ranges of the world began during the late '60s with a plan to traverse the Southern Alps of New Zealand. I have always felt that a true mountaineer should be a back-country jack of all trades — a person who can cope no matter what the hills throw up:

To be able to climb difficult rock and ice is only part of the story — one needs to be at home with the earth's wild places when a storm is tearing down the tent from around you, when the rain floods the rivers and makes a fire in the cold subalpine forest a work of tenacious patience:

The complete mountaineer should be able to ski anywhere, climb anywhere and walk anywhere. Of equal importance perhaps, unless he wants to go solo, he should be a tolerant and understanding companion. Jill Tremain and I succeeded in traversing the Southern Alps during the winter of 1971. This superb adventure took nearly 100 days and whetted our appetites for further similar trips — beyond the blue horizon lay the other great ranges:

The Alps, the Rockies, the Andes and of course the very roof of the world — the highest and broadest mountains of all — the Himalaya. Tragically this is where Jill died — killed by an immense avalanche on the Milam glacier in India during May 1974.

During 1978 Pete and I climbed together in California's spectacular Yosemite valley. Although we had both independently thought about the traverse of the Himalaya this was the first time that we had discussed the journey together. On the vertical walls of Yosemite our explosive relationship and the traverse of the Himalaya took root.

During early 1980 after Pete's desperate accident on the south-west face of Amadablam we committed ourselves to a programme in the Himalaya. Stage one would be the traverse, followed by alpine-style attempts on the highest mountains in the world.

During May 1980, while on an Air India trip to the Garhwal Himalaya, I made overtures to the key men of the Indian Mountaineering Foundation (IMF) in Delhi — the president, Harish Sarin, the astute civil servant known as the right hand of Indira Gandhi; and vice-president Captain Mohan Kohli, famous for his leadership of the highly successful Indian Everest expedition of 1964. Both men were keen on the concept of a lightweight fast traverse of the Himalaya, so long as Indians were involved.

So the initial agreement was made — a team of two Indians with Pete and me would attempt the traverse during 1981. "Alpine style" had arrived in India.

We decided that such a mammoth journey required a support group and as we had no idea what the Indian Mountaineering Federation could provide in this line we decided to take our own group. My friend Corrina Gage had

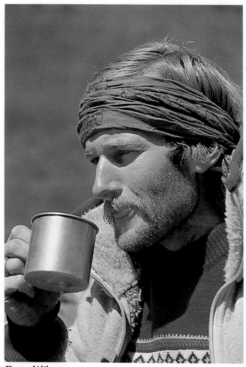
Doug Wilson

been involved from the beginning. Although not yet a high climber she was a keen tramper and skier, and had done quite a lot of rock climbing with me (although she will never admit it). I knew that her moral support would be of immeasurable assistance to me, both before and during the traverse.

Corrina is a member of the Ngati Tuwharetoa tribe from the Turangi area. She is a natural athlete blessed with good looks, big flashing eyes and dark skin that inevitably meant that she was claimed by nearly all who met her in India, Nepal or Pakistan as a true native. It was Corrina who suggested that we invite Doug Wilson and his lady, Ann Louise Mitcalfe, to form the remainder of the support party. Pete readily agreed although he later had second thoughts about this decision. It was clear that from a psychological aspect I would have a greater degree of support than Pete. I felt that it was Pete's prerogative to have a girl friend in support if he wished but just because he was suffering it didn't mean that everyone should.

About the time that Pete went off to Nepal to join his father on a filming trip, I wrote to Doug and Ann. An excited reply came back:

> Dear Ding,
> Hello sunshine. Well, I haven't slept for three nights now — the ol' brain has been going chick, chick, chick.
> I have been talking it over with Dave and saying that I am thinking it over, but I am deluding myself — in fact I have thought it over and decided that if you still want us we'll come.

16

I am pretty freaked out that you are prepared to put that much faith in a pretty unproven ability to get things organised, and like I said, pretty flattered that you've asked.
So, the short answer is yes, damn right we'll come.
If I have to resign from the Ranger Service too bad...

Both Doug and Ann were interesting characters. I had first met them at the Outdoor Pursuits Centre while Doug was a ranger at the Tongariro National Park. He had retired temporarily from his profession as lawyer and was blowing off a few physical cobwebs in the outdoors. He quickly turned into a competent skier and all-round mountaineer.

Ann Louise was also a strong all-rounder. She could be a frightening little bundle of aggressive enthusiasm: sometimes student of law, clothesmaker and mountain lady, commuting between Wellington where she worked and studied and Mt Ruapehu where Doug lived. They had been together for nine years and it seemed to me that their combined skills were just what we needed in a support team that would be required to dash from one rendezvous to another — steering a loopy course through the Himalayan foothills with new supplies of food, film and equipment, and relieving us of exposed film, articles for the media and worn gear. They would need to be prepared to wait for long boring periods in grotty Indian villages, to know when it was reasonable to stop waiting and to start searching for us. They might be called on to join in with the traverse if one of us was injured and they would need to be able to cope with delicate bureaucratic difficulties that would sometimes blossom into problems of nightmarish proportion. Also of considerable importance, Doug and Ann had a good practical knowledge of mountain first aid.

Corrina and Ann Louise

Soon after my invitation had been accepted by Doug and Ann, a letter from Mohan Kohli brought further relief to us. The IMF undertook to sponsor the traverse, and to provide two members, including the leader.

I communicated the first successes to Pete. He replied with enthusiasm but airing some doubts about the support team. He was concerned about the financial burden that the group would incur and wanted to reduce the size of the support party, or else have the members contribute $2000 each to the budget. This the trio agreed to. Then came the good news that Hallmark International had agreed to underwrite the adventure to the tune of $30,000.

On the Indian side the IMF had named the traverse leader — a mountaineer who was well known to us. Major Prem Chand, an immensely strong and honest hill man with many successes to his credit, including Kanchenjunga. Prem visited Delhi about a month before our anticipated arrival and when he found that no organisation had been done he told the IMF he wasn't available.

The first I knew of the other member was when a cable arrived from my old friend Colonel Balwant Sandhu (Ballu). It read: 'Will join for expedition send letterhead — Colonel Balwant Sandhu.'

I replied requesting an explanation and received back an aerogramme. I opened it with eager anticipation to be greeted by an ominous message. The page contained nothing but Ballu's measurements. Unfortunately all the equipment for the Indian side was procured with these two men in mind.

We were always aware that we had competition to be first to do the traverse. From Europe, Reinhold Messner, one of the world's greatest mountaineers had been making overtures to key people in India. From America the threat came from Arlene Blum, perhaps the most successful American woman mountaineer. The real challenge came from an unexpected direction.

Our first inkling of this competition came a few weeks before our projected departure when a telex arrived from the IMF explaining that they were experiencing difficulties obtaining the relevant permissions from Defence. Soon a letter came from a friend in Kathmandu which explained all.

The Indian Army was mounting their own traverse of the Himalaya — a plan which bore a remarkable similarity to our own plans, which coincidentally had been described in a media kit sent to India only a few weeks before. It was similar even down to the terminology: 'alpine style', 'lightweight', 'fast moving', 'space age equipment' and so on. Terminology that was still not properly understood in Indian mountaineering circles, but was now being used authoritatively.

Meanwhile in my little Hallmark office I battled with the hundreds of letters requesting assistance for the undertaking.

During November we organised a crucial expedition meeting. Pete hated these meetings. Once again he aired his doubts about the support team.

Diary: 20 December 1980 (my office Hallmark International). I've decided that the modern mountaineer needs to be a bit more than a bloke with a pack, an ice axe and a pair of boots. He needs to be a bureaucratic jack of all trades to cope with mountains of paper work and negotiations with quasi and real government departments. Add to this the need for fund raising and you have a formidable creature closely resembling Henry Kissinger, Golda Meir and Ed Hillary rolled into one.

By Christmas we still didn't have permission so I began to frantically try to telephone Harish Sarin in Delhi. On one occasion I lodged the call at about 3 pm and settled down to several hours of frustrating waiting. The New Zealand operators were remarkably patient but they could not get beyond Bombay before the line went dead. About 10 pm a very worldly operator came on the line. She explained how she had experienced this before and had beaten it by putting on an Indian accent. This she did and miraculously I was immediately connected.

Harish explained that he had only recently heard of the army attempt. I asked if perhaps we could join forces but he said that he had already made this request without success.

'What about starting from Pakistan?' he suggested, but there seemed two main problems with this. First, the authorities probably wouldn't look favourably on us if we had just come out of Pakistan; and secondly we would be going straight into the teeth of the monsoon, whereas going east to west we at least stood a chance of outrunning the dreaded rains.

'We'll just have to beat the bastards,' I breathed.

'Beg your pardon?' asked Harish. 'This is a very bad line!'

Diary: 27 December. What a Christmas! For forty-eight hours Corrina and I forgot the bloody traverse at Uncle Hori and Auntie Pol's farm near Taumarunui. The hangi contained pigs, chickens, sheep, spuds, kumaras and pumpkin. The Christmas dinner table was at least twenty feet long and loaded. And the celebration went on with scarcely a break for forty hours. When we left everyone cried as if they'd never see us again. Uncle Hori reckoned we 'oughta take some of that rotten corn to those Himalayas.'

How many times during those hard months ahead would we remember the fabulous food and genuine warmth of those wonderful people!

Two weeks after my phone conversation with Harish a telegram arrived from Mohan saying: 'Postpone departure one week.'

This I did but then another arrived. It read: 'Do not plan for India.'

It was too late. We were committed — I refused to comprehend or acknowledge the ominous message. On 22 January we flew to India.

There was no one to meet us at Delhi airport. We found our way to the YMCA hostel and in the morning I rang Harish who was noticeably surprised to hear me.

'Oh, so you are here,' he responded. I assured him that we were.

Delhi was unusually cold and damp. A kind of disgusting yellow smog hung over the city. We moved from the city centre out to the new IMF

Ann Louise and Doug.

complex on the outskirts. An immense stone fortress that we were shown around by Mr Motwani, the secretary. He proudly showed us lecture halls, equipment halls and sleeping halls that echoed to our questions like a medieval castle. He told us proudly that we were the first guests and in the loos proceeded to show us how the shiny new taps operated.

The first tap came off in his hand, covering him with brown water. The taps never worked again while we were there.

We immediately moved into our spartan ways — sleeping on the concrete floor and cooking dehydrated food on a primus. The main tortures of Delhi were not, however, these mild physical hardships. During the days we battled with the most nightmarish bureaucracy on earth in an attempt to get our show on the road. Harish and Mohan seemed to be our only friends and it seems unlikely that we would have got anywhere without the quiet genius of Harish.

One morning as we sat in our concrete box amidst heaps of shiny new equipment, a dapper little man with short black hair and a moustache and wearing a three-piece suit strutted in and introduced himself.

'Chamoli, Indo-Tibetan border police,' he said with obvious pride. 'I am to accompany you on your expedition.'

He didn't look at all the type, I thought. 'Oh well,' I stumbled, going for breathing space. 'What should we call you?'

'Mr Chamoli.'

I was now sure that he wasn't for us and began desperately trying to dissuade him by telling him how painful the journey would be.

'How will you live.. what will you eat?' he asked with high-pitched incredulity.

'Oh, we have some freeze-dried meat,' I said, pointing at a nearby hillock of foil packets.

Suddenly his voice took on a note of panic. 'But, I am a vegetarian!'

We talked for a long time — mainly S.P. (as I had now discovered his initials were) asking questions while I attempted to answer them. My answers were all pretty woozy, mainly because that was the way the trip was. We didn't know what we would have for breakfast on 5 May or even where we would be. But many Indians wanted our projected plan down to the last detail. We would have to play most of it as we found it. After a time Doug and Pete had an appointment to attend so I invited S.P. to join me on an ascent of the IMF complex — only the evening before we had driven a line of pitons up its new monolithic north wall. S.P. agreed quickly and had soon exchanged his three-piece suit for a nylon pile suit.

The ascent was mainly successful and by the time we had safely returned to ground S.P. had a position in the team.

That evening we met Harish and Mohan again. Harish explained that permission for our journey was proving very difficult through political complications in the country's corridors of power.

On 5 February, Corrina, Ann Louise and I said farewell to Doug and Pete and headed for Kathmandu. As we drove away from the IMF Pete scowled through the taxi window: 'Lucky bastards.'

Our job was to dump off the Nepal equipment and food in Kathmandu and to get my permit to cross Nepal. Theirs was to get permissions, etc for Indian territory in New Delhi. We would meet again in Darjeeling on 13 February.

We sped towards New Delhi railway station in one of those 1954 Morris Oxfords that the Indians proudly call Ambassadors. This particular projectile was driven by a fierce-looking Sikh who drove nearly as fast as Alan Jones, the famous racing driver (but with much less control) — partly because this was normal but mainly because I had made the rash promise of a small bakshish if we got there in time for the train.

The car, apart from being old, was in very bad repair and was one of that relatively common variety with the dreaded delayed steering. To avoid an obstacle the driver needs to be something of a clairvoyant in that he must anticipate his next move by several seconds, no small task when the over-riding traffic rule is "the law of the wild" — mainly, small gives way to big. Coming from every direction are ox carts, motorised trishaws, sick-looking buses, trucks, other cars and people pushing carts. To avoid these the driver flings the wheel vigorously and several seconds later the vehicle veers roughly in the desired direction. At one roundabout our taxi was cornering quickly, leaning at an alarming angle when the driver saw ahead a Sikh temple. He removed both hands from the wheel and clasped them together in front of his face in salute while at the same time closing his eyes for a moment and bowing his head. The heathen car discontinued cornering and departed the roundabout, apparently down the correct outlet.

We arrived at the railway station, paid the bandit on wheels, fought off a determined attack by would-be porters and stumbled under our 300-pound load to the train. No one can consider themselves educated or well travelled until they have journeyed second class on an Indian train. The grottiness and crowded chaos only add charm — old travellers say that third class used to be something else — these days third class is on the roof.

Our journey via Muzzafapur and Raxaul to Kathmandu was punctuated by the usual cocktail of dysentery (bad news on a crowded train), colourful station stops (where food and drink peddlers pushed their grubby wares through the windows), waits in the hot sun on station platforms (surrounded by bevies of disfigured beggars), rickshaw stacked high with our kitbags, mechanically unsound buses (with hard seats designed for short-thighed Asians or yoga experts) and barricades arranged on roads by angry students. Finally a short bus journey took us across the plains of Nepal where the land shot upwards in a tangle of contorted forest-covered ridges. After two or three hours of diesel-scented climbing our old bus burst across a high ridge and there ahead in breathtaking splendour were the white buttresses of the Great Himalayas thrusting up into and above the towering cumulus clouds.

Kathmandu tingled with its usual colourful clamour — and it wasn't a great surprise to find that the king, having just returned from overseas, had proclaimed a three-day holiday. Therefore, because all offices were closed we had to cool our heels. On one of these days Corrina and I were trying to return to our flat by rickshaw, but at the end of each street tried by our rickshaw-wallah we were stopped by the police. The king was about to drive along the crowd-lined main street, and to get home we needed to cross this street. As I was keener on getting home than watching the king, I removed the protesting rickshaw-wallah from his seat and sat him beside Corrina in the back. Then having taken over his position at the controls I sped us down one of the previously blocked streets. Steering a slalom between shouting policeman and rifle-wielding soldiers we rocketed into the main street and waving regally to the cheering crowd we pedalled along to the desired exit and disappeared into the wall of happy Nepalis — our little rickshaw-wallah was nervously delighted.

After the holiday I began the old Kathmandu run around — moving dejectedly from one office to another in search of an "All Nepal Permit" until I eventually found the appropriate office. At this office I was discouraged by two men but found a third who was more helpful.

'Do you want your permit today or tomorrow?' he asked.

'Oh, today please,' I blurted, unable to contain my delight at getting the permit so easily.

'That will be 1150 rupees.' Cheap! I thought as I paid with more thank-yous than necessary. I returned later that day to collect the invaluable document which now needed only the chief inspector's stamp. Soon he appeared, looking grim.

'You cannot do this,' he said. 'There are many treks in one here!'

'Why?' I asked innocently.

'We can only issue one trek at a time,' he replied.

I began to stick my toes in. 'Can I see the regulation please?'

Immediately he produced his book and stabbed a dirty finger at the problem regulation. It read: 'A permit may only be issued for one trek at a time.'

'But I am only doing one trek,' I protested. 'It just happens to be a big one.'

A small grin creased his face and a few moments later I was shaking his hand and departing triumphantly clutching my permit.

On the evening of 12 February I said goodbye to Corrina and Ann and departed for Darjeeling by bus. They would do a trek into the Hellambu before meeting Doug and S.P. Then they would all do the first resupply at Kunde.

During the last week Doug and Pete had been having a desperate time in Delhi. However, they had received permission for the first part of the journey. With the necessary documents they travelled across India by train until they reached Darjeeling in West Bengal.

Darjeeling at nearly 7000 feet was cold. The hills were shrouded in mist as I walked up to the Himalayan Mountaineering Institute — the school established by Nehru for Tensing Norkay to promote mountaineering in India. After a short search I located Pete, Doug and S.P. We were all very glad to see each other and lost no time in going off to a cafe for a beer.

Our main task here in Darjeeling was to locate a Sherpa called D. Lhatoo who had apparently been directed by the IMF to accompany the traverse. Next day we did find Lhatoo, a delightful, sophisticated man with all the charm of a well-bred and educated Sherpa. However, we were shattered to learn that he had only heard of his inclusion twelve hours before and could not get away at such short notice. Luck was on our side though. Lhatoo reckoned that he knew a man who would be keen to go with us — Chewang Tashi, like Lhatoo was an instructor at the mountaineering institute. He was obviously a well-respected mountaineer and despite the short notice, his large extended family and other commitments, Tashi was keen to go. As we stood telling this tough-looking Tibetan of our plans we had no idea just what a great man we had just recruited. His boyish face disguised his forty-two years — only his lined brow gave any hint of his toughness. At five foot seven, he looked tall and although both his parents were Tibetan and he was born in Kathmandu, he called himself a Sherpa. One of the most amazing things about Tash was his grasp of languages. For starters he spoke two Tibetan languages, English and Hindi fluently, Nepali (his mother tongue), Bengali and Garhwali, and he understood and could speak some Sherpa and Urdu. Tash was the most superb gentleman and was perfect for the journey — although we didn't realise it, we had stumbled across the one factor that would lead to ultimate success.

At the border-crossing point in eastern Nepal, a bird is silhouetted against the rising sun.

Peter on Ratong La at 17,500 ft, with the Yalung glacier behind.

2

Into Sikkimese Himalaya

IT WAS WITH a feeling of reluctance that I left the great cleft of the Ratong La, the exhilaration of the thin air, the piercing cold of the wind that funnelled its way from the Yalung glacier far, far below into the venturi of the narrow pass. Rimmed on either side by imposing walls of rock and ice that rose abruptly for over 5000 feet, the Ratong La is a no-man's-land with Sikkim to the east and Nepal to the west. I suppose my reluctance was pure reaction to our surroundings as a more inhospitable place you would have difficulty in finding. We had striven for this moment, the beginning of our rather preposterously ambitious traverse of the Himalayas, for eighteen months: and with monotonous regularity, the future of our dream adventure had been threatened. It would have been good to cross the border at the Ratong La, but without a permit that was not on. And now, under my own volition, I was descending from this slot in this great Himalayan ridge back to our camp at the upper limit of the sparse alpine vegetation. Keeping a wary eye on the tiers of green ice-cliffs latched precariously to the mountain walls above me, I set off down the flank bounding from boulder to boulder until the giant granitic blocks gave way to glistening glacier ice. Here and there etching on the ice by the others' crampons indicated their passage and that they were still ahead — that much closer to hot tea and food and comfortable sleeping bags. For them there had been little hesitation over leaving the chilling cold and gusting winds of the Ratong La.

As darkness fell, I reached the silver hut and was greeted with a hot cup of soup, and a slap on the back by a beaming S.P. It was 6 pm and we were all very tired, dehydrated and footsore. While I sipped from my bowl one of the succession of hot drinks that we consumed, I thought of the morning and our departure... the traverse would begin in earnest. Just Tashi, Graeme and I, three little people heading off on a very big adventure. The Karakorams of Pakistan seemed an impossibly long way off, like an unattainable goal. There was so far to go, so much to survive.

With what we all agreed was a suitably slow start to the previous energetic day, we wound ourselves up into a state of tremendous industry and activity, writing diaries and important communications, sorting food and equipment and stuffing our gear into our nice new packs. We must have looked a band of fair-dinkum "freshers" with our impeccably new gear and clothing, its flashy colours a symbol of our almost childish impatience to get moving.

Due to the political restrictions imposed by the border we were unable to cross the Ratong La directly into Nepal so we planned to follow the border, the Singalila ridge, to the low country and a border-crossing point. We would rendezvous again with S.P. and Doug in Darjeeling before crossing the border into Nepal at Karkarvitta. From there Tashi, Graeme and I would trek north into the mountains again on the Nepalese side of the border so that we could continue our westerly traverse across the spine of the Himalayas. Doug and S.P. would return to Darjeeling the way we had come in. With large packs and S.P.'s rhetoric on how he had never carried a big pack before and that we must understand that he was not used to such tasks, they slipped out of earshot and eventually out of sight as they followed the meandering track across the winter-locked alpine meadows.

Cloud had risen out of the valleys early and the ridges and peaks were shrouded in mist as we climbed from the valley on to the complex system of mountains, passes and ridges that forms the Sikkim-Nepal border and one of the Himalayas' great radial ridges, the Singalila. For days we would follow this immense ridge from near the foot of Mt Kanchenjunga down to the heat of the Himalayan foothills where we would strike west into Nepal. We crossed over the first ridge and dropped down into a small isolated valley nestled beneath a perimeter of tall cliffs and smooth rock slabs with Fray's Peak, an elegant rock and ice tower appearing briefly through the mist. As we descended from the ridge at about 15,000 feet, we surprised a flock of burrel, blue sheep, who picked up their heads from the dry, wind-burned grass, their solid gnarled horns silhouetted against the grey clouds as they assessed the intrusion, and then ran further up the windswept ridge and disappeared in the swirling mist.

Once down on the valley floor we set about making a camp. All we had was a tent fly, and Tashi wore a look of resigned apprehension. 'And just how are we going to handle this.' He had already shown some reserve in his confidence in our collective ability to traverse the Himalayas in the lightweight, do-it-yourself style that we intended and even as to Graeme's and my credibility... perhaps we were all bravado.

26

We dropped our packs and rushed around searching amongst the moss-covered boulders beside the stream for caves or bivouac sites but, finding none, we hastily repaired a broken-down rock enclosure left by some shepherd, and draped the tent fly over the top. Voila! The mould was set and with hot food being cooked on our tiny kerosene stove the first of nearly 300 days was all but over. It was very cold that night. Our especially light sleeping bags were not enough despite wearing all our clothes to thwart the late winter cold of February. Like three cocoons we lay beneath the tent fly in an insomnia-haunted vigil until dawn.

With an early start under our belts we climbed abruptly out of the little valley and on to yet another of the subsidiary ridges of the Singalila. It was a perfect morning with the northern sky filled by large snow-white shapes as we began a series of climbs and descents into deserted valleys with cold brooks tumbling through the alpine flora and the occasional timid flock of burrel. Again a bank of thick grey cloud rose and engulfed the mountain environs in which we moved; following snow-covered tracks and scrambling over windfall trees and branches in the veil of mist and wind. It was all rather "spooky" as winter imposed a hush, a quiet, that was quite uncanny; then there were the tall ghostly shapes of firs and cedars rising into the mist and sets of tiny footprints in the snow. The track emerged from a tangled forest of rhododendrons and crossed a bare hillside where a fire, many years before, had destroyed the trees, leaving only stark evidence of what once was. Turning downhill the track led us into a magnificent stand of tall firs. There was a rustle above and clumps of snow fell from the disturbed branches making a dull, insulated thud as they hit the deep snow at the base of the tree. Looking up, we caught a glimpse of a strange opossum-like creature hurtling from this tree to another large fir about fifty feet away. Clasping a slender branch with all four paws, it stared unflinchingly at us. We returned its gaze, but with a great deal more surprise and bewilderment than the extraordinary, furry aerobat. Then suddenly, as if to complete its display for the incredulous humanoid viewers, it sprang off the branch, and in a gliding dive swooped silently into the mist with the abandon of a fighter pilot on a mission of no-return. Astonished by the little creature's capacity for flight, we discussed our observations as we continued through the fir forest eventually agreeing that the "little fella" was a flying squirrel. 'Jonathan Livingston squirrel,' quipped Graeme with a laugh.

The day's gloom intensified as we skirted the flanks of huge ridges and crossed steep spurs that fell away below into the oblivion of the mist. Our black and white copy of an American Army 1:250,000 scale wartime map (the best we could get for most of the journey) indicated we were entering the valley of Bokto, a place filled with eerie gloom, a frozen, snow and ice-choked silence and an air of abandonment. We marched towards our destination for the day with apprehension, expecting something intensely dramatic — a bear attack or a large, white snow leopard to bound across the track... or even a mystical yeti to appear. Without speaking, cameras at the ready, we approached the deserted houses of the old Bokto mine, the dilapidated village now having, in our minds, the atmosphere for a wild west shoot-out. I peered into one of the dark and ramshackle buildings, lowered my 75 to 150mm zoom and bending low, went inside. It was dark and dirty and disused, and many of the roughly split planks that made up the roof were missing. Without further ado, we opted for a small conglomeration of huts 1000 feet below in a narrow valley, quite obviously sunless at this time of year. We crashed through spiny bushes and vines and drifts of snow that littered the ground below the lofty deodars. Perhaps, we surmised, we had been watched by a snow leopard despite not seeing one on arriving at Bokto. Thus, we decided, our feelings of expectation may not have been so frivolous after all!

The three huts sat in a clearing by the river with snowclad firs and pines all around; there was plenty of firewood. In the valley behind, steep slopes striated by the narrow threads of frozen waterfalls welded a line between the ceiling of grey cloud and the snow-covered valley floor. The huts were used during the brief monsoon season when yak-herders and shepherds would bring their animals to the high pastures to graze. Both the men and animals had been living in the simple huts, and it showed. Our hut had walls of split timber and woven bamboo mats, split wooden planks which overlapped on the roof, leaving plenty of gaps, and a carpet of leafy juniper stems. Where it was particularly sordid the monsoon season incumbents had lain down more of the slabs of roughly split deodar. It was shelter and once a warming blaze was burning before us, the hut quickly became our home… and a cosy contrast to the night before.

Again in mist and cloud we pushed on, plugging through the snow that covered the vague pathway. After a long steep climb we moved quickly

Off course during our descent of the Singalila ridge.

Tashi looking south along the spine of the Singalila ridge.

along open ridges at about 15,000 feet until a combination of visibility problems, map scale and massive snowdrifts stretching across the high alpine meadows and obliterating much of the track led to our inadvertently descending a spur that plummeted more and more steeply to the valleys below. By the time we realised that it was not just another minor ridge but that we were moving off the Singalila ridge itself, it was too late. It seemed better to keep following the track we had found on the spur in the thick cloud. We might come across some villagers down in the valley who could advise us on how to regain the ridge and describe the route ahead.

It proved a knee-jarring 9000-foot descent right down, it seemed, to the banana belt. Feeling somewhat demoralised we sat by a stream sipping some orange drink from my water-bottle and trying vainly to philosophise on our error. Ke garne? What to do?

Just then a group of wiry Sikkimese gents came along the path. They halted on seeing us and looked quizzically in our direction. Tashi called over to them and asked if they could help us. With broad smiles and inquisitive eyes, they studied our packs and equipment and told us how to regain the Singalila ridge. But, they warned, the track is very complicated; you will need a guide.

At 6.30 am the following day, we arrived at the little village of Chandri where, after much calling out to villagers we saw collecting water or tilling their terraced fields, we found our guide, a strongly built young man called

Phu Tsering. Phu Tsering had more than a good strong back... he had a very pretty wife who Graeme, in his incorrigible way, sat smiling blissfully at while she served us Tibetan tea (a tarry mixture of black tea, rock salt, and yak's butter... often a little rancid) and insipid boiled turnips. Smiling was not enough, the moment would be captured for all time. Under the amused eyes of Phu Tsering, Graeme photographed the young wife peeling boiled turnips, holding the baby, pouring more Tibetan tea into our cups and returning with water from a stream nearby.

It was definitely time to go, so we heaved our loads on to our backs, and climbed the uncompromising steep spur behind Phu Tsering's house at an excessively fast pace. Eventually, Phu Tsering halted for a short rest before continuing onward and upward at a more leisurely rate. It had been sound advice to get a guide, for the route followed an intertwined series of insignificant tracks and mere mentions of tracks that pushed through thick jungly undergrowth, bamboo groves and, finally, beneath stands of giant deodars. Occasionally, we heard large animals running through the bush making abrupt barking calls; Himalayan tahr, we were told.

As the magnificent deodar forests began to give way to the alpine rhododendrons, it began to snow and strong gusts lashed at us. The weather was deteriorating rapidly, so we sent Phu Tsering back to his village (and his wife) while we put on more clothing and continued up the spur to the Singalila ridge and Dhund. It was one of the worst storms of our ten-month traverse. The wind increased till it shrieked and snow was plastered all over us, leaving us like snowmen and in this part of the world, abominable snowmen at that. We climbed through the rhododendrons and on to the precipitous ridge top. I couldn't help thinking of the reception we might receive from some local people should we happen upon an inhabited house in this storm. It would soon be dark, and this was no place to be caught in a violent storm. We plugged furiously onward in the deep snow that blanketed the ridge, peering ahead from beneath our waterproof oversuits, hoping for shelter from the storm. By some good fortune, amidst the blindness of the blizzard, we came upon a very broken-down and snow-filled shepherd's hut. But then, it is curious how, once you have found something along the lines of what you sought, there is this tendency to want something better. We continued on and into a forest of rhododendrons through which the wind roared. For a while we clambered over branches, trying to avoid patches of ice. Then we stopped. What the hell were we doing? We returned to the shack higher on the ridge and while the wind tore at the old building as if it was bent on blowing it to pieces, we improved its weatherproofness and collected some firewood from dead trees that stood above the blanket of snow.

It was a miserable night curled up in our sleeping bags with spindrift being blasted through the gaps in the walls and roof and covering us and our sleeping bags with a dusty layer of powder snow. With only our noses protruding beyond the tightly secured sleeping bag drawstrings, we suffered out the night. Periodically, I crept a little nearer to the obstinate fire and blew on it till I felt dizzy and a flicker of reluctant yellow flame rose from the frosted wood transmitting the pretence of warmth through the windblown and sleety cold.

The morning was calm and clear, not a sign of the night's ferocity other than the sculptured shapes of trees plastered with ice and snow. To the north rose a majestic shape, like a throne, something aristocratic and arrogantly defiant amidst a maelstrom of wind-contoured clouds — Jannu, one of the most uncompromising of the Himalayan giants. Jannu is rather special to Graeme as in 1975 he went on an expedition to attempt the first ascent of its incredible north face. They were plagued by bad weather, terrible conditions and bad luck. They went high on Jannu, doing some extremely difficult climbing, but the summit eluded them. For some reason that Jannu experience has left a lot of bad feelings among New Zealand mountaineers, both members of the expedition and others. It was a large and very expensive expedition, and they needed to reach the summit to bring in the funds that would pay for the climb. They missed the summit and on returning home found they had huge unpaid debts. But looking at the mountain, I could easily see what attracted them to it — a mountain so difficult and magnificent posed a superlative challenge.

As the rambling ridge descended and the day warmed the snow receded until we found ourselves dripping perspiration. Over the ensuing two days, we followed the undulating crest of the mighty Singalila ridge from where we had an almost constant view of Jannu seated impudently to the left of Kanchenjunga, perhaps the most massive of all mountains. Westward spread a skyline of snowy peaks till a cluster rose like disproportionate warts above the next — the great armchair of Makalu, the colossal white flank of Everest's Kangshung face and the dark rock wall of Lhotse. At the tiny ridge-top village of Singalila we stopped for lunch. We asked a man if we could buy any food; he shook his head with a wry smile. I took an immediate dislike to him not because he couldn't or wouldn't sell us any food, but from his attitude. He was a tough-looking character and I suspected a fairly nasty individual. While we cooked up a large and thick brew of sustagen milk drink, he led a cow over to near where we were sitting. By the time our brew was ready, and we were enjoying it in the sun, he was ready too. Clumsily, he and his equally repulsive offsider killed the cow, looking repeatedly across at us with gleeful smiles apparently in search of some mythical European blood-lust feedback. We hastily packed our loads. Do you want some fresh meat? No, thanks... the lovely scent of daphne flower filled the air as we left Singalila.

At Sundarpur, a cluster of hotels and guesthouses, we halted for the night and the next day walked the short distance to Jonbari and the road end. Sititng in the sun on the steps of a shop in the small Tibetan town we sipped tombas (a fermented millet mash on which hot water is poured; you drink the alcoholic liquid using a bamboo straw with slits in the bottom to sieve out the millet grains) and waited for an antiquated Landrover to be repaired. Half of the vehicle was spread over the partially cobbled street — the main (and only) street of the ridge-top town. However, the vehicle was supposedly fixed when it came chugging along the road, and we jumped

31

Tashi beneath frost-covered rhododendron on the Milke ridge.

Tashi lighting a fire at 14,000 ft on the Milke ridge with Makalu towering behind.

Tashi amongst burnt forest on the Milke ridge.

Graeme on the Milke ridge as clouds engulf Everest and Makalu.

aboard. Away we went, down into the thick, hot, dusty air of the lower valleys over the four-wheel drive switchbacked roads to Simana Bazaar and finally Darjeeling where we again joined Doug and S.P. The five of us travelled together by bus to Karkarvitta, the Nepalese border-crossing town and there made our official entry into Nepal. Having fulfilled our obligations to the authorities we bade farewell to S.P. and Doug who continued on to Kathmandu from where they would trek into the Kumbu, the Mt Everest area, where we would have our first rendezvous. They would bring in spare clothing and footwear, tents and equipment, dehydrated foods and drinks, film and diary gear. As for Tashi, Graeme and me, we would take another bus and head north to the town of Ilam and the road-end just west of Jonbari, on the Sikkim/Nepal border. A long, dusty and windy ride ensued along roads that, although remarkable in many ways as feats of engineering, were only partly completed. The state of the roads — and our bus — had us wondering whether we would have to walk to Ilam through the heat. The huge hills of lowland Nepal slipped by the grimy windows. Intensive agriculture on terraced land supported a large population.

The scourge of all travellers who use Asian buses — *sorus bottus* — was about to become serious as we reached Ilam. Dragging our cramped, dust-covered and dehydrated bodies from the iron-hard seats we stepped out into the hill-town's main square. The square was paved with stone and surrounded by two-storied buildings; the ground-floor rooms were shops that opened out on to the square, providing the simple goods the hill peasants would require or could afford. The upper stories with their tiny verandahs, some with pots of flowering shrubs, were the residences of the shopkeepers. The arrival of the bus was a special event with many of the townspeople just coming to watch, porters standing by in case of work, and the storekeepers crosslegged amidst the chaotic piles of their wares smoking pipes or bidis (a conical cigarette rolled in a leaf instead of paper) and chatting to other village gentlemen, all of whom appeared to have plenty of time on their hands. It was immediately clear to us that foreigners were not common visitors here, let alone ones wearing green plastic boots and sporting silky-blue running shorts with long white hairy legs protruding from them and considerable crops of funny-coloured hair.

We climbed up the hill, heading north-west towards the high Himal we had left only days before, but on the other side of an invisible boundary dividing Nepal from Sikkim. Our plan was to travel westward to the Milke ridge, another large radial ridge like the Singalila, where we would follow its crest north as far as we could go. From there we would turn west again, ascend the Barun valley to the foot of Mt Makalu (fifth highest mountain in the world) and cross three very high and difficult passes in order to reach the Kumbu, the Everest area. There we would be met in a little village at 13,000 feet by our support team at the house of my father's sirdar (foreman). I was looking forward to reaching the Kumbu immensely. For me, it was familiar ground, a part of these magnificent mountains that I knew well from five previous visits on the aid work expeditions of the Himalayan Trust, an organisation headed and operated by my father. But all this was far from Ilam. We had a great deal of rugged country to cover and a full five days' march before reaching the Milke ridge alone.

From a river we climbed a short distance up the hillside winding our way through terraced fields all brown and dry, passing groups of villagers returning to their homes after a long hot day of toil in the fields and the forests. A cheerful people, their lives are tough but then their expectations are not high and disappointment is not a word they know. Recognition of their lot gives them the capacity to enjoy the simple lifestyle and not to demand more... a more they could never have. We halted at the first village, perched on a knoll beneath a huge shady pipal tree. True to our resolution that whenever it was possible to eat well we would, we ordered a chicken shakpa (stew) from the weedy-looking character who claimed to own and, what's more, operate the local teahouse.

The long-awaited shakpa was served to us in the darkness of the dingy trackside teahouse as if to mask its contents. It was certainly chicken, but the fashion of butchery left something to be desired. With furrowed brows and looks of intense concentration, Tashi and Graeme would chew briefly, then spit out the door into the blackness of the pathway. They had been blessed, it seemed, with a similarly constituted ladle of shakpa as the one I was dealing with. It was as if the whole chicken had been diced with an axe, bones and all. 'Enjoying your splinter stew, fellas?'

For two days we followed the dusty track through the foothills, sweltering in the heat as we lugged our loads of cold-weather clothing, down sleeping bags and dehydrated high-altitude rations. At Phidim, a district headquarters, I arrived ahead of the others and, feeling hot and thirsty, located a little teashop run by a comely wench with a gold ring in her nose, a red tikka on her golden brown forehead and red tassels braided into her long black plaits. While I sat in the shade of her poky little shop gulping copious quantities of tea my companions were still sweating on the outer edge of town. It was 6 pm and time for the local constabulary to sound the bugle. At this moment, Tashi and Graeme came ambling along the track that passed the barbed wire-cordoned camp, and no doubt foremost in their minds was a cup of tea. The bugle call sounded and two officious young Gurkhas posted at one of the camp entrances shouted at them to halt, cocking and aiming their bayonetted rifles at them as they did so. Reluctantly they stopped, too tired to protest or run. They sat down untidily until the bugler had completed his duty. Then, as the rifles were uncocked and returned to a less alarming upright position, they continued towards a cup of tea.

The sign of authority is so often barbed wire, military force, red tape and prisons built conspicuously for all to see. The broad well-built path leading out of Phidim passed through the luxurious shade of a line of pipal trees, a holy tree to Hindus, and beneath the Phidim gaol, a high-walled square with coiled wire fringing the top of the wall. We descended to a river below Phidim, leaving authority behind, and followed it across dry hillsides and fields to the junction with the Tamur river, a massive body of jade-green water flowing swiftly southwards. We turned up the Tamur valley, following the river to a large wire cable footbridge. Here we crossed, gasping in the unrelenting heat and, feeling exhausted and dehydrated, we clambered through rubble to the boulder-strewn bank of the river. We gathered some driftwood and lit a fire to brew a billy of tea. In the populated parts of these mountains we never drank the water unless it was well boiled as a host of unpleasant diseases and parasites could so easily be picked up. I consistently observed on arriving and departing the hill villages — an observation difficult to avoid — the state of the local people's faeces and far from the presumed natural immunisations to dysentery and diarrhoea and other consequences of limited hygiene, they have simply learned to live with it. We lay panting in the heat, and through my day-dream of 'only mad dogs and Englishmen go out in the noonday sun' came a friendly Nepali gentleman wearing a jacket with several pens in the breast pocket, traditional Nepali trousers cut tight at the ankle, the long sleeve cotton shirt that is fastened at the side and atop his head a multicoloured Nepali cap. How he could have worn all those clothes in the heat I do not know, but throughout the journey we found the local people were able to wear many layers of clothing in hot conditions without displaying any signs of discomfort. A hill-country man could never masquerade in shorts as we did, no matter how hot it was. It would be beneath his dignity, improper and a display of low caste and class. This man was on his way to Taplejung, a large town further upstream, and although we would be turning off the main track before Taplejung, he

Graeme and Tashi at 15,000 ft on the Milke ridge.

Graeme and Peter in one of the bivouacs on the
Milke ridge, attempting to escape its winter-locked confines.

Looking west from the Milke ridge at Lhotse and
Everest, Makalu and the Arun valley below.

assured us he was happy to show us the way to where our two paths separated. So along with him we went, climbing above the Tamur river feeling much better for a cup of tea.

However, it was not long before we were again sweating profusely and gasping for each breath in the hot, dry air as we climbed several thousand feet above the river to a village. Sitting in the blissful shade of the verandah of a farmhouse, we sipped from small brass cups sweet, lemon tea, and greedily consumed yoghurt and popped-corn served by a buxom lass who skilfully divided her attention between two demanding young children and three demanding expeditionaries. It was a welcome break to relax and enjoy the peaceful atmosphere, watch a hen with her chickens foraging around the courtyard, a boy bringing the water buffaloes in from the hill and tethering them in a field by the house, the old grandmother peering down at us from an upstairs window and the large dark eyes of the two children as they watched unabashed as we drank our tea and chatted. Our destination for the day was Pokhari of which this farmhouse was apparently part. The village is a sprawling agricultural region spreading 2 or 3000 feet up the hillside to the ridgeline. We zigzagged, traversed and climbed, enquiring at every opportunity as to the whereabouts of the village centre. Without exception, everybody pointed upward. The village centre consisted of a number of shops and a school, all of which were closed. Out of the woodwork slipped the local schoolteacher, who directed us to the house of a kindly old woman who ushered us into her home. Seated on the smooth earthen floor, we drank tombas in large wooden mugs while the old lady began cooking our meal by the fire. A couple of boys played beside her, the flickering light of the fire on their faces as she deftly positioned pots above the flames and adjusted the firewood and dried cow dung so as to burn only what was necessary of the valuable fuel. Her husband had died and the old lady was supporting her family by selling tombas and chung to the local gentlemen. As far as possessions went she probably had very, very little. With no welfare system for the needy, her children were her best investment for the future, for her old age.

Determined that we should not be subjected to "splinter stew" for a second time, Graeme attended to the creation of our chicken stew. The result was the antithesis; instead of having chips of bone we had a chicken, roasted intact, then cut into three pieces. Wrestling like primitive men with our large hunks of meat in the dimly-lit and smoke-filled room, we savaged the chicken noisily with relish and abandon, accompanied by the hysterical giggles of a group of children who had congregated to witness the spectacle.

I awoke slowly as the sun crossed the dry mud yard and shone warmingly on to the verandah where we slept. Tashi, as always, had been up early and we were soon drinking bowls of piping hot tea. It was then that I noticed a strange tick-like creature crawling over my sleeping bag. With the well-practised nonchalance coming from much time in the hills, I flicked the tiny trespasser off my bag, and continued sipping my tea... I spied another tick, then another and before long my casual approach had become a frenzy as I searched through my clothes, inside my sleeping bag and on my body for the despicable little brutes who had dared encroach on *me* and *my* possessions. Having extracted about twenty ticks I set off up the hill above Pokhari as if I was being pursued by an army of... parasites.

A long climbing traverse took us past small stone houses, plastered with clay and with thick thatched roofs; past bare, terraced fields awaiting the monsoon and another season of crops. We were all perspiring heavily with our heavy packs on our backs and our strangely incongruous plastic boots. The track wound through the lower limits of the rhododendron forests. Already there was bloom on a few trees, splashes of bright red amongst the deep jade-green of the leaves. The track climbed more steeply through the trees till it led into a large yard surrounded by several two-storey buildings. The sounds of children's voices echoed into the yard as they learned their lessons by monotonous rote. We suddenly found ourselves engulfed by kids, bright brown faces with wide inquisitive eyes. The word had got around that something strange was in the school yard, and we found ourselves being scrutinised, quizzed with their latest English phrases and the subjects of considerable amusement.

'What is your country?'

'Where... from... you come?'

'Why have you come to Artrai Sunrati?'

We left their beaming and enthusiastic smiles and questions, ascending the short distance to the ridge-top bazaar of Sunrati, the last major town with shops on our way to the Mt Everest area and our rendezvous with the support team. We purchased provisions from some of the dark, cramped cubicles that passed as shops with their dusty wares all brought to Sunrati on the backs of men; poorly paid porters who labour along the hot and steep foot tracks of Nepal. Tashi decided to have a wash at the village water tap in the middle of the bazaar so he removed all but his shorts and doused himself with the cold water and soap. Feeling refreshed he walked up through the bazaar to where Graeme and I were sipping cups of hot cargati tea (a lime juice and tea mixture) forgetting his wristwatch which he had removed before the wash. By the time he remembered it, it was gone, and no one knew anything about it. The watch had been given to Tashi a long time ago. 'It wasn't a good watch,' he lamented, 'but my mother gave it to me and it... ah... was special to me.'

With mixed feelings about Sunrati we marched off along the track that crossed a vast hillside and entered a large valley scattered with hamlets and terraced fields. The track remained near the ridge line so we were well above the valley floor, giving a sensation of floating above the gigantic hill folds of rural Nepal. We traversed around the valley, climbing through the forest at its head to a pass where, according to vague indications on our map, we should find a major path that would take us on to the Milke ridge. There was no track, but there was a view of the mountains, spectacular snow summits piercing the hazy veil of cloud that had persistently enshrouded them during these late winter days. We walked through several gullies thick with the seductive scent of mauve and white daphne flowers; a deciduous daphne, a skeleton of twigs and lean branches ablaze with clusters of flower; a

fragrance so glorious that as we sauntered through their perfumed presence, I tried to re-word Wordsworth's efforts with daffodils.

We found a minor and little-used track which soon trifurcated and then bifurcated. Eventually we found our way on to a main path using a little commonsense, some luck and Tashi's inquiries from a man we met along the way. 'Oh, yes this is the right track,' we were told. 'He's just saying that,' reproved Tashi. But the path did lead us on to the Milke ridge, now cloudy and cold and there in a bleak and miserable hollow on the crest beside a grimy and decidedly greasy pokari (little lake) was Gopa — a handful of dilapidated and depressed shacks where we would be spending the night. From Gopa we would leave the beaten trail and make our way north along this colossal radial ridge system, the watershed of both the Tamur and the Arun rivers (two of the largest in Nepal) till we were as high as we could go. From there we would turn west to Mt Makalu.

Tashi was told that a pig had been recently slaughtered so we went in search of it, finding it in a dark shanty. Large hunks — butchery is not a well-developed skill in these parts — hung on bamboo twine from the roof. It was difficult to see in the poor lighting and smoke of the building but what was obvious was that there was more fat than meat. So with several bags of the 'soggy pig', as we labelled it, we returned to our spartan abode. In the cramped room of the lady who ran the dirt-floored, dosshouse we cut the pork into cubes of the tallow that it really was, and boiled it in saffron for two hours. Fortunately it was dark by the time dinner was ready and plates of ghastly, yellow, fatty meat were handed round. 'When in Rome do as the Romans,' I thought as I closed my eyes and chewed.

The remainder of the pork was wrapped up in plastic bags, ready for stowing in our packs to accompany us up the Milke ridge in the morning, to supplement our meagre rations of dehydrated stews.

We walked quickly up the gradually ascending, frost-covered Milke ridge. At a saddle covered with golden winter grass we dropped our packs and ecstatically, with cameras in hand, groped for the shutter buttons. Clear, supreme, indomitable, rose Jannu, with the colossus of Kanchenjunga emerging beneath a storm of grey lenticulate clouds that swept its summit to a smooth facsimile of a summit dome. With the sweet scent of daphne in the air and glimpses of the mountains through the rapidly rising cloud we continued up the grassy ridge — a rampart high in the sky — over the monsoon pastures of herds still far below in the valleys. We passed a group of sinewy porters carrying blocks of suka, a raw crystalline form of unrefined sugar, of which we purchased a large block for 10 rupees (80 cents). Tashi asked them about the route ahead. As became the norm for the entire trans-Himalayan journey, the local people would nearly always give an answer, advice or directions, perhaps in a desire to please, when as often as not they knew little or nothing of what we had asked. So with what we considered to be additional information and a piece of the delicious new sweet we had just acquired in our mouths, we munched our way along the ridge.

Through a forest of gnarled rhododendrons and holly we reached a deserted summer village of rickety bamboo and wooden sheds that lay above a small tarn. Just then the awesome towers of cumulo-nimbus that billowed and crackled thousands of feet above our heads boomed and thundered ominously. Heavy showers of hail rained down on us as we retreated to one of the more inhabitable sheds where we began to prepare ourselves for the night. While Graeme lit the fire, Tashi and I went to collect water at the tarn amidst the flurries of white, airborne shrapnel that fell from the black sky, carpeting the ridge in large white hailstones.

A bowl of piping hot tea does a lot to ward off the chill of evening; and 'soggy pig'... it can ward off almost anything. I've never been an enthusiast for eating fat, although Graeme relishes it, and Tashi will eat just about anything, but when there is nothing else, you know your body requires food and energy, you know you will be expending plenty of energy in the days to come, you know there is no alternative... you eat the saffroned soggy pig.

We continued up the ridge with early-morning cumulus already rising on the east side curling upward like mushrooming cornices of powder snow. Atop a rise in the ridge we caught an unexpected and brief glimpse of the destination for this section of the traverse, a great pyramid of sweeping rock ridges and ice-fluted faces: Makalu with the indistinct massifs of Lhotse and Everest behind. Much elated by what we had seen we continued along the track in steadily thickening cloud and mist.

The path led through forests, most of which had been severely damaged by the local people during the monsoon period as they collected firewood and burned off areas for pasture. Pasture that without the binding roots of the lofty Himalayan firs and rhododendrons was destined for the rivers far below and eventually the silt banks of the Bay of Bengal. Using a series of compass bearings we reached what we estimated must be a deep saddle in the main ridge. Both the ridge and the tenuous foot track dropped away ominously into the rhododendrons and the mist. To ensure we did not take the wrong route and descend off the Milke ridge, as we had done on the Singalila, we decided the prudent measure was to halt and camp. We pitched the tent in a grassy hollow and began cooking dinner over a very smoky fire while sleet fell from the heavens above, the ice pellets stinging noses and fingers that protruded from our one-piece overalls as we tended the uncooperative fire... source of heat... food... life!

While adjusting a branch on the fire Tashi accidentally upset one of the two billies; it contained the last of our rice (the other pot contained the last of our soggy pig — a mixed blessing). There was little hesitation, the three of us fell on our knees in our maroon one-piece suits, sleet beating on our backs, our spoons carefully scooping the precious rice from among the coals and ashes of the fire, back into the billy.

We squeezed into the miniscule two-man tent, all three of us, and bent almost double as we sat in the tent, we consumed our evening repast; a sumptuous mixture of grey, barbecued rice and the last of our old standby, the saffron soggy pig.

Graeme, then Tashi, then I emerged carefully from our cocoon-sized abode to minimise the inadvertent kicks, accidental elbows and upper cuts

43

Tashi and Graeme climbing at 19,000 ft with
Mt Makalu behind.

*Our tiny camp at 19,000 ft, with Makalu behind,
en route to Far East Col (20,500 ft) and the Everest area.*

from raised knees, that we dealt each other. The cold and wintry atmosphere outside helped us to get moving as did the brilliantly clear views of Makalu and Everest to the west. We descended on to the saddle below us, crossing a line of mysterious footprints in the deep snow as we did so. They appeared to be of a barefoot man and they were fresh. The footprints had joined the track somewhere below our camp spot and as we reached the saddle they again disappeared. 'He must have tough feet — *it* must have tough feet,' I called to the others, who smiled.

We would have liked to have met somebody so as to confirm our route and receive any information he might have on the ridge ahead. But if the somebody was a yeti, then the onus might be more on his meeting us. Thick cloud with light snow falling was soon the order of the day as we hiked up above the saddle and across a high-alpine meadow, at over 14,000 feet, studded with tarns (pokari), alpine juniper and rhododendron bushes and tussocks that pushed through the drifts of snow. We meandered across the meagrely vegetated slabs in thick cloud, searching for a semblance of a track or route along the progressively more rugged and precipitous ridge.

Scanning our inadequate map for fine details as we went, we reached a small col deep in the mirk and wind with rock bluffs all around. We decided that it could be construed with a little imagination to be the same minor col marked on our map. So, when a little further on we found vague snow-drifted impressions that could correspond to a track we were delighted. Climbing over a small roll in the ridge flank, we looked below into a hollow where, sheltering from the weather, was a flock of mountain sheep. They were stocky beasts and incredibly agile with short, stubby horns and thick coats. They ran ahead across the snow-covered rock slabs, disappearing into the mist while we followed their tracks, finding their chosen route to be also the best one for us. On an exposed rib we pitched the tent. The light was already dim, and we rummaged around in the snow, the cold wind, the fierce winter isolation, looking for firewood. While we laboured over the fire, trying to protect it from the wind, I looked up towards the ridge-top skyline. Silhouetted against the golden glow of the western sky were the magnificent outlines of the flock of blue sheep, watching us from high on a rocky outcrop. No doubt they felt secure with 1000 feet of bluffs and rock slabs separating our campsite from their freezing winter tower at over 15,000 feet.

It was a dark and stormy night and Graeme said to his mate: 'Tashi, spin us a yarn,' and his mate began as follows... And the snow fell, and the wind blew, and the temperature plummeted below zero, and we huddled together and we shivered aloud, and we cursed the world asunder! What earthly good can there be in these hills; a man has to wonder.

A wild red sky greeted us as we reluctantly emerged from our cold haven into the threatening world. To the east Kanchenjunga and Jannu stood majestically, bathed in a haze of mist and clouds with a scarlet sky above them; the message was clear: 'You shouldn't be here... not now.'

I headed up the mountainside to get some idea of the way ahead before the inevitable storm and its disorienting clouds arrived; smearing all into a white oblivion broken only by a few confusing dark shapes that had resisted a coating of snow or frost. Tashi and Graeme were still taking down the tent as I plugged uphill in the crusty snow till I reached the outcrop above our camp. I began to skirt around it beneath the wall of bluffs that rose to a craggy summit.

With my thoughts on escape from the winter-locked Milke Danda, the rock that skittled down 'the cliff above and crashed into the snow before me gave me a frightening start. Anticipating an avalanche or rockfall, I looked upward readying myself for a hasty retreat. What I saw astounded me. The flock of blue sheep were descending the cliff by way of a very steep slab of probably 70 degrees. One by one they made their descent in a series of controlled slithers, tiptoe manoeuvres on miniscule ledges and crack systems, followed by measured athletic leaps and bounds to the next point where they could find some purchase and regain control of their descent. In a short time the whole flock was off the cliff face (about 300 feet high) and rushing together across the broad snow-covered rock slabs below where I stood. I didn't know whether to dig into my pack for my camera, or call down to the others... in the end I simply stood where I was, dumbfounded.

Their descent route was over some difficult rock, and it would not have been easy climbing by any stretch of the imagination for Graeme, Tashi or myself. Our earlier speculations as to the route of ascent that the animals took to reach the top of the outcrop were beginning to look a trifle shaky. If they descended the way I had just witnessed, surely such an ascent route would also be feasible. But perhaps they were in a hurry and didn't have time to use the easier ramp we conjectured there must be on the far side of the outcrop. A few minutes later that hypothesis was well and truly laid to rest. The far side of the outcrop was an overhanging buttress about 1000 feet high. They must have climbed the same route they descended. A fairly effective way of dispensing with aggressors I would say!

Feeling rather inferior to the magnificent blue sheep, masters of their cold and inhospitable environment, I continued on across a broad snow face to the crest of the ridge to get a view of what lay ahead. All three of us had agreed that retreat from the Milke ridge was highly desirable. The threatening weather, the already difficult conditions and the daily white-outs were making progress tediously slow. We thought we would climb down one of the many ribs and spurs into the valley to the west of the ridge and proceed to the mighty Arun river and thence to Mt Makalu. It seemed such a good idea as we scrutinized the 4½ miles to an inch map in our tent that morning but such splendidly reasonable rationale does not always concur with the Himalayan reality.

I reached the ridge and climbed into a narrow nook between the stark rock pinnacles and peaks that now composed the jagged ridge-line and looked down to a snow-filled basin on the far side. Beyond the basin, I could discern several spurs that dropped out of sight into the valley below and indeed, where we wished to go. However with the shining brilliance of hindsight on my side, I now know that we had not only misread our map but that we intended to break a rule that both Graeme and I had long held to be true and which I had once again been warned against breaking while we were in New

Delhi. Doug and I retreated occasionally to the airconditioned atmosphere and the delicious, cool ice creams of a restaurant when both the meteorological and psychological temperatures of our Delhi sojourn reached extreme limits. There we met Ewald Ruf, a vey fit German mountaineer and adventurer with a great deal of Himalayan experience. He had hiked along the Milke Danda some years before, and he too had made an error. 'Believe me,' he said, 'don't descend any spurs or ridges where there are no tracks.'

Tashi and Graeme were soon standing with me in the nook in the ridge at over 15,000 feet now becoming swamped by cloud. We were fed up with the conditions: 'Let's get out of here,' I grumbled, and together we climbed down off the ridge and towards the snow basin only partially discernible in the mist below. We down-climbed steep bulges of water ice where we chopped pockets for the toes of our boots and then lowered ourselves down, using our ice-axes driven in above for purchase. From the basin we rushed about in the veil of swirling cloud following tenuous leads indicating human presence during the monsoon season — wood choppings or vague tracks. All the while we hoped for a sure path down the dizzy spurs to the valley somewhere in the mist. We descended lower and lower until all human signs had ceased and we continued like obsessed men, lowering ourselves down through the thickets of bamboo and stubborn rhododendrons, over heavily vegetated precipices dripping and wet, and into the cold, damp confines of a narrow gully. Plugging steeply downward in wet granular snow, slipping on sheets of exposed water ice, we descended 5000 feet into the bowels of a deep and practically impenetrable gorge flanked by bluffs and cliffs, huge boulders and thick bamboo and rhododendron jungles. We abseiled, doubling our rope around a clump of bamboo stems, down a verglassed bluff, beside an elegant frozen waterfall into a chilling hellhole where everything was frozen and coated with smooth ice. Clambering out of the ice-clad ravine we re-entered the jungle feeling despondent and demoralised. This wasn't freedom!

Just above a major stream junction — the roar of its waters we could hear but not see — we stumbled upon a remarkably dry overhanging rock. There was room for the three of us beneath it with a little work and since we had been on the move for eight hours without food or rest, we granted ourselves an early halt to ease our tired limbs and shelter our bodies from the penetrating cold and wet of the drizzle and the unrelenting bush. It rained all afternoon and then all night, as we cowered in our sleeping bags beneath our giant moss-covered boulder, waiting for the morning.

We set off into the cold, wet alpine jungle heading downstream until yet another gorge forced us to climb. I was keen to climb out of the gorge, regain the high pastures and attempt to rectify the matter from terrain that we could move around on more easily. The others agreed and without further ado, we set off up a spur that rose abruptly into the laden clouds. The spur was a little less densely vegetated and thus our progress through the bamboo and rhododendron thickets was better. The day was developing into a cauldron of wind, snow and pure unadulterated misery and as we climbed higher the weather became worse. Eventually Tashi suggested we bivouac, so as we

*Graeme and Tashi at over 20,000 ft on the Lower
Barun glacier, with Makalu behind.*

climbed we searched for shelter on the steep, narrow spur. He was very cold and wet as he had not put on his extra clothing.

A tall rock prow leaned out over the precipitous snow-covered spur, its craggy top only faintly discernible in the falling snow. Beneath it was a small sheltered area. We placed our packs inside this bivouac and while Graeme and Tashi collected some firewood, I climbed up the spur above the rock to where it narrowed. Here I found an old track that came from nowhere and followed the narrow spur further up into the cloud and more thickets of wet snow-covered bamboo. I traced the old track for a couple of hundred yards to ensure it didn't peter out as miraculously as it had commenced and with the sure knowledge that we had at last found a route, I returned to help my friends collect firewood. We collected a substantial pile of wood, enough to last the afternoon and the long night, and set about the task of lighting the fire in difficult conditions.

We were crammed under the rock with only enough room for the three of us to crouch. On the outside a large log fire was raging; behind we were confined by the overhang of rock that sheltered us from the big, crystalline snowflakes that landed gently on the garden of elegantly curved bamboo stems surrounding the bivvy. These afforded a barrier between us and the flank that dropped away through clinging vegetation to the gorge.

Strangely, we all slept well, squeezed together in a variety of postures. Nor did we lose anything… or anyone… in the fire that we spent the night slipping into. Clad in our one-piece suits, looking like Apollo astronauts we struck out into the jungle of white. As we brushed by bamboo, the snow that had built up would be knocked off and the stems flick upright. Taking turns to plug the steps in the snow we climbed until, as the cloud began to drift in, marring visibility, we looked across into a basin where we could see a track traversing its flank. Graeme pointed to the ridge above the basin. 'Isn't that where you climbed from the other side of the ridge, Tashi?' Tashi nodded. A full four days before he had scrambled up there to scout around and look for a route. Now after our escape from the ravine, we were perhaps 300 or 400 yards from that point on the west side of the Milke ridge.

In the rapidly gathering mist we crossed into the basin, and at the base of the track had a quick lunch of tea. Our supply of dehydrated stews was getting low and we needed to conserve what we had left for the high crossings in the Makalu area so, as we had done for several days already, we went hungry. We plugged along the snow-covered track and into the cloud until the inevitable happened. In the mist, we were unable to find a continuous trail, across the semi-pastoral maze of aimless, snow-covered animal tracks. Once again, disappointed, we stopped at a large overhanging bivouac rock that had been used before by the monsoon herdsmen, to await the morning and that brief interlude of clear skies. How to get off the bloody Milke Danda? We were trapped and our food resources were now very limited. There had been people up here so there *must* be a route other than retracing our steps along the ridge to Gopa.

A starry sky peered down on our frozen camp and our near frozen bodies as at 4.30 am we began to get ready to dive — come hell or high water —

down the big spur opposite the bivvy. To the west the ghostly shapes of Makalu and Everest loomed huge and white in the moonlight as we lit the fire, scoffed some tea and stew before stomping off across the frozen snow towards the spur on which our hopes were pinned. According to the map there was a track on it.

Once on to the spur, we scrutinized the map's complex, tiny-scaled impressions. A terrible realisation came over us as we pinpointed where we were. We weren't on the spur that we had thought we were on, but on another large spur to the south of it. Resigned and still utterly determined to escape from the Milke Danda, we decided to force a route down this spur into the populated valley below. There would be tracks part way up so if we persevered we would certainly make it. Down the spur through the bamboo, around great bluffs and tiers of cliffs went the intrepid trio, following incipient paths that meandered, disappeared and re-appeared... Then the air filled with the glorious scent of giant white magnolias and pretty pink daphnes, the track — or tracks — became more substantial and we more optimistic.

Over a sharp downturn in the spur we came face to face with four burly Nepali men, who moved gingerly and very swiftly up the steep track, puffing on their leaf-rolled cigarettes. Tashi, who is a keen smoker and had long since run out of cigarettes, was soon smoking one of their leaf-rolled variety and trying to communicate with them. It wasn't easy as they were Limbu people, and spoke only a smattering of Nepali; however, Tashi gleaned that they were from the village of Phukum and it was at the bottom of the spur. Elated we bade the four men (who were the first people we had seen for a week) farewell and continued to descend... and descend we did, down the outrageous pathway that barely zigzagged or turned from its direct, plumb-bob line to the river at the base of the valley. A full 8000 feet of knee-jarring and muscle-quivering descent lowered us swiftly from the frozen tops to the muggy valley depths — a radical temperature transition none of us enjoyed.

We were saddened by the way the local people had chopped, burned and abused their mountain homes. They have to go continually higher to find pastures for their animals in the delicate alpine environment, even higher to fetch bamboo, firewood and fodder for their animals. As we descended towards the village down a stretch of hillside pitch-black and denuded by a recent fire, I wondered how high could they go, how long could these mighty mountains sustain the onslaught?

Feeling sure we had reached Mecca we entered Phukum with beads of sweat on our brows, a big thirst and insatiable hungers. From house to house we wandered trying to buy food, even water... anything. We received nothing. Tashi went into the courtyard of one house having taken off his pack and trying to make himself more presentable to ask the woman there for water. In simple Nepali he made his request; she looked back at him uncomprehendingly. Tashi returned to the track and together we descended to the lower edge of the village. Here a local school teacher befriended us, sold us some of his precious rice (a scarce commodity in these parts) and directed us to a house below his school where we could cook a meal and get some tea. The man of the house offered us a rooster to have with our lunch. We accepted the offer with alacrity and asked where the tasty morsel was. 'In the yard, you'll have to catch it,' we were told. 'Right, are you ready Peter?' Graeme commanded as he marched for the door. Flailing our ice-axes and using all the cunning acquired during a sound secondary education of travel on municipal trains, dodging extra drill and reducing the length of long school runs, we chased the wily rooster round and round the house till he got tired of our desperate antics and took off across some fields. With local insipid vegetable to flavour our lunch we munched silently through the mounds of white rice we had steaming in our bowls.

A good deal more alive than we were when we had reached Phukum, we trooped off down valley. Tashi led at a strong pace till we reached a village where, as the sun sank, we stopped at a house by the pathside. It was like being admitted into the land of milk and honey as this house and the friendly family that lived there seemed to have everything we could want! Alcoholic tomba, then milk followed by a main course of chicken, rice and vegetables with pancakes and butter and honey for dessert. I smiled as I lay comfortably in my sleeping bag thinking of Tashi's incredulity the night before as he gazed into his bowl at his meagre share of stew. 'Do you always eat so little on expeditions?' he had queried unhappily.

For two days we marched across country to the village of Num on the banks of the Arun river. From there we would climb to reach the Barun valley and then Makalu basecamp. After the challenges and tensions imposed by an experience such as the Milke ridge there often seems to be a period of introspection and deflation. You have striven so, put all you had into something, and then when the challenge has been overcome it's not always a sense of satisfaction or victory that one feels rising in your chest, but an anticlimactic disillusion. For us, we were free of the Milke Danda, but there was the Makalu/Everest area to come and beyond that over 4000 kilometres of Himalayan horizons.

Perhaps one of the most difficult things for me to come to terms with was the very essence of the trip, its length. Ten months of driving oneself was outside normal human perspective. There were no weekends coming up in a tangible two or three days and having been on the move for only about four weeks, the prospect of a further eight months was, to say the least, daunting. In many ways, I felt very much alone and it was thoughts of my family that helped give me strength and a feeling of purpose. Perhaps of primary importance was the realisation, probably the result of recently losing close friends, of how important the special people in my life were to me. I would be separated from them for nearly a year, living a different life and almost completely out of touch with them. In some ways, this aroused a morbid sense of isolation...

We passed groups of well-dressed people, wearing brightly coloured clothing and toothy grins, as they headed down valley to the Saturday market. There were a couple of men who carried home-made muskets complete with ramming rod, flint and lock, and there were plenty of cheeky comments and loud, raucous laughter at the extraordinary foreigners. Tashi asked some of them about Num so as to confirm the existence of some shops and a means of replenishing our very depleted food stocks. 'Oh, yes, Num is a big town.' With impressions of a row of shops down either side of a cobbled main street we reached Num. There was a disused school and a closed-up building near-by from the back of which appeared a slender Nepali man with whom Tashi spoke.

'This is Num,' Tashi transmitted, 'and that's the shop.'

'You must be joking.' I was furious as I had had some uneasiness about a last-ditch effort at restocking with all we needed for the very high and glaciated passes ahead; now my fears were realised. We would have to do our best but we needed ten days' food if we wanted to complete the journey by the high route. Disappointed, Tashi asked the man, whose name was Krishna and who was the Num shopkeeper, to search the village for what he could get. We too roamed the village succeeding in purchasing five chickens which we dressed and cooked to take with us. We were served a delicious meal by Krishna's wife who had Graeme grinning like a Cheshire cat each time she served him food. With full bellies we went to bed more heartened than we had been on our arrival.

Krishna had organised a porter to carry our extra provisions for a few days — never an easy thing to organise. After considerable negotiation the so-called porter informed us that he was the local mail-runner and that he could not work for us.

Who, then, was or could be our porter? Eventually a burly Tamang fellow (Tamangs are well known for being strongly built and hard workers) willing to carry our load appeared, although not well clad for going into the mountains. He wore the remnants of a cotton shirt, a black cotton waist coat, a multi-coloured Nepali skullcap and a kind of jock-strap. Still he was willing and the first couple of days would not involve any real cold or any snow so off we went down the hillside towards the Arun river, a great brown snake that sliced through the mountains carrying the murky melt waters of the Tibetan Plateau and the Himalaya to the sea. Just above the river we stopped at some houses where we bought more food for our journey and further diminished our monetary reserves by ninety-five rupees. We had a little over 200 rupees ($18) left and the porter still to pay. Despite having several hundred dollars in travellers' cheques, which were of no value whatsoever in the mountains, we had badly miscalculated the amount of Nepali currency that we should have been carrying. With the funds remaining, we were cutting a very fine line; there was little in hand for emergencies.

At one of the houses where we purchased rice and eggs the two sons of the house were wearing white and their heads had been shaven. 'Their father has died,' Tashi told me. The oldest son was an amiable chap. He attempted to demonstrate his grasp of English which easily eclipsed my slender grasp of Nepali. Then, with a degree of pride, he pulled from a pocket an official-looking piece of paper. Typed on it was his name and CLASS SIX... FAILED. He smiled lugubriously at me.

The twin-cable suspension bridge spanned the foaming brown waters of the Arun and, one at a time, we stalked carefully across to the western side and the way to Makalu. For two hours we climbed the hillside through prickly heat and tropical jungle, then past tired and leached fields till we reached the lower perimeter of the village of Sedoa. The sky was black with thunder clouds; and as we approached a house with broad verandahs on two sides the heavens let loose and rain began to fall with monsoonal ferocity.

The lady of the house, who coughed and sneezed and looked tired and miserable, said we could stay for the night but that we had to have our dinner early as some sadhus (holy men) were coming to conduct a puja to rid her of the evil spirits that caused her ailment. Two sadhus duly arrived and set about building a small altar out of bamboo and flowers. For seven hours they recited incantations, they chanted and danced and beat on a drum and a brass plate. At two o'clock in the morning, the ritual reached a crescendo outside on the porch with the woman kneeling, her head lowered, and a thread of cotton leading from her head to the roof and the pale moonlit night outside (presumably the route for the evil spirit to retreat by). The sadhus beat the drum and the plate furiously to a hectic rhythm and performed a violently energetic dance as if they were actively doing battle with some invisible demon, jumping and hopping from side to side in a frenzy of intense spiritualism. Then almost imperceptibly one of them indicated to the woman, mother of twelve, to go inside which she immediately did, closing the doors of the house behind her, leaving the two sadhus to continue their foray with the spirits of evil on the porch. Satisfied the spirit had been vanquished, or certainly evacuated, they ceased their chanting and their dancing and the wild rhythms they beat on the drum and the brass plate. A clear sky stood silent vigil over the village.

The lady of the house looked as bedraggled as when we first met as we paid for our lodgings and trudged up the hillside above the house. Much of the day was spent aimlessly following animal tracks in wet bush, just short of Tashi Gaon, the last little village we would see for two weeks. Here our scantily-clad porter informed us he would go no further as stories of snow beyond Tashi Gaon from porters returning from jobs for mountaineering expeditions had worried him. With good reason: he stood a fair chance of losing more than his toes through frostbite. Fortunately a young Tamang who was more suitably equipped for the conditions ahead was keen to work for us and carry our extra food provisions for three days beyond Tashi Gaon. We had the choice of splitting the extra load between the three of us, or hiring a porter, but we preferred to carry only medium-weight packs so as to assist our acclimatisation and not overstress our bodies. With a porter who knew the way into the Barun valley that leads to Mt Makalu we would not waste any time route finding.

It took us five and a half days to reach Makalu basecamp in the deep snow conditions and inclement weather. From Tashi Gaon we climbed through conifer forests to the snowclad ridges above and in light snow and hail decided to halt early beneath a huge overhanging rock, lined with quartz lenses and stippled with red garnets. It snowed heavily all afternoon so we sat tight drinking brews of green tea while looking out at the large white flakes that chased one and other down in thick flurries. Every so often we would hear muffled voices as a group of porters descended past our bivvy in the snowstorm following the line of footprints back to their villages. They had been carrying loads for the three expeditions presently at Makalu basecamp, our young porter told us.

The following day we climbed the snow-covered tracks of yesterday's travellers to the ridge-top. In the deep, fresh snow we puffed our way to a 15,000-foot pass from where we descended steeply into magnificent fir and rhododendron forests. I was travelling slowly as my right ankle, one I had damaged in a mountaineering accident two years before, was giving me considerable discomfort. It was beginning to worry me as to whether I would be able to cross over into the Mt Everest area by the high passes or even whether I would be able to complete the traverse. The pain that I had experienced all day had been quite acute at times, diminishing my enjoyment of the journey. So somewhat depressed, I limped down to the base of the new valley where a jade-green river flowed over a slabby rock base down the constricted valley floor. Just short of another bivvy rock where we would spend our second night, I was met by Graeme who was on his way back to meet me. 'I've got a surprise for you,' he said, obviously anticipating a reaction. I grimaced. 'We're in the Barun!' he exclaimed.

For some reason, we hadn't expected to reach the Barun valley, the way to Makalu basecamp, so soon, nor as easily. I followed him through a stand of tangled alpine rhododendrons as it began to snow again and beneath a very sizeable bivvy boulder was Tashi lighting a fire. I sat on my pack inside the bivvy, a colossal boulder propped up by lesser boulders and creating the recess in which we crouched. I watched Tashi blowing on the fire. He was always quiet and self-effacing, almost impossible to draw into conversation. I had tried but with his refusal to talk of his family or friends, or to give any opinions it made communication difficult. I suspected he still had reservations about the feasibility of the mammoth challenge we had set ourselves and perhaps still some reservations about Graeme and me. After all, Graeme and I knew each other before the expedition, and Tashi hadn't known either of us from the proverbial "bar of soap" until just a few weeks ago. I suspected his original very spontaneous decision to join the expedition would take some time for him to fully accept, or even to justify to himself.

Tashi is very tough and determined with a wealth of mountaineering experience, and he possesses the tremendous asset of being able to live in uncomfortable and harsh mountain conditions without complaint. Graeme, in many ways, is the opposite. Far from being reticent, he uses his lack of rhetorical inhibition for similar ends, although he, I suspect, barely realises his cover. I thought I had known Graeme quite well before the expedition, but in retrospect, I know our relationship was based on many fairly brief associations as opposed to this already lengthy one. The tensions both during the organisation of the trip in New Zealand and in New Delhi and over the past few weeks in the mountains had been high and not conducive to the early development of a relaxed relationship between us. Consequently, I found that instead of getting to know him better my knowledge of him remained the same. Perhaps only our similar mountaineering aspirations were what had brought us together. Graeme's highly competitive nature possibly helped to cause a difference between us. But then, I know, I'm hardly exempt from a sizeable barrage of idiosyncrasies myself. In a way, we were an ideal team for the rigours and stresses of the journey: all three determined to reach the other end, and each for his own reasons.

We all have our idiosyncrasies. There were small things that irritated me and possibly affected a finely-tuned, lightweight effort such as ours: Graeme's propensity for losing and misplacing things; first his toothbrush, then his spoon and finally this evening beneath the bivvy rock in the Barun valley, he melted one of his plastic climbing boots which he was sitting on while he cooked dinner over the fire. An essential piece of equipment for what lay ahead.

Despite the melted boot which Graeme pressed back into reasonable shape before the plastic cooled sufficiently to set we had a meal, the usual insufficient titbit. Our food fantasies soared to previously unsurpassed heights. We talked at length of what we were going to eat at Kunde or Kathmandu or of Graeme's passion for pork and crackling. Then the words of one of the mountaineers who accompanied Eric Shipton and my father on the Mt Everest reconnaissance came to mind. Food? 'That there should be some.'

It had been another cold night. Feeling stiff and unrested we prepared to leave our first Barun valley bivvy rock. I was sitting on my loaded pack beneath the low sooty rock ceiling, psyching myself into a suitable frame of mind to don my load and begin trudging onward and upward when a small group of porters arrived. They were returning down valley after their load-carrying jobs with the expeditions ensconced above at Hillary basecamp. (Hillary basecamp, as the Sherpas refer to the more popular of two Makalu basecamp sites, being the camp my father first used in 1961 when he led an oxygenless attempt on Makalu after an extensive physiological programme in the Everest area.) There was one young Sherpa and three Sherpanis (young Sherpa women), one of whom had no shoes or socks. Most of her toes were badly frostbitten and blood seeped out from around her toenails; it was obvious that she was in considerable pain. Still, as she warmed her hands over our fire, she put on an impressive show of smiles and laughter at her lot. With another two days of snow-covered country ahead, she stood every chance of losing her feet and in the unhygienic conditions of a hill-country village, with the warm and wet monsoon not too far off, a rampant infection with fatal consequences could well be on the cards. We asked her friends to help her. 'She's holding us up,' they replied.

'At least share your footwear with her.'

'It's her own fault,' came the callous response.

'That may be, but she is your friend so you must help her, she needs your help.'

'We don't know her well. She comes from a different village from us.'

Feeling exasperated and positively hostile towards the three shod, insensitive and inhumane people before us, Graeme gestured to the young Sherpa that he deserved a good hiding. 'She is not my sister, she is not my cousin, nor my mother, nor my wife,' he pleaded pathetically. It was obvious that, whereas we were convinced our humanitarian argument was true, they were satisfied with leaving consequences to fate, the laws of the wild... to God. They apparently decided the warmth of our fire was subdued by the hostility, or perhaps unreasonableness, of those who attended it and stumbled off through the deep snow.

Feeling quite depressed we set off up the valley. The steep forested flanks of the river rose abruptly on both sides to spectacular rock spires, plastered with glistening frozen waterfalls. Higher still were peaks of 22,000 feet, unnamed and unclimbed. I was thrilled to be in the Barun valley, for as the crow flies the Kumbu, the Everest area, is only a short distance to the west. Once we had reached there we would have made a very considerable step in the direction of K2 in Pakistan, our journey's end, and given the whole expedition a real boost of confidence. However, there was some very high country dividing us from the Kumbu... In a way this would be the test for our lightweight and minimally equipped venture.

The valley broadened into snow-covered river flats and pastures with clumps of tall firs scattered along the perimeter. Cloud massed above the forbidding rock walls that bordered the spectacular valley; as time wore on the mist settled on to the treetops and showered us with snow and painful pellets of hail.

At Ni, a conglomeration of tree-covered morainic boulders that afforded shelter from the blizzard, we halted. Leaving our packs beneath the best of the overhanging boulders we went foraging for firewood in the snow-covered forests around the 13,000-foot high bivouac. As we finished our dinner a group of porters arrived from the Hillary basecamp. They were a cheery, tough lot, all wearing the usual cotton shorts, long wool socks and gymshoes in the knee-deep powder snow. Their high spirits and good humour soon failed to inspire us, however, as they nonchalantly removed over half of our firewood including that which was already in the flames so as to light their own fires. My good humour subsided into a dark and irritated state as I fended them off in an attempt to preserve some wood for our planned early-morning departure.

It was still snowing unabated as I rose at 4.30 am to light the fire and prepare breakfast. As the first light began to filter through the cloud to where we lay in our sleeping bags beneath the bivouac rock, I peered out beyond the glistening curtain of icicles that rimmed the overhanging rock, at the flurries of silent but persistently falling snow. At times I could make out the shapes of the tall firs on the other side of the narrow valley, inundated with pillows of snow, just 100 yards away... and I began to wonder whether forging up valley to basecamp would be wise. It was still a full day's march and another 3000 feet to climb. We would arrive wet and cold and with only our tiny tent for shelter it seemed prudent to remain where we were. We swallowed our breakfast of sweet boiled rice without much relish and then watched incredulously as about a dozen porters cooked their food over our fire using the firewood we had collected. Seating themselves unabashed on our gear and sleeping bags they forced the three huddled members of the Himalayan Traverse Expedition further and further from their fire. Eventually they left us to the quiet of the Barun valley, the gently falling snow, the smouldering remains of our fire and our cold, spartan bivouac rock.

The inclement weather was a real concern as our food and fuel reserves were very limited, we counted each and every one of our potatoes and assessed the quantity of uncooked rice. We estimated just how long we could spend in the Barun valley before we would be forced to retreat the way we had come. The alternatives were far from desirable as a low-country route would not only be a less attractive challenge but it would take longer. With our depleted cash reserves we would be reduced to dependence on charity or starve. At the very best, which meant consuming the very least, we could stretch out our rations to last nine days. We needed an acclimatisation period of several days; we needed fine weather for the high passes ahead; we needed reasonable snow conditions and we needed luck.

It was cold all day and with the night even colder. I lay in my bag and watched the moon rise, casting its milky light into the bivvy and causing the domes of powder snow that built up on rocks, branches and tufts of grass outside to glow. Tashi tossed and turned and in the early morning put on his jacket and wriggled nearer the fire place to begin breakfast. For the first time he sat inside his sleeping bag while he cooked our meagre meal. Watching the flames lick higher, I felt warmed by the scene if not by the physical heat of the fire.

'Well, that was a really cold night,' I said to my taciturn comrade.
'Grunt.'
'Did you sleep well?' I continued, a little taken aback.
'Yes.'
One last try. 'Were you warm?'
'Quite O.K.'... End of dialogue.

We walked in deep, cold powder snow, climbing abruptly up through the fir forests into the juniper scrub and then the snow-covered high pastures. The cloud gathered overhead early and we were soon engulfed in white as we plugged on. Occasionally we halted briefly to brew bowls of hot tea and to remove or put on clothing, for temperatures raced from stifling to freezing as the cloud cleared periodically exposing the azure sky. Where the Barun valley veered to the north at about 15,500 feet we halted for an acclimatisation stop below the basecamp. It was interesting how the higher valley enjoyed longer spells of clear sky, with less snow. The temperatures and the ferocity of the winds did not ease in the same way. A freezing cold night followed, with little sleep for three large men squashed into a slim-fitting two-man alpine tent. There was plenty of time for contemplation: my bodily functions and requirements when under extreme conditions and altitude seemed an appropriate field of inquiry. I calculated the amount of fluid I had consumed — I estimated I needed about six litres a day at these elevations and under our present work intensities. Had I eaten sufficient of certain vital foods, salts, and so on; had I taken my vitamin pill; when was my last bowel movement (...now let me see); do I have any altitude-sickness symptoms and are there any ways other than the devious, of lightening my load, decreasing the consequent stress on my acclimatising body and my troublesome ankle?

Eventually we wriggled out of the little tent into the sunshine where we thawed ourselves and set off for the last two hours separating us from the basecamp. Huddled together in a lateral moraine trough, beside the Barun glacier, we found the basecamp at 16,400 feet. A mosaic of brightly coloured tents comprised the three resident expeditions. It was here that many of our sumptuous food fantasies were to be realised. We marched up to the first group of tents: 'Hello.'

There was a muffled, obviously querulous response in German. A man wearing immaculate saloupettes and a smart ski jersey emerged from the largest of the tents.

'Hello,' said he, 'you have just arrived here?'

'Yes,' and we went on to explain why, and why there was not a cavalcade of porters, cooks and high-altitude Sherpas trailing along behind us. Suddenly the tent behind began to shake as somebody made a frenzied attempt to extract himself. A very unhappy and unwell man stumbled out and oblivious to our little gathering, pushed past us. He disappeared behind the tent from where groans and pained sounds of dry-reaching emerged. 'He is sick; he has the altitude sickness.'

They were planning to take him down to a lower elevation in the morning. He desperately needed the change as soon as possible. We were invited to dinner — no doubt we looked at least as hungry as we felt — so we left the friendly Germans to go looking for a site to pitch our tiny tent. It was with some incredulity that the members and Sherpas observed us as we pitched the tent and rolled out our lightweight sleeping bags to air.

'This is all you have?'

A large noodle stew was served up by the reluctant cook to Franz, Luis and Martin, our German hosts, who displayed a distinct lack of enthusiasm for the meal.

'We don't like this type of food. Next time I will bring *all* the food from Germany!'

We all laughed... Graeme, Tashi and I had finished our second large serving of the "sumptuous" noodle stew while they sat twiddling their forks, twisting noodles around the prongs, psyching themselves with apparent difficulty into each mouthful. After the evening's repast, the first large meal we had enjoyed for many days, we sauntered through the camp, hands in pockets, bellies distended to where the Anglo-Polish expedition's camp was. They were attempting the formidable and unclimbed western wall of Makalu. We stood outside chatting with Alex MacIntyre and Voytek and their team-mates until the fading light drew the silver column of mercury in their thermometer to below the $-15\,°C$ marking. We all filed towards one of the tents. Before going inside I stood in the biting cold air and looked north, across the broad expanse of the moraine-coated jumble of ice of the Barun

glacier to Makalu's immense south face. Just a brush of pink tinged the summit pyramid nearly 12,000 feet above me as the sun shone for a brief last instant on the few rock and ice summits that penetrate the exclusive 8000 metres echelon. The basecamp site is an awesome place — huge glaciers and moraines, and even more gigantic are the mountains that surround it, making the scale difficult to grasp. A shrinking of self by mammoth grandeur.

There was a large selection of music cassettes with a compact stereo tape recorder to render incongruous sounds to the cold mountain air, a few nips of Polish vodka, a whole plate of delectable chocolates that held our eyes firmly until we felt satisfied. Rowdy debates and discussions continued till 11 pm when the batteries in the tape recorder became weak from the power output and the intense cold. We meandered, rosy cheeked, back to the nylon sardine-can of a tent into which we fitted ourselves for another cold and cramped night.

We spent three more days at the Hillary basecamp below Makalu's massive pale gold south wall, preparing ourselves for the highest crossings of our whole trans-Himalayan journey. We needed to acclimatise so as to increase our performance at over 20,000 feet on Far East Col and West Col and to minimise the dangers and discomforts of altitude sickness. Graeme had a slight headache, the most common symptom of cerebral oedema (a type of altitude sickness) and we would all need the absolutely minimal few days at the basecamp to give our bodies a chance to adjust. One's haemaglobin count increases with proper acclimatisation and facilitates a more efficient absorption of oxygen from the less dense air. This process would not be complete in three days, but it would be under way. Being pressured to get moving by our diminished food resources and being a week overdue for our rendezvous with the support team in Kunde village in the Everest region — just beyond the lofty snowclad barricades above the Hillary basecamp — we could not delay for too long. Living at altitude is a rather extraordinary experience as the effort involved in all physical exertion is grossly magnified. Crawling out of our little tent requires a bout of deep breathing to regain breath; talking has to be liberally staccatoed with deep breathing and any very energetic activity like climbing or running requires deep and rapid inhalations and exhalations — not unlike hyperventilation — and lengthy periods of deep breathing to regain one's breath. Once accustomed to the thinner atmosphere it is no longer an alarming sensation; in fact, I find the thin, cold air exhilarating and coupled with the setting of the world's highest mountains, an ecstatic experience.

There was plenty to do. The stove needed attention and all our grimy kerosene fuel had to be filtered through precious sheets of toilet paper. Boots needed drying, clothing and sleeping bags had to be aired, crampons checked and adjusted and the rapidly diminishing food stocks reassessed.

It interested me how my passion for eating, although unaltered as far as my desire to consume was concerned, had suffered a complete change in emphasis. Whereas at home eating is for taste and pleasure because food is so easy to procure, here food is survival and the quality seldom causes one to wax lyrical. As if these philosophical thoughts were being portrayed clearly on a 'day-dream cloud' floating just above my head Franz came over and told us we could have some food from them if we needed it.

'Well, actually, Franz... yes.'

'I'm sorry we can't give you much,' he added apologetically and returned to their mess tent to sort some rations for us.

I looked into the large cardboard box with disbelief. Salamis, muesli, canned peaches, biscuits and so on, all of which qualified very definitely for a celebration... haute cuisine! In classical ancient Roman style we gorged shrunken stomachs till my uncontrolled gluttony led me aside to squat ashamedly behind our tent and deliver a partially digested epistle on the evils of greed to the alpine tundra.

With our food dilemma solved for the time being, we counted what money remained in order to pay Franz for the food. It was an optimistic exercise as the coffers were all but bare. Thirty-nine rupees ($3) wouldn't pay for even half a salami so we insisted that we would see them in Kathmandu, repay them there and go out on the town for a dinner together. Our running short of money was nothing less than very poor organisation, and I was annoyed with myself, with us, for our having been so remiss on a commodity as vital and useful as "cash in the hand". Money was really the only backup we had if some gruesome contingency arose... an accident where a lot of manpower and money was needed to evacuate the injured.

We worried for the Germans a little as their Sherpas were the most belligerent and uncooperative lot I'd met for a long time. Their sirdar resented our being befriended and the cook on purpose wasted as much food as he could so that when it all was gone he could go home — which he wanted to do as soon as possible. He made enormous containers of rice, dal and potatoes and persistently threw about half of it over the moraine wall to the glacier 500 feet below. The waste was particularly upsetting to us as on such matters as food we had become very frugal. We took turns at scraping the pots for tit-bits and licking the wrappers of our dehydrated food supplies. So embittered did the Germans' Sherpas become towards us that their sirdar attempted to solicit Tashi into abandoning us on the high passes — possibly to our deaths — and return to the basecamp where he would pay him a large sum. Fortunately for the young sirdar, Tashi didn't recall this story until we were a day's march beyond the basecamp. Even then Graeme and I wondered if a quiet chat with the pathetic young man was not in store.

On the second day we headed up the Barun glacier's lateral moraine to the Japanese Baruntse Expedition's Camp I at just over 17,000 feet. A superb day with Lhotse and Lhotse Shar dominating the head of the valley and Makalu's spectacular pyramid form towering above us... an unreachable zenith... an abode for gods. It was mid-afternoon when we returned from our acclimatisation climb, our minds laden with the distinctly non-cheery discussions that Graeme and I had been having. Our personalities and our feelings were far from synchronised and there was considerable discord between us which made Tashi unhappy and sullen. The altitude, our acclimatising, our having had only small meals before reaching the basecamp, the generally poor weather, our cramped tent all made us scratchy and irritable. In addition Graeme had lost alarming pounds for someone not over-endowed with weight in the first place.

On the fifth day after having reached the basecamp we took down the tent, packed our few chattels into our rucksacks and retraced our steps along the cairned route on the Barun moraines to the Japanese Camp I. Light snow fell with shafts of sunlight beaming through a patchwork of transitory blue above, highlighting the large flakes as they floated lazily to the bare morainic boulders. The Japanese doctor was at the little camp and allowed us to use one of their spacious dome tents for the night and thus help speed our departure the following day. Our stove continued to give problems and we were apprehensive about its functioning over the next few crucial days. I spent much time that night pondering the gruelling nature of our journey — how different it was from the more orthodox Himalayan expeditions. The standard expedition comes to a single objective, a particular route on a particular mountain and spends never more than three months, often less than two months, on the objective. There's always a tangible end in sight. The activities are usually vigorous for only a few days at a time, spaced out with periods of comfort and leisure at an established basecamp. Our journey across the Himalayas was long — very, very long; the end was so far removed that it was impossible to visualise an end to the 5000-kilometre quest to cross the world's highest mountain range; with most of the journey still to come, I began to wonder if we ever would. Day in, day out we drove ourselves onward, westward. Often short on food due to our load limitations; cold unending nights in our tiny tent; scavenging for firewood when dead-tired at the end of a long hard day or coaxing the obstinate stove to burn; this marathon adventure was lining itself up to be the toughest undertaking of my life.

I was extremely cold. I lay in my sleeping bag sneaking glances at my watch, waiting for the fateful moment when I would have to rise and coax our obstinate stove into life and somehow create an early morning cuisine. As the minute hand moved towards half past four I tugged at the toggle of my sleeping bag and stuck my head and shoulders out into the biting cold, trying to console myself that at least I had something to do. Anything, surely, was preferable to reclining in my sleeping bag like an Egyptian mummy, chilled, watching the luminescent hands of my watch troop stoically around its face waiting for the sun's warmth to thaw the tent — a hall of frozen condensation. I groped for the matches and one of the two candle stubs we possessed and lit it. The waxen light filled the Japanese dome tent and immediately made me feel a little warmer with the prospect of the stove's roar and a piping hot cup of tea to come. I lit another match and primed the belligerent contraption before easing the fuel valve open. A burst of yellow flame leapt from the burner, filling the frozen tent with a golden glitter refracted through the innumerable condensation ice crystals coating the inside of the geodesic dome. The stove coughed and spluttered and my mood turned from a pleading wish for combustion to annoyance and an oath. I mean, just as we planned to attempt three of the most difficult passes of the journey, a crossing which, with our food and monetary situation we could ill afford to fail upon, our stove decided to bring its short but colourful history of Guy Fawkes spectaculars and its long line of quirks and idiosyncrasies to a crescendo... and at 4.30 am at over 17,000 feet and I-don't-know-how-many-degrees below zero!

With the burner surging and dying, I melted some snow in the billy and produced a cup of tea for my mates, who lay in apparent rigor mortis beside me, and then heated some cold boiled potatoes. We wanted to devour most of the heavy foods to lighten our loads for the climb to the Japanese Camp II site at 19,000 feet where we intended to spend the night before crossing the 20,500-foot Far East Col and the West Col en route to the head of the Hongu valley. From there there was one more difficult pass and we would be in the Kumbu, land of Mt Everest and the Sherpas.

The sun, like a wave of good news, spread its warmth and enthusiasm over the tent at 6.10 am and from it we crawled to attend to the calls of nature and to pack away our gear. A last look around to check we had all our few chattels and we began, solemnly, the hike up the boulder gully to the next camp. Like well-disciplined troops we climbed in single file making the deep, regular breaths that must accompany any exertion at altitude, each of us drifting off into his own daydream mesmerised by the constancy of our pacing forward and upward. As we climbed, Makalu's west ridge elongated and sharpened, its direct, razor-fine line sweeping down the centre of Makalu's majestic south-western aspect. I could see that the wind was blowing strongly high on the mountain and from those lofty ramparts came the fearsome roar of wind on rock and ice... and in the lee, like a graceful mime of wild energy, hung a plume of flowing wisps, undulating in slow unhurried motion; a great mountain's elegant banner.

Graeme developed a headache as we approached 19,000 feet, Tashi was as usual 'Quite O.K.' and I was more than happy to halt and unload a couple of cans of sardines that the Germans had given us for an en route snack. It was a magnificently clear day with the mountains all around set against the blue sky, clear as a bell. Another 100 metres up the slope we plugged in the wind-blown snow to where the angle of the slope lay back into a glacial basin and there before us was the Japanese Camp II.

A cold westerly wind blew as we huddled into the camp cook-tent where the resident cook, Gurung, offered cups of tea and told us of the Japanese expedition's progress. Today, we were told, they were hoping to establish a route to the Far East Col and beyond on to the lower Barun glacier. We were delighted at this news as it would mean that much of the route we would be taking was already plugged through the deep snow. With luck, it would hasten our crossing of the two big passes we planned for the next day. As we enthused on our good fortune, Gurung filled bowls with a delicious noodle and vegetable concoction and handed them to us.

'What's this?' we asked a shade too anticipatory.

'Break-a-fast. Members not much liking. Not eating.' We most assuredly did.

To one side of the camp the three of us dug out a platform in the snow on which we pitched the tent; retreating then to its restrictive but sheltered confines for an afternoon of R. & R. and retreat from the incessant blast of the westerly. By evening the members of the Japanese team returned to the camp tired and wind burned, their faces red and blistered. We all crowded into the cook-tent while we were told of their six-hour dilemma plugging in thigh-deep snow to the Far East Col. There were open crevasses and the possibility of our taking two days to reach the Hongu. But the leader, a tough, martial-looking man, assured us that with the good meal he was going to give us behind our belts, we would have no trouble reaching the Hongu valley in one day. It was a super evening and it confirmed yet again for me the tremendous rapport between mountaineers, people involved in extending themselves physically and mentally, partners in a game of calculated risk.

I suppose it's a finely drawn line that separates your physical condition from your psychological state, but whatever it is, it was right. I felt strong and elated. I took the lead plugging the steps above the camp, up the little glacier towards Far East Col. The wind had blown strongly all night and the Japanese team's trail of the previous day had been drifted in with wind-blown snow. By staying on the same line I found I only sank into the snow six or twelve inches — most of the time! Graeme had a bad headache and looked off colour; Tashi was hardly a ball of uncontrolled energy so I cheerfully took it upon myself to break the trail and get us all to the Hongu.

Two hours of steady plugging and climbing saw me sitting on a slab of pale, coarse-grained rock, studded with hornblende crystals atop the narrow Far East Col with steep 100-metre drops on both sides. I sipped from my waterbottle and waited for the others to ascend the fixed rope the Japanese had put in the previous day, spanning 100 metres of precipitous bluff above the glacier from where we had come. To the west I gazed longingly at the Kumbu. Yep, I was headed back to old and familiar and much-loved country. Across the broad snowy sweep of the West Col rose Tangnag Tsen (Peak 43), Kangtega, and a maze of unnamed summits, all white frosted and fresh against the blue morning sky. Tashi, followed by Graeme, climbed the fixed ropes and emerged before me on the narrow col. We all sat briefly gazing eastward at the formidable triangular bulk of Makalu, then west at the halo of delicate snow and ice peaks that encircle the head of the winter-bound Hongu valley from our 20,500-foot-high vantage point on the Far East Col. Then it was all action — the freezing cold wind left little choice in the matter — as we hastily strapped crampons to our boots for the descent down the western, icy flank from the col. At the base of the steep flank we jumped across a partially snow-filled bergschrund and waded in deep snow on to the lower Barun glacier, a colossal stretch of gently undulating, unbroken and untouched white.

'The snow looks horrendously deep,' and that astute observation proved to be quite correct as I plugged across the smooth roll of the glacier's snow-bound surface. There was a long way to go to get to West Col and in these conditions and at this altitude progress was destined to be slow. A degree of urgency had entered our crossing of these two high passes as Graeme was developing symptoms of pulmonary and cerebral oedema: he felt weak and listless and had a piercingly painful headache. Tashi also was feeling off colour and as I felt O.K. a sense of mission filled me as I realised the onus was on me. I forged a meandering line of steps through the deep wind-crusted powder snow following a line of bamboo marker poles, posted sporadically across the glacier by a previous Mt Baruntse expedition. The conditions were very cold; the bitter wind forced us to don our one-piece oversuits and the freezing powder snow kept my toes only in vague communication with my master-switch. I took as many photographs as I could of our journey across to West Col, of Graeme and Tashi, their forms obliterated from their thighs down by the drifting snow and Makalu towering over our insignificant presence with cold impartiality.

Graeme was dragging his feet from plug hole to plug hole, his mirror glasses, perched on his burnt nose, down turned and his hollow cheeks draped with his frozen beard. I really was becoming concerned, both about Graeme and the expedition as a whole.

At the broad, smooth plain of West Col I watched Graeme stagger over the pass and, unerring, plod downward toward the frozen Arctic expanse of the head of the Hongu valley. There was one thing in his mind... go down, go down. Tashi followed while I packed away my cameras and then set off after a last gaze at Makalu. The wide and fortunately firm snow slope steepened rapidly and we were soon backing down, foot first, on the front points of our crampons. Looking down between my boots, I could not see the whole face as it arched ever steeper below me for 2000 feet. I caught up with Tashi who was moving very carefully, and as I came alongside him he muttered: 'Stay with me'.

'God, I hope he's O.K.,' I thought. This was not the place for problems. I looked down again at Graeme, his body superimposed against the glacier 2000 feet below, as he descended, then traversed left towards a rock outcrop that protruded through the steep ice. He seemed all right. I chatted to Tashi as we kicked in our front points, driving our ice axes into the firm snow and ice above our heads for security before taking another step downward — nearer the Hongu valley, one step closer to lower altitude. Then I heard a noise. Looking down Graeme had stopped and gesticulated with one hand for us to move further left. He didn't move. We descended till we were off to his left side hanging on our front points and axes on fifty-degree water ice with an annoying dusting of powder snow frozen to its icy surface.

'Can you give me a hand? My crampon has come off.'

I crossed carefully to where Graeme clung to his axe and one useful crampon hold and, poised tenuously on my crampons, chipped out a small and narrow step in the green ice for his foot so that he could rectify matters. The crampon was soon lashed on to his boot properly and we continued our descent into the vast basin of winter-whiteness and silence, the Hongu. Once on the glacier, we stopped to nibble biscuits and sip the last of our water and stare up at the West Col blazing against the blue sky 2000 feet above. Graeme still had a bad headache but was feeling much healthier than he had an hour earlier. This he proceeded to demonstrate by wading out in front down the glacier, pushing his way through the bottomless powder snow. All I could think of was skis and wide, lazy giant slalom turns as we meandered down towards the snow-covered moraines and frozen lakes of the valley. With the sun dipping behind a serrated skyline of peaks we pitched the tent on a frozen pond on the glacier, squeezing inside with a glowing triumphant feeling about the day.

As we made our way down the glacier, we realised we had simply not spent sufficient time acclimatising at Hillary basecamp and we were now paying for it with pain and discomfort and reduced physical performance. We decided to spend another night in the Hongu near one of the frozen "panch pokari" lakes which would be at a lower altitude and would hopefully prove beneficial for our altitude-induced discomforts. Following one behind the other we had been wending our way through the moraines, folds of ice and deep moulins when Tashi, in his usual indirect and uncomplaining way, queried us about sore eyes. A quick look at his eyes was sufficient for even a layman's diagnosis of snow blindness as they were red and swollen. He conceded that they were uncomfortable so without further ado Doctors Dingle and Hillary taped up the sides of his snow glasses and administered eyedrops to ease the suffering.

Another hour and we reached the far side of the glacier where we camped by a frozen stream near one of the frozen lakes. The day was still young as we melted snow over the stove that was cooperating rather better as Graeme had dismantled it — almost a pre-use ritual now — and cleaned the components. Again our food reserves were getting very low and we had only one litre of kerosene fuel left for the stove. What with our minimal thirty-nine rupees and forty paise, our particularly isolated location in the frozen snowbound wastes of the remote Hongu valley I felt a growing sense of commitment to our intended crossing of the difficult Amu Laptsa pass the next day. If the weather turned foul and forced us to retreat down valley, life would conceivably become very miserable as even by the low route there would be two high, although easier, passes to cross to reach a semblance of civilisation. We would certainly run out of food; a day and a half of light, yet sufficient rations remained. Our fuel in snow conditions would last perhaps three days and when we did reach habitation we had only "chicken feed" cash reserves with which to purchase food. Added to that the discomforts and ailments of Graeme and Tashi and our present isolation left us with only one conclusion. We must cross the treacherous Amu Laptsa pass and we must cross tomorrow.

At a quarter to three, with my red windsuit on and feeling as if I was bundled in a cocoon, I plugged steps up to a little pass above our camp leaving Graeme and Tashi to the comparative spaciousness of our slim-fitting two-man tent without the third occupant. A layer of grey alto-stratus spread a drab and rather introspective mood on the day as I climbed up to the pass past a large cairn that stood in lonely vigil amidst drifts of deep snow. A hundred metres beyond, nestled beneath a ring of low hills and razor-edged peaks as level as a bowling green, lay the albescent stillness of a frozen lake. No waves lapping on the shore, a hush broken only by the chilling westerly draught that streamed across the hibernating waters, tugging at my windsuit and encouraging me to keep moving. I thought I would go as far as I could, plug a line of steps we could use tomorrow, identify the pass and the route to take to reach it. Conditions would have to be abominable before I would turn back on tomorrow's attempt to cross the Amu Laptsa.

I forged on in the deep, wind-compacted snow across the southern end of the lake and up the far side over mounds of treacherous snow-covered boulders to the crest of a gentle rise. On the south side the snow petered out and I moved quickly, skirting an old morainic hillside till I was due south of the Amu Laptsa, the final barrier between us and the Sherpa villages of the Everest region. There are many stories about this pass; of fatalities, its steepness and difficulty and of avalanches and rockfall. My quick appraisal of the rocky niche in the jagged armour of craggy peaks that divides the Hongu from the Imja Kola was that although it looked quite steep it did not look too difficult.

It would be dark soon so I retraced my steps to the tent. All the way I kept looking behind me and around any large boulders as I had a strange and uncanny feeling that I was not alone. No footprints, no sounds... just the wind and the drifting snow. The tent appeared before me in the dimming light, a speck of yellow in the monotone landscape and as I drew nearer the aromas of our evening meal wafted from within.

I coaxed the stove into life in the early morning darkness, melting snow to fill our water bottles and to make tea and porridge. The tea wouldn't be very strong as we were re-stewing yesterday's tea-leaves since our supply was exhausted. By 7 am, we were following the tracks I had made the previous evening and climbing towards the frozen lake. We traversed the hillside beyond and dropped into a series of shallow vales and troughs all well endowed with very, very deep wind-crusted snow. I would try to raise myself on to the heavy crust but once my thigh reached horizontal, I would crash through the collapsing plates of crust, sinking in up to my waist... again. Across another frozen lake at the foot of the pass I crashed through the deep and obstinate snow using the same demoralising and exhausting technique. When it was too deep to get my foot on to the crust, I used my whole body to break the crust and then plug a route along the hollow my body had made. On a large boulder at the base of the rubble screes leading to the pass I waited for the others. Graeme was looking very ill. He had a pounding headache and felt weak and lethargic.

'How are you feeling?' he asked me. We had about 2000 feet of moraines and steeply inclined rubble to climb to reach the Amu Laptsa and it was going to be hard work at this altitude.

'Pretty good,' I replied.

'Do you think you could take some of my gear?'

I could hardly believe it, as for Graeme to concede his physical condition was less than par, regardless of the odds, was unheard of. I knew he must be very sick... we had to cross this pass and reach lower altitudes.

Up the moraines and on to the slopes above of tumbled blocks of rock we climbed infatuated with our own breathing rhythms; sucking in a lung full of air and blasting it out with a hiss. One's mind locked on a repetitive track, careful not to upset the rhythm and throw the delicate respiratory balance into disarray — a spate of gasps to rectify any imbalance. As I approached the top of the pass, I was able to look from the Arctic scenes of the Hongu across at the greatest mountain wall in the world. The lofty ridge connecting Mt Nuptse and Mt Lhotse stood naked and imposing exposing its folded and faulted geology, too bold and steep for any burden of snow. The huge wall stands 27,800 feet high and is five miles long, making man's building efforts like the Great Wall of China seem in comparison like a flimsy bamboo trellis. The blackness of Lhotse's jagged summit was pitched starkly against the blue sky with a constantly distorting scarf of rushing white cloud whipping from its crown. Dumbfounded by the aura of this savage mountain I drew my eyes away and looked about me. The horrendous stories about the Amu Laptsa (19,000 feet) suddenly began to make sense. The pass dropped vertically from where I stood, the angle easing out progressively, into a steep snow-filled gully that spilled out on to a small and broken glacier about 3000 feet below.

'How the hell do we descend this?'

Looking west along the ridgeline I saw a possible descent route. A steep arete dropped away into the gully below. It didn't look an easy descent but after scrutinizing all other possibilities — and they were a vertiginous bunch — it was clearly the only really feasible route. The others reached the pass so

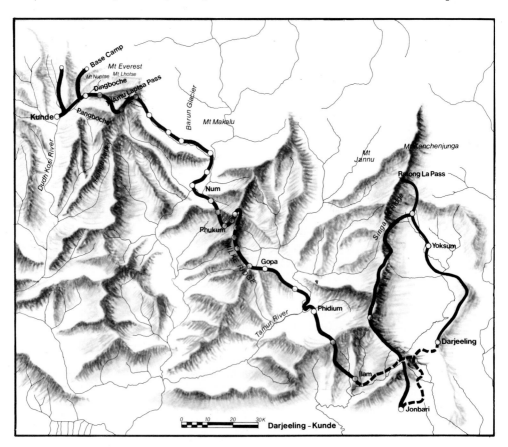

we sat on the knife-edged col with the vertical drop to the north and the steep rubble plummeting below to the frozen Hongu valley to the south and finished the water in our bottles. We prepared ourselves for the descent strapping on crampons and donning oversuits and mits with our technical climbing gear at the ready. Following the divide ridge we scrambled along until we were directly above the steep arete where, using the rope, I set up a belay.

First Graeme, then Tashi lowered themselves gingerly over the corniced lip of the ridgeline, and with the rope taut reversed down the steep face, kicking their feet into the slope and sending waves of cold, dry snow down into the gully. Then it was my turn; but I would have to descend the top section without a top rope and as any belay from below would be superfluous, I would have to rely on my holds and the toeholds left by the others. With my arms over the top of the cornice, I lowered my feet towards the face that plunged away below for 3000 feet. Steady, Peter, steady. I felt the snow beneath my boots and scratched with my crampons to locate the steps made by Tashi and Graeme. Carefully, I lowered myself into them and with a sigh of relief sunk the pick of my axe into the slope. Looking down there was Tashi, holding the rope, and Graeme looking up watching the descent. I reversed down the face to them and together we descended into the gully.

The gully was windslabbed and every so often our footprints caused large plates of surface snow to break loose and slide rapidly down the slope and out of sight. There was a definite avalanche danger so we kept to the perimeter so that, should the slope break loose, we stood the best chance of jumping clear. Towards the bottom the gully opened out into a fan that spilled over a large bergschrund and on to another long slope, crevassed in places, that led to the glacier below. Down one side of the bergschrund we found a twenty-foot section down which we were able to climb, lowering ourselves down the seventy to eighty-degree ice with our axes, holding our weight on the front points of our crampons. A final jump from the ice wall over the crevasse at the base and we reached the glaciated slope that would lead us to the glacier and the valley floor.

We moved quickly down the snowslabbed slope, winding around crevasses and avalanche debris. I paced across a steepening in the face and could feel the hollow thud of my steps on the windslab surface and... thwack! The slope around me broke loose, catching both Tashi and me. I lost my footing and fell among the blocks of windslab that gathered momentum as it slid down the slope towards the glacier still far below. We were both swimming in an attempt to stay on top of the small avalanche; wondering what would happen next. The slide rumbled towards a rock outcrop; it might either be stopped there, enabling us to escape, or we could be scraped over the rocks. Still floundering on the slabs we hit the outcrop. Much to my relief the avalanche slowed and then halted, setting solid as it did so. Both Tashi and I extradited ourselves from the chaos, took a glimpse back up the slope at the clean break in the snow crust which had caused the avalanche and decided that the best thing for us was to keep moving!

We joined Graeme who was off to one side and had watched

apprehensively as his mates were being swept away before his eyes. Reunited, we rushed down to the glacier, happy that the windslab had not been far larger and much faster... as the debris of other avalanches in the vicinity indicated some had been.

On the far side of the little glacier and out of harm's way, we sat on the lateral moraine rubble and removed our crampons. We had done it. We were in the Kumbu and in one piece. With luck, we would find the support team somewhere in the Imja valley in which we had just arrived and Graeme felt we would find them quite soon. The thought of it was a treat. Food, money, letters and good vibrations. They would probably be worried about us, initiating a search perhaps as we were now eight days overdue. We stumbled on over the moraines and on to the high, sparsely-grassed pastures, scanning the valley ahead, searching for any signs of tents or people. Eventually, we reached the vast Imja glacier that flows east-west along the base of the Nuptse/Lhotse wall. Then we struck west following the vegetated lateral moraine trough. Nowhere did we see any signs of recent human visitation. We moved mechanically, our throats dry and limbs tired; we needed rest and plenty of it too. Yet foremost in our minds was relief — we had left the claustrophobic confines of the narrow Barun and Hongu valleys, we had crossed the three passes that barred the Kumbu from us and now we could reach Kunde village for a well-deserved rest.

By a chuckling stream of fresh, cold water we pitched the tent on a grass-covered flat in the lateral moraine valley. Graeme was completely exhausted and both Tashi and I were close to being on our last legs as we lay in the tent slurping down our dinner before drifting off into a deep sleep beneath a bright, starfilled sky and the ghostly shapes of great mountains, the mountains of the Kumbu.

A fresh, clear day sparkled around us as we dried and aired the tent and sleeping bags and, feeling much better for a good night's sleep, prepared ourselves for reunion with the support team — presumably at Dingboche village just two hours' march away — and humanity in general.

We washed our faces in the freezing cold water and tried to scratch some of the pot black off our grubby hands with river gravel; and we combed our hair with the communal comb. Looking positively dapper we slung our packs on to our backs (they were now only ten to twelve kilograms in weight) and marched briskly down the Imja valley. No more worries about weather and high passes for the meantime and a night at only 16,000 feet had all three of us in high spirits. We passed porters and yaks laden with firewood and equipment for a Spanish expedition attempting Lhotse Shar, passed the summer village of Chukum and pressed on through scented alpine pastures scattered with juniper and azalea bushes. As Dingboche village came into view our pace quickened and we scanned the dry, brown potato fields with their fragile dry stone walls for the support team's tents. Not a sign.

'They could be staying in a hotel or a house,' I suggested. 'I think I'd rather stay inside a cosy house,' I added, momentarily forgetting Graeme's sensitivity about his tents.

Enquiries at Dingboche produced many possibilities: they had gone to basecamp, they had gone up the Imja, they left yesterday, they had never come here, they are attempting Mt Everest... it seemed that all foreigners fitted the description of our support party. There was only one sensible path of action for us to take — the path down valley to Kunde village.

An early lunch of boiled potatoes and tea put us in good form for the race down valley, following the turbulent course of the Dudh Kosi river. As we pounded along the dusty, tourist-infested track towards Tangboche, I made another fiscal computation: we had seventeen rupees and forty paise remaining. At Duwoche, below Tangboche monastery, we stopped for tea at Ang Kanchi's teashop. While Ang Kanchi's elderly mother plied us with cups of sickly, sweet tea a tall, lanky fellow strode through the door.

'Aaah! I thought those three packs meant something?' It was Mal Clarborough, a friend from New Zealand, presently directing the establishment of the Sagarmatha National Park, the park of the Everest area. He assured us that the support team was indeed ensconced in Kunde village at Mingma Tsering, my father's sirdar's house, and that they were a little concerned about our whereabouts as we were long overdue. S.P. especially had consistently pleaded for e.t.a.'s, detailed route plans and schedules. He considered this alpine-style business a joke... like a passing phase of adolescence.

Fortunately, Mal paid for the tea so, still with a few coins in pocket, we continued up the hill through the birches to Tangboche monastery, a large two-tier building with red ochre walls, surrounded by prayer flags and walls of mani stones inscribed with Buddhist prayers. We crossed the broad green pasture before the monastery, the centre of the Sherpas' Lamaistic Buddhist religion. Passing conglomerations of brightly coloured trekking tents and groups of tourists parading in fancy tight-fitting knickerbockers, fairisle jerseys and gaudy duvets we descended, without delay, the 3000 feet to the Dudh Kosi river. Up the far side of the valley we climbed with our now only five rupees and forty paise, three small sachets of dehydrated food and one match stick only, regaining 13,00 feet. In the dimming light and cold of evening we reached Kunde Sherpa village. A maze of stone-walled, two-storied houses with slabs of stone and wood for tiles on their roofs surrounded by bare, brown paddocks cordoned off with dry stone walls. Above, a forest of firs that gave way to junipers and then to the desiccated hues of golden brown grasses; dark rock buttresses loomed above the village nestled in the hollow of a long departed glacier. We marched across a field where some boys were playing ball when one of them hurled himself at me, throwing his arms around me, hugging me enthusiastically. 'Temba!' My father's sirdar's oldest son, the deaf mute, the artist, the happy face. Temba led us jubilantly along the narrow path through the potato fields to Mingma's house, where the hugging routine really swung into action. S.P. threw his arms around us and grinned from ear to ear. 'Well done,' he cried. A welcoming hug from Ann Louise and Doug's 'look a man in the eyes and wring him by the hand'. Corrina emerged from the house with tears in her eyes and sidled up towards Graeme and then came Ang Dooli, Mingma's wife, with tears in her eyes too. She reached out her hands and touched my cheeks, 'You not coming; we not knowing,' she said softly. Tiny Ang Dooli, with her long black braids, striped woollen aprons and turquoise jewellery, who I've known since I was seven years old, has long been like an aunt, my Himalayan aunt. It had been a long and hard thirty days since Karkarvitta and it was wonderful to be with them all again. We went inside and sat around a cosy fire sipping tea, chatting excitedly, reading mail — contact with another world — and as it grew late, we retired to some comfortable beds knowing there was no need to go anywhere in the morning.

Mounts Amadablam, Kangtega and Tamserku dominated the horizon with their spectacular forms as we pitched tents and made ourselves thoroughly comfortable. There was repair work to be done on some of our gear, and a lot of sorting through our support supplies. I pitched my tent in front of Mingma's house on the stone tiled porch and then walked across to the house. I opened the heavy wooden door with a screech, and stepped carefully into the darkness, walking past the family's yaks that munched away on leaves and grass in their basement home, waiting to be taken out to graze, and clambered up the steep flight of steps that led to the top storey. There was a walled-off kitchen, in part open to the sky and a haven for catching warm sunlight, a large communal room, dimly lit, with an entire wall shelved and cluttered with the family treasures. Locked chests and magnificent brass and copper water vessels, pots and pans. A long settee lined the opposite side beneath the windows. In the corner sat Temba, his head bent low as he concentrated on a painting, making the fine and time-consuming dashes of his paintbrush that characterise Tibetan Lamaistic Buddhist art. Over his legs was draped a heavy wool blanket, he sat cross-legged and intent on his work, a shaft of light penetrating the dusty window to where he worked. He was oblivious to my presence until I called loudly his name, 'Temba.' 'Ahaah!' he responded and grinned happily, gesturing for me to come over and look at his work. I've seen his paintings improve over the years, and it's a thrill to look at his present work, the pride he takes in it and his success at selling it, giving him a sense of worth and security. In Sherpa society people like Temba are called 'kooa' and are treated like fools. Temba is a highly intelligent being who is deaf and consequently has not learned to speak. I looked through a window that opened into the main kitchen/living room and Mingma and Ang Dooli's bedroom. A cosy enclosure in the corner of the house where the warmth of the juniper, fir and yak dung fire is concentrated, the seats are soft and comfortable, covered with beautiful Tibetan carpets. Ang Dooli was cooking by the fire so I went through to join her. She smiled as I entered while she stirred a pot on the clay and stone wood stove. We chatted about the traverse, about her sons and their education and about when my father Ed, and Mingma, were due in Kunde.

'I thinking, soon coming,' she said.

Later, I worked in my tent in front of the house listening to Temba going off to the water pipe to collect water for the household in a five-gallon jerry can. Later in the afternoon, I heard him herding the yaks back from the pastures above the village and into the basement of the house, the place where the winter's firewood is kept, the yaks live and a year's supply of potatoes are stored in deep pits in the ground. With a growing season of barely three months, production and storage of food is of vital importance.

Over the days we spent in Kunde we attempted to iron out the teething problems of the expedition, coordination of the traverse party and the support group, overdue and emergency procedures and what we expected to have waiting for us at each rendezvous. High on my list of priorities was cash reserves, in small denominations of local currency! Numerous meetings ensued where we discussed objectives, policy — not unlike the parliamentary process — and expressed our various points of view. The meeting sessions seemed to confirm my fears; talk breeds talk rather than action. We were getting nowhere with decision-making and tempers were raised and yet, despite the volatile atmosphere, we ploughed on demonstrating an increasingly great capacity for procrastination.

Perhaps it was all a subconscious attempt to stall the inevitable continuation of our journey. Graeme had lost thirteen kilograms and we all needed lots of good food and rest. But with about 4500 kilometres to go convalescence had to be kept to a minimum. The endless philosophical and logistical rhetoric continued with greater than ever fluidity; would there ever be an end to it? Like waves in a bathtub radiating across the surface of the water they reach the far side where they rebound unchanged and obstinately intent on reaching the opposite side... again. I felt particularly isolated and lonely. The expedition divided itself into exclusive cliques within which all members of the cliques had to share identical views. There was a natural pairing off for Doug and Ann Louise and for Graeme and Corrina, but I doubt whether they realised, most especially the latter couple, how their exclusiveness and tendency to jettison an "esprit de corps" affected the other expedition members. I don't believe that the presence of women in itself contributed to our problems but, with any interaction between human beings, there must be compromise and sensitivity to the other's feelings. On both counts, in my view, we were all very selfish, refusing to offer an olive branch, so to speak, because one had not received it from the other. This hard attitude could regrettably, and quickly, lead to animosity and disharmony.

Graeme and I had already found during the early stages of the expedition that we were very different people. It was as if we were sociologically alienated and both too stubborn to relent. Graeme is extraordinarily competitive. However, I found it very tiresome. Also, we were a small traverse group, the going had not been easy... we had a long way to go.

I desperately needed some alternative company as companionship had ceased to be part of our language. For me who better than my Uncle Rex and my father who arrived in Kunde on our third day there. Dad and I made our usual reserved greeting to one another and slowly began to chat and catch up on news. Sometimes, we must initially appear no more than awkward acquaintances. Life warmed up considerably with the large group of people my father had with him on his Himalayan Trust work party. They were

77

renovating and enlarging the Kunde hospital, the Thami village school and doing some work on the Khumjung village middle-school. The evenings became noisy with talk, helped along with a little rum and large plates of hot food. I doubt I've ever consumed as much: three huge helpings of rice and shakpa (Sherpa stew) and riggis (potatoes). I talked with my father about the expedition and the discordant atmosphere and loneliness.

'Often expeditions are lonely,' he said, 'and you feel you can't talk to anyone. It's one of those difficult things that you have to put up with.'

A couple of days later my Aunt June arrived, making it a Hillary family reunion with myself being the sole representative of the offspring. Many long talks ensued, all of which assisted my resolve to complete the traverse despite many of my reservations. To traverse the Himalayas had long been a dream for me; now that I was attempting to fulfil it the nature of the trip and the personality problems were far more severe than I had anticipated. There would be much 'grin and bear it'...

We had decided to make a short sortie into the Mt Cho Oyu and Mt Everest glacial valleys, to climb a 20,000-foot peak, Kungchang, that was first climbed by my father twenty-nine years before, and then return to Kunde from where we would again set off across the high passes and valleys of the Himalayas. Ever westward, ever closer to Mt K2 in far off Pakistan. As we prepared ourselves for our brief diversion an old friend arrived with a group of heavily laden porters. Phu Tenzing had been my sirdar on the Amadablam expedition two years before and we had become close friends. We greeted each other warmly and he pointed, with a grin on his face, at my beard.

'Gawa!' he said laughing, for it is Sherpa for "old man". 'Small one now having, O.K. You marrying, no beard having... After... big one... O.K.'

He gestured in a way that could only suggest a beard of the luxuriant proportions of an ancient Greek philosopher, or perhaps Jim Wilson, a close friend who drove one of the jet boats up the Ganges in 1977 on an expedition that my father had led.

It was a fabulous day as I packed my load and set off down the track to Khumjung village. Tashi, S.P., Graeme and Corrina had departed a little earlier and we had agreed to meet at the small village of Dole from where Graeme, Tashi and I would sally forth to make our attempt on Kungchang Peak the next day. We wandered up the track towards the immense whiteness of Cho Oyu's eastern flank, boulder hopping across the freezing waters of the Gokyo river to the deserted summer village of Na not far below the Cho Oyu glacier's terminus. Climbing on to a boggy alpine tundra we marched across, avoiding the more waterlogged areas and enjoying the view of a coronet of peaks all around us with layers of grey cloud accumulating among them. Earlier I had noticed S.P. was unhappy, so I decided to ask Tashi if he knew what troubled him.

'In the mountains, you know, you always get this thing. There is only one thing to think about. If you are in the town you can do this thing, you can do that thing, you can go to the cinema, you can gamble or talk with the ladies. In the mountains you have none of these things.'

A little further across the boggy meadow, from beneath a huge morainic boulder sprang a European man wearing a red parka who came scampering across the spongy ground towards us.

'Do ya need a place to camp?'

Somewhat astonished we looked about us. There was no shortage of camping sites here. 'We're going to have a cup of tea, would you join us?'

'No thanks, I don't eat *anything* cooked.'

'Would you like a lemon drink?' I persisted.

'No. I have plenty under the rock over there,' he replied, accepting some raw peanuts as he said so. He told us some frightful stories about trekkers perishing on one of the nearby passes that he had just crossed and went on, since he had noticed our climbing equipment, to mountaineering feats. Apparently he had reached 8200 metres on Mt Everest's West Ridge during winter, at the same time a British team were attempting it, along with a Sherpa called Gorak — presumably from the summer village of Gorak Shep, we decided in a jocular appraisal of his stories. Prior to that he claimed he had climbed Amadablam via the South Ridge with a Sherpa... probably called Gok from Gokyo or perhaps Nam from Namche or even Kat from Kathmandu.

He scurried back to his rock and all his uncooked food. 'Wonder what he's going to climb tomorrow?' 'Makalu!'

Near the base of Kungchang Peak we pitched the little tent and spent the night readying ourselves for an early start. With cloud filling the lower valley we set off for the peak following an old lateral moraine trough. Walking on sparsely grassed ground and frozen streambeds we reached a tarn, frozen solid, that lay at the bottom of a tiered glacier which led us to a col. On opposite sides of the col were the two peaks of Kungchang with cloud whirling around them as the weather deteriorated rapidly. The vague ghostly image of Cho Oyu appeared periodically to the east until visibility reduced to such an extent that we could see little further than 100 metres.

After some deliberation we decided to continue for a while up the narrow convoluted ridge over fractured rock outcrops and snow bulges until we reached about 19,500 feet. In a flurry of snow and wind and negligible visibility we decided the climb was a futile waste of time in the conditions and descended a steep gully to the frozen tarn. A little despondent we returned to the tent, packed up our camp and retreated from the inclemency of the weather on the high tundra to Dole where S.P. and Corrina were halted for the night.

Next morning we returned to Kunde. While S.P. and I sat in the sun among the trackside rhododendron trees waiting for Tashi who had stopped to talk to some Sherpas, S.P. commented on Tashi: 'He is a very good mountaineer,' wobbling his head in that unusual Asian manner of affirmation, 'but he is a very sensitive fellow. He says very little, but he feels even the most tiny thing.'

After eleven days in the Kumbu we decided it was about time, conflicts or no conflicts, harmony or disharmony, organised or disorganised, to head off west across the Himalayas. We had a raging farewell party where alcohol-induced boldness had Mingma proclaiming great truths as we all shrieked with laughter. 'You plenty talk doing, no work doing. You plenty walking doing. You finishee getting; O.K. plenty talking doing... see!'

The day scheduled for our departure began with an unpleasantly volatile meeting, so when Graeme and Tashi said that they were ready to depart I told them to continue and I would join them in the evening. Feeling depressed and dejected I sat by the charcoal burner in Mingma's house writing. Dad came in and we talked over the problems. I appreciated his concern and encouragement then, for without it I would not have joined Graeme and Tashi as planned but fragmented our team by continuing on separately with a Sherpa. Then Mingma had a talk with me. 'You plenty writing, thinking doing. This thing you must finishee, see. You finishee and I very happy.'

It was evening, time to imbibe hot rums, dinner and noisy chatter with the members of the work party... and it was 7 pm, time I was on my way. A wave of emotion rushed through me as the reality of my imminent departure sliced through the warmth of the charcoal burner, the friendship and happy chatter and there I was standing by the door. 'Well, I'd better be off.' With the proverbial frog in my throat and tears welling in my eyes, I slunk into the veil of darkness outside where I farewelled Dad. It had been wonderful to see him and I had enjoyed and appreciated his company so much. In an uncommon gesture for us I gave him a hug which he returned and I headed off along the track. Just as I was going out of sight, I looked back... there was my father's tall form, standing still in the waxen light of the full moon watching me walk away. 'Bye,' I whispered to myself, waving my hand at him. 'I hope this year is going to be worth all this.'

Graeme on the Tesi Lapcha pass at 19,500 ft.

3

Tibetan Country

WE HAD PLANNED to leave Kunde on the 18th but Pete wasn't ready so Tash and I agreed to go on and to wait for him above Thami. There are few things more demoralising to a party than unnecessary delays when there's a long way to go. Waiting around saps the resolve — it's a bit like jumping into cold water. It's really better to get it over with rather than to get involved in thinking about it. The resupplies tended to have this effect. Even Doug, Ann and S.P. were eager to get going and had begun walking that morning to Kathmandu. Corrina was going to stay for the farewell to the New Zealanders, Mal and Margaret Clarborough from the Everest National Park — a sad event as this marked the end of New Zealand's involvement in the park. The park had been set up by Kiwis and was having a vital effect on the Sherpas and the area. The party promised to be one of those memorable Sherpa affairs.

S.P. had wanted to accompany us on the next section but although I had no objection to him coming on this stage, Pete held out vigorously for a traverse party of Tash, himself and me. Late in the morning Tash, Corrina and I left Mingma's house and walked slowly through the brown fields of Kunde. Pete said he would leave later in the day and meet us at the camp above Thami.

Behind the stone walls the happy Sherpa women sung and chatted as they planted the crucial crop of rigis (potatoes) for the year. Rising beyond the fields, the sparkling fluted whiteness of Kangtega, Thamserku and Kwangde showed that spring had only just arrived. Only two days before the vertical ice hanging down the north gullies of Kwangde had fallen off with cannon-like reports — this was the annual signal to put in the rigis.

At the village boundaries we passed the long prayer wall with its hundreds of carved mani stones and began up through the rhododendrons to the low ridge. At the top I looked back at the neat rows of stone and mud houses and sadly remembered the many good, often chung-befuddled hours I had passed in them — how long would it be before we returned?

Above Namche Bazar where the track forked to go up valley to Thami, I had an even sadder task — to say farewell to Corrina. I couldn't just turn my back as I had on Kunde, but there were no words to say. She hugged me with big tears running down her cheeks, turned and hurried down towards Namche. Tash and I walked quietly up the good path towards Thami feeling strangely close for perhaps the first time. Thami was the last permanent village and so here we ate an enormous meal of boiled potatoes and Tash had his favourite — sen, a tasteless millet flour which he kneaded into little balls before eating.

Beyond Thami we climbed on slowly among the mist-shrouded rocks. Before long our world was softened by falling snow as we climbed up into a high flat near the glaciers. The scene here was Siberian. Hairy yaks, breathing jets of steam and covered in frost, nuzzled about the frozen ground for something to eat. From the grey valley where streams of ice still waited for spring, ghostly buttresses rose into the grey sky. In the middle of this desolate scene a rock house offered some warmth.

We were invited in by an old Sherpa man, as rugged as the landscape. His pretty little girl, dressed in rags, said nothing as she poked twigs into the fire to boil us some tea. In the corner of the hut a nak had just given birth to a furry little bundle which made a noise like a sick London bus. Its mother would answer with a rude but more refined snort. The old man explained that even in broad daylight the calves get eaten by snow leopards, so they are kept inside for several days after birth.

Despite the house, Tash and I slept out in the tent in case Pete arrived late, but he didn't arrive that night. He eventually arrived about mid-morning in a very grumpy frame of mind. After a brew we packed and wandered up to the foot of the climb to the Tesi Lapcha. Here we stopped for lunch, but a host of petty tensions continued to build up between us. We even "blew up" over some biscuits Pete had brought from Kunde! At the glacier we stopped again and Pete shared some chung, scroggin, boiled potatoes and biscuits. Despite this the tension between us had me just about at the end of my tether.

Home for the night was under a boulder at about 16,000 feet. A platform just large enough for the three of us to stretch out was overhung by a large boulder. Mist once again had blanketed any view but by evening this began to dissipate and the frost radiated down out of an inky sky studded with stars. We were keen to get on to the Tesi Lapcha early. It was a pass with a bad reputation. Before we left Kunde, Ed had explained how he had nearly been killed here. And on another occasion how Mingma and some of his mates had been cleaned up by an avalanche near the pass. Battered and bloody they had dragged themselves home, where they were scarcely recognised by their wives.

So I was struggling with the primus at 3 am making the brew, while still as far as possible in my sleeping bag. We left the bivvy at 5 am and stumbled upwards. I felt quite spastic and tripped over regularly on the rough and loose ground. Many of the falls must have been most comical but the faithful Tashi didn't snigger once — just plodded on behind. Once on the steeper snow, going seemed easier; or was it the psychology of gaining height more quickly? Pete was going well and had soon disappeared amidst the broken ice of a short icefall. The danger was painfully obvious as above swept the vertical walls of the unclimbed Tengi Raggi Tau.

If rock or ice should frivolously break off the wall it would rake the gully up which we were forced to climb. There was also a slight danger of a serac avalanche but this wasn't too great. We climbed as fast as the thin air of 19,000 feet would allow. Above the icefall a large neve stretched endlessly to the pass and up this we plodded lethargically. I was most relieved to finally reach the pass at around 9 am. All around us spread a scene of unbelievable grandeur. Behind, the graceful peaks of the lower Kumbu shimmered in a hazy blue distance. Nearer, the walls of Kwangde and Teng Kangpoche rose to crenelated ridges. Above the pass rising to 23,000 feet Tengi Raggi Tau stood like a fortress, its summit a difficult plum for someone to pluck. Below us like a slow icy conveyor belt out of Tibet flowed the massive Droiamboa glacier surrounded by so many good-looking peaks that we almost got tired of looking at them.

Shortly after we began the descent Tash fell into a crevasse, winding himself and painfully bruising or breaking some ribs. We tied on to the rope and continued with greater care, down an easy icefall, then left down the Droiamboa. The glacier flowed south for several miles, plunged over an icefall before turning abruptly west. Below this corner the ice was covered in rocky morainic debris for many miles until the glacier finally ended at a large moraine lake, not far above the Sherpa village, Na.

We plodded down the left side of the glacier as the sun softened the snow and seemed to make the air harder to breathe. After an hour's steady progress the glacier steepened. Below us somewhere, the millions of tons of ice spilled over a cliff. Remembering the firm advice we had been given to 'stay out of the icefall at all costs', we descended suspiciously, as if a big bogey waited for us over the edge. We kicked down the steep icy slope craning our necks to see over the cliff below. Suddenly, as if by magic, a very Germanic head (but not wearing a Kaiser Wilhelm helmet with a point on top) poked up over the brink. It looked not the least surprised to see us in this icy wilderness and immediately ordered:

'You must put an ice screw in zer!'

We did what we were told, fixed our rope to it and abseiled over the edge. At the foot of the cliff we met about fourteen porters. Apparently the Germans had been climbing this icecliff for two days — cutting large steps and fixing rope to assist their heavily-laden porters.

It all seemed a bit of an overkill simply to cross the Tesi Lapcha but they had their style and we had ours. One of the two Germans at the foot of the cliff greeted me. 'You must be the New Zealanders,' he said with amazing perception.

'Why's that?' I asked.

'Because only New Zealanders carry such big loads, have no porters and go out in zee storms.'

I looked up at the perfect blue sky, then at the porters, then back to the German.

'How far to Na?' I asked.

'Three days!'

'Shit!' I exclaimed. 'We were hoping to get there today.'

He peered at me questioningly. 'Vot are you superman or something?'

Below the cliff two other Germans were helping a third man up the slope.

'Our friend, he is very sick,' said one.

'Yes, we can see that... this man has high-altitude sickness and must go down immediately,' we warned.

'Vee have told him this, but he will not go.'

The sick man popped another headache pill and poked one of his assistants with a ski pole. 'Up,' he ordered as an indication that he wished to be dragged on.

Mt Gauri Shankar with a terraced hillside below.

'Vot are vee to do?' pleaded his friend. 'He is zee doctor!'

We shrugged and continued on down.

Somehow the Germans managed to cross the pass but at great expense. Four days after our meeting and just on the eastern side of the pass the doctor tore off his clothing and dashed about in a last frenzy of activity before dying. A victim of high-altitude cerebral oedema and a reluctance to turn back.

Below the icefall the glacier was a tedious mass of undulating ice and rubble: dotted here and there by small green lakes set amidst rubble-covered ice pinnacles. In the distance we could see the big lake at the terminal of the glacier. Looking back up at the shambles of ice which was the icefall we wondered how the Sherpas ever managed to get their yaks up there and over the pass.

'One thing for sure, they wouldn't do it this year,' said Pete.

We wondered whether in fact they would ever do it again. Apart from the glaciers getting more difficult to travel as they shrink the need is not as great as in the past for these tough mountain people to commute across such high dangerous passes. They can supplement their incomes from trekking and mountaineering and by walking down valley for one week they can catch a bus to Kathmandu to trade or work.

Over a late lunch of "dehy" in the middle of the glacier, we debated what

Peter walking through the barley fields in central Nepal.

side to travel down. After eventually opting for the traditional right side we really put on the pressure for the next three hours, determined to reduce the Germans' prediction of three days to half a day. In the evening we dodged flying rocks as heavy limbed we scrambled up the dangerous moraine wall above the terminal lake. A spectacular sunset dyed the snows a warm peach as we hurried down towards the promise of the 'big smoke', but an hour above Na we met some friendly Sherpas and a South African and took up their offer to share a fine cave. We soon lay in our bags staring out at the stars and before long a perfectly round moon rose above the peaks.

'Our third moon,' said Tash.

I called out to the South African: 'Is the Springbok tour of New Zealand still on?'

'Don't ask me... I only knew Reagan was shot a few days ago when I met Russell Bryce down at Na.' (Russell was well known to us as a respected mountaineer in New Zealand.) You might think that we were keen to shut off the "bad old world" as we lived close to nature, but the opposite was the case. We craved news and were nagged by the possibility of something important happening without our knowledge.

We knew tension was mounting in Europe over Poland and as we moved westward towards the tension areas of the third world we became more and more concerned that a major confrontation would take place. Perhaps one of

85

our worries was that such a flare-up might cut us off from home. I think in New Zealand we forget that much of the world lives continually under this smothering blanket of tension. My diary for April 21 reads:

'We ambled on down the old grassy moraines to the river flats and down these to Na — a beautiful summer village: typical neat Sherpa houses arranged about a monastery: potato fields fenced with rock walls: happy Sherpa people, snorting yaks and barking mastiffs — the village walled in by 20,000-foot-high mountains. We found a house that could sell us potatoes and these we boiled and ate in the hot spring sun.'

We were in Beding almost before we realised. The school, built by Ed Hillary's Himalayan Trust and now taken over by the government, emerged from the mist like a spectre — sadly it was empty and with an air of disuse. We were made welcome in the house of a "new-rich" Sherpa who had made his money from trekking; then Tash and I went off in search of goodies — rakshi, chung, biscuits, cheese — anything tasty to supplement the usual potatoes or "dehy". After trying several houses unsuccessfully we discovered an old lady with chung and tsampa (barley flour) and while she went off in search of biscuits we drank plenty of her chung.

By morning the mist had cleared. We were fortunate to see the lower peaks of the mighty Gauri Shankar rising to 23,000 feet up behind the monastery.

As we wandered down the beautiful Rolwaling valley I worried myself about Pete's and my relationship. We were two ambitious people whose interest in mountains had brought us together. We had climbed together in India and America and although we had been together on two trips in the New Zealand mountains, we never actually climbed a mountain there together. Although we liked each other on a social level it was now clear that we had only known each other superficially before this trip and on reflection it was easy to see that there had been a high chance for big problems between us. Having committed ourselves to the journey it was now painfully obvious that there were many things that we didn't like about each other and these went much deeper than just disliking the way the other spoke or sniffed, or stirred his tea or picked his teeth — they were basic social differences. It wasn't easy for him to be the son of Sir Edmund Hillary. And in 1979, Peter was badly injured and a close friend killed when they were avalanched on the south-west face of Amadablam. I nurtured a hope that as the trip progressed we would learn to like each other and finally finish up the best of friends. One thing was obvious — we were both obsessed with individually completing this marathon. Perhaps herein lay our main problem.

The beautiful fir forest of the Rolwaling finally began to give way to fire-ravaged hillsides — a clue that people and lunch weren't too far away. Before long we picked up the scent of smoke. In a clearing stood several shelters made of bamboo matting. Around them grazed goats, and zums (a cross between a yak and a lowland cow). Two frightened kids ran into a hut and we followed. Inside, sitting crosslegged, a woman fixed a basket while her man tended the small fire. 'Is milk available?' we asked.

'Yes,' came the answer.

After a good lunch we continued, sidling the great hillsides, climbing and descending through cool forest of fir, maple, oak and rhodondendron. About mid-afternoon we came into a clearing. And rising from the grass at one end of the clearing were two beautifully shaped breasts. Behind the breasts rose a friendly American lady followed fairly closely by her large boyfriend.

'Where have you guys come from?' he asked.

'Sikkim.'

'Where are you going?'

'Pakistan.'

'Hey we've heard about you guys...'

We sat in the sun having a great old natter for an hour or so then began down — Pete and I feeling closer than ever before. We spent the night in the village of Simigaon and were about to leave in the morning when a strong-looking Sherpa stuck his head through the door.

'I'm Rin Norbu and I was with Ed Hillary as mail-runner during the 1960, '63 and '64 expeditions... please have breakfast with me.'

We reluctantly agreed.

After the first two bottles of rakshi we were beginning to warm to the idea of breakfast with Rin Norbu. We told ourselves that a good blowout was exactly what we needed. I have no idea how much of the firewater we drank but the sun was high when Pete advised me to go outside to be sick. I must have been in pretty good form because I hadn't realised myself that I wanted to be sick. The chore was successfully completed beside Rin Norbu's house; then we went back inside for a solid lunch of noodles before setting off for the day. Tashi had kept himself well in check but Pete and I were walking write-offs. Our path descended very steeply through cliffs to the Bhote Kosi river and on a number of occasions we nearly stumbled over the edge — each occasion bringing forth greater peals of laughter than the previous one. At the river I decided that a swim was crucial and plunged in fully clad. Tash was quite sure I would drown and sent Pete to rescue me.

As we descended the valley we slowly sobered up and this change was completed by a climb of about 2000 feet up to a village on the western side of the valley. Here a wedding was in progress and everyone was quite drunk. 'How disgusting,' said Pete, smirking.

The next few days were hot, long and dry as we crossed ridge after ridge on our way to Barabise. We were, however, rewarded with magnificient views of Gauri Shankar to the north-east. This mountain had repelled several strong attacks until it was finally climbed by a powerful American expedition spearheaded by the formidable John Roskelley, in 1979.

On the morning of 26 April we descended several thousand feet to the Sun Kosi river and the first road that we had seen since entering Nepal nearly two months before. Only that morning we had decided to go down to Kathmandu for various business (mainly some steak and beer at KC's restaurant but also to see the Germans who had been so kind to us at Makalu basecamp.)

Corrina was waiting for us with many goodies at Lamosangu, a grotty little town a few miles from Barabise. She was delighted with the news that we would accompany her to Kathmandu. So was Tash; he didn't stop grinning for the entire four-hour bus journey. Psychologically Kathmandu was good for us. This was Tashi's birthplace and it was his first visit back for twenty-two years. Within minutes of arriving he had bumped into some Tibetan friends and gone off happily with them.

We had a good time with our friends the Germans. Sadly they had failed on Makalu II but were not too disappointed. They had had a good trip and were eager to return.

We were very keen to hear about the progress of the Indian Army team so S.P. paid a visit to the Indian Embassy. He came back to announce proudly that they were making great progress and were about to enter Nepal and reach Taplejung. 'A bit lower than 10,000 feet,' said Pete referring to their claim that they would not go below that height. Taplejung is in fact about 3000 feet.

Meanwhile Tash had made his own enquiries. He had been told that the Army would not reach Taplejung before 26 May. They were at least two months behind us which gave us little breathing space, particularly if they were going to take a lower route and have no problems with bureaucracy. The monsoon was due in eastern Nepal during early June — we had no time to lose.

Well watered and fed we began again. After taking the bus back to near Lamosangu we began up the bountiful Balepi valley, heading north towards the Jugal Himal. It was May Day and the sun beat down from an azure sky.

Graeme dives into a mountain stream.

A change of style — we dispense with mountaineering paraphernalia, and travel light with gym shoes and umbrellas.

Peter and Tashi marching down the Langtang Valley.

After two hours' walking we stopped beneath a Banyan tree. Pete wiped his brow and moaned: 'Let's get back to the mountains where we belong.'

A couple of hours later we walked into the beautiful medieval town of Jalbire. Under the sacred pipal tree women pounded the husks off rice. The narrow paved streets were hung over by solid and ornate buildings. We drank our morning tea while the village idiot hovered nearby, curious about the newcomers.

Beyond Jalbire the rich river flats began to shrink as the river steepened and the hillsides closed in. It was soon back to the old up and down sidling game — a good thing it wasn't always on the same side or we might grow one leg longer than the other, I thought. As we began the grind upwards we were tantalised by the view of distant mountains at the end of the Balepi gorge. While we climbed Tash talked about Tibetan history which we really enjoyed. We were particularly interested in the war between Tibet and Nepal 200 to 300 years ago. The Tibetans had good cavalry but the Nepalese infantry were too good for them. Tash reckoned that it was following this war that the Sherpa people came to Nepal. The Tamang people were also Tibetans — descendants of the Tibetan cavalry.

Late in the afternoon, under an inky sky we entered one of those flat-roofed Tamang villages, Pukerapu — perched on a steep hillside, the dark-coloured houses clustered close together behind the terraced fields lush with

89

their new crop of grain. Beyond Pukerapu our route continued a crazy getting-nowhere ballet of ups and downs and drastic changes of direction as we crossed major side valleys. We did have one really fortunate meeting.

While we were resting by a steep stream a formidably bronzed and muscular man accompanied by one porter came thundering down one side and was disappearing up the other when he saw us. I clambered up to him and he held out a great ham of a hand. 'Kim Schmidt,' he said, bright blue eyes sparkling out of his handsome face. I felt hopelessly white and puny as I offered my hand. I knew the name well — a famous American climber. He was in a hurry having apparently been held up carrying a sick Sherpa for two days. (He looked to me as if he could walk at normal speed even with a Sherpa on his back.) During our brief conversation I learned that he and John Roskelley had attempted our route on the north face of Jannu some years before and that a party of New Zealanders were at present camped below Tilman's Col.

But more importantly he told me that our best route into the Langtang was across the 17,500-foot Tilman's Col at the head of this valley. Kim generously gave us his old maps and then rocketed onward down valley. We plodded on upward jealous as hell and wishing we were so strong.

The next day we began the first of a series of long climbs to reach the elusive Tilman's Col. A very vague and exceptionally steep track climbed through fir forest until on top of a high narrow ridge we discovered an old camp. A black sky threatened rain but there was no shelter. Tash and I discovered a roomy hollow log while Pete pitched his nylon poncho. Tash stayed in the log but my end was too similar to a coffin for my liking so I slept outside, keeping my ice axe handy in case the landlord, Mr Bear, returned during the night.

Dinner had been the usual rice and "dehy" stew and breakfast followed ten hours later — tsampa and a brew. With hollow stomachs we began upwards again and were soon in snow, wallowing kneedeep through endless basins. As the mist came in and it began to snow gently we had that old lost, Milke ridge feeling.

By lunchtime we had long since lost the vague steps that we had been following and we were soon blundering about again, navigating by the seat of our pants. But this time by dint of some skill and a generous smattering of luck we climbed on to the correct pass. This was followed by several more 'correct passes', each higher than the previous one until ahead of us was all downhill — at least for the meantime. The weather had now cleared and ahead, up the Balepi glacier, we could see a wall of peaks blocking our way. A neat gap in this wall was Tilman's Col.

We plunged downward towards the river again — bum-sliding down the steeper slopes and moving quickly in an attempt to reach the New Zealand camp. Our imaginations had turned the camp into a comfortable little embassy. But we were too late. By the time we reached the river there was little light left. We spent the remainder of it collecting some scrubby sticks of wood from under the snow. Beneath a leaden sky we lit a fire and prepared some lumpy spots to sleep on. With our skimpy food supply and no tent we realised this was no place to be caught by bad weather and more snow — especially because we had now adopted a new lightweight approach. We had pruned back our gear to the absolute minimum — speed had become the theme of the traverse.

'Move fast, eat little, sleep rough and think big,' Pete had said. This we were doing. We had perhaps taken it to extremes — no technical gear, no tent, no crampons, no spare clothes and perhaps most interesting of all, no boots! Our plastic boots were fine up high but hard to move fast in below the snowline. What we needed was a light boot that we could climb in but which we could wear for fast valley travel. Tashi had managed to buy some in Kathmandu but Pete and I made do with our Adidas road shoes. Ironically Tash now had a superficially frostbitten left foot.

During the night the sky cleared and the 5th dawned a brilliant day. We packed quickly and sauntered up valley towards the Kiwi camp. Just below the terminal of the glacier, beside a bubbling stream we found it — a great spot dominated by views of the spectacular peaks, but sadly deserted. We had a drink and continued up towards Tilman's Col, climbing a moraine rib which seemed endless but took us up steadily.

The crux of the ascent was a steep icefall but someone (probably the New Zealanders) had made steps up a gully on the right so progress was pretty steady. Above the icefall we made quick work of a broad neve and about 1 pm we were greeted by a freezing wind blowing over Tilman's Col.

Pete wrote: 'The beautiful morning had turned Jekyll and Hyde and we descended the broad glacier in a maelstrom of wild gusts and blasting sleet. We peered through the veil of the storm at the ghostly shapes of the Jugal Himal peaks that loomed about us — huge white domes and fluted faces, serrated ridges and monstrous precipices dropping on to the soft smoothness of the high neves and spilling in icy confusion to the moraine-strewn glaciers.'

Once the glacier was behind us we took our own routes through a confusion of scrub and boulders, linking up to cross the milky Langtang river. On the flat above we were delighted to meet the New Zealanders — Dave Bamford, John Nankervis, Kevin Helm, Dean Stotter and John Cox. What a great natter we all had. They shared their food and whisky with us and this also helped to clear the air between Pete and me.

We proclaimed 6 May a rest day. After tramping down broad flats for three hours we halted at a monastery below the peaks of Langtang Lirung. Here we feasted our eyes on a pretty Sherpa girl and our stomachs delighted in her chips, omelettes and rum. The bill for our debauchery was a shocking 442 rupees and a slight headache — normally living expenses for more than a week. An hour further down we passed through the rustic village of Langtang then we dropped into a deep forested gorge.

In the early afternoon Pete stumbled off the path and twisted the ankle which had plagued him since his accident on Amadablam. He asked Tash and me to carry on to the next village, Syabru, and to let him continue at his own pace. We continued through dark primeval forest and were lucky to see a musk deer standing on the path. It stared at us with big brown eyes then,

Village children in the Langtang region.

not the least alarmed, ambled slowly into the forest.

Syabru was an amazing town arranged along a narrow and steep ridge top. The people were Tibetans and their houses had finely carved woodwork, particularly around the doors and windows. We were now on a main trekking route so we found someone who sold beer and sent one bottle with a porter back to cheer Pete up. He arrived soaked by a recent rain shower but holding the empty bottle in his right hand and sporting a big grin.

> *Diary: 8 May:* Today we stuffed about in Syabru waiting for Pete's ankle to mend. He had the top off his first bottle of beer by 9 am. He was so depressed that he is talking about going out to Kathmandu, going back to New Zealand or missing this stage and meeting us in Jomoson. Life is so difficult with him that part of me hopes he does pack it in but despite this I encourage him to carry on.
>
> Horrors, the monsoon appears to have started early. It is raining heavily every day. The house we are staying in is called the "Langtang Hotel" and is run by a happy couple. The wife is very cheeky and pregnant — the man, one of those strong silent Tibetans. They have a pretty maid — a kind of Cinderella dressed in rags. At night she sleeps in her dirty clothes, huddled into a little bundle on the bare boards without even a blanket.
>
> *9 May:* Today we descended the short distance to Syabru Bensi at the junction of the Langtang and Bhote Kosi rivers. It is an important day for Nepal — the first ever election... well, elections after a fashion. From what Tash says it seems that the people can vote for the king's

A local man smoking a pipe in the Ganesh Himal.

party or one other that doesn't even have a constitution. All of the election officials appear to work for the monarchy. Tash has been wandering about, listening to the conversations in Tibetan — he reckons that the party stooges are moving about paying people to vote — in some cases more than once. I guess it's not much different to what happens in the west but here the corruption is a bit more blatant and less sophisticated.

Our host today is an interesting bloke — a kindly pixie-like face with little hair, big ears and sparkling brown eyes. He had fled Tibet to Bhutan during the Chinese invasion and had worked there as a porter. Later he secured a job in a Sikkimese hotel and then he came to Nepal with plans to set up his own hotel.

As a foreigner he couldn't set up business near Kathmandu so he tramped into the hills and set up a series of hotels in the Langtang. These were either closed by the jealous locals or the police. They cut down bridges to stop trekkers reaching his hotel and on another occasion the government made the area he was in a National Park so he was moved out, without compensation. Finally he established himself in Syabru Bensi where he and his pretty young wife ran the Tibetan Horse Hotel.

After a delicious meal at the Tibetan Horse we fell asleep but were soon awoken by a noisy celebration. The locals had lit a fire in the street and an amazing night of singing and dancing began. During the singing there was lively competition between men and women — both were very good but the men's drunken gusto could not match the sweetness and skill of the ladies. Usually a man would start the song to be joined by the other men. When their verse finished the women would come in with enthusiasm, building up and hanging skilfully on one note before bursting forth again while the men stamped in time. There was a fair bit of fraternising between the sexes and from time to time a couple would sneak away from the firelight into the shadows.

On 10 May we crossed the Bhote Kosi and headed into the Ganesh Himal. Hot dry ridges led to Gatlang where we tried in vain to buy food — it was one of the few occasions when neither love nor money would buy anything. Above Gatlang, as we climbed up through the fir forest, we were caught in a fantastic deluge. We sheltered in a hollow tree and then continued. After 500 feet we saw our first deodar monkey. The grey-coloured animal with a white beard was the size of a small man. It sprung up the nearest tree with unbelievable agility and disappeared in the top branches.

The days were beginning to pass more slowly — a boring montage of ridges, passes and grotty villages. We skirted the high peaks of the Ganesh, eager to reach the mighty valley of the Buri Gandaki and some more high country at its source.

On the 13th something happened that came close to changing the whole course of the expedition. We were heading uncertainly up a valley towards Kading. Pete had gone ahead while Tash and I tried in vain to get directions from the locals on how to get across to the Buri Gandaki. It seemed that they never travelled in that direction so consequently most had little to offer. Eventually we met a man working in a field who told us that we must cross two passes and then climb up to a place called Yarsa. He emphasised the distance and climbing by saying over and over, mate mate mate (up, up, up). Pete had long since disappeared from our view but as we came up the main path of Kading he came raging down on us. He had walked himself into a terrible tizz and shouted at us. Both Tash and I were nonplussed.

'But I haven't done anything,' said Tash defensively.

'That's the trouble... you never do anything or say anything,' shouted back Pete. I stood silently with perhaps a hint of an "oh God, here-we-go-again" smirk on my face. This infuriated Peter. With a push he knocked me off balance. I was pretty fired up but felt that if I hit him we had reached an irreconcilable point. On reflection, a good dust up is probably what we needed. I had never had to cope with such behaviour from a so-called friend.

'Don't ever hit me again,' I tried to say firmly and without emotion; but it was impossible. I was trembling with fury.

'If I do you'll never move again,' he retorted. I considered three actions in this order. The first was to bring my brolly down firmly between his eyes. The second was to give him the old Dingle haymaker in the ear and the third was to grin at him.

Tash presented me with a fourth by saying quietly and firmly: 'I'm going out to Pokhara.'

'Okay I'm coming with you Tash,' I replied. Tash was already trying to find a porter.

'What will you tell the others?' asked Pete, already coming back to earth.

'I'll tell them I had frostbite and couldn't go on,' replied Tash flatly. His frostbite was in fact healing quite well.

Pete and I sat down, backs against a stone wall, and I began to tell Pete the things about him that really upset me. When I had finished I expected (and wanted) him to do the same with me but he said nothing — apparently quite shocked.

After quite a time of sitting in the hot sun surrounded by locals Tash and I began up the hill. After a while Tash stopped and said: 'I've decided, Graeme, I'm going to Pokhara... today he attacked you... you can strike back... what happens if he attacks me? If I hit him I'll probably be arrested.'

'I'm coming too then,' I repeated. I had already worked out an alternative plan. We would catch up with the support group, who by now would be walking into Jomoson, and we would form a new traverse team.

When we reached the pass Pete asked Tashi again what he was going to do.

'I'm going on. I cannot do this to you two,' replied Tash coolly.

He had simmered down and decided that his action might jeopardise the success of the traverse.

So the show was still on the road. It was raining again and the leeches were reaching frantically at us from the jungle. A part of my heart was relieved but I felt disappointed too, that the status quo had been maintained. Decisions were going to be just as hard to make. But as we slid down towards another valley through jungle fresh with rain, the sun peeped through and I decided to put all my energy into making the traverse a happier experience than it had been so far. One thing I was keen to do was to involve the support group more. They had been forced to feel like an ugly appendage and this had the effect of making even the resupplies unpleasant.

Tash was soon feeling better. As we passed through a jungle clearing he gave his little chuckle of delight and said: 'One day soon, I'm going to a pasture like this with my wife — and we'll have some yaks.'

At lunchtime we all tried to find little rocky islands where the leeches could not get at us while we ate our tsampa. I found a new way to make the bland stuff more interesting — I chopped soft-boiled eggs into it and beat it into a yellow mush.

After crossing the pass we descended steeply through dense forest where orchids grew in profusion — hanging in purple and white veils from the trees. The knee-shattering descent was at least 6000 feet and it was followed by a steep climb of about 3000 feet. At the top we discovered the poor but friendly little village of Yarsa. 'Yes', the locals told us, 'tomorrow you'll reach the Buri Gandaki — perhaps even the big town of Rumchet... if you go quickly.' So Rumchet became our next objective.

A good track took us sidling around the end of the huge dividing ridge. As we went we paused from time to time to pick wild yellow raspberries and Pete nattered about flying and all the things he was going to do when he got back to New Zealand. Before long we crested the ridge and slowly entered another valley system — the long-awaited Buri Gandaki. Thousands of feet

Rhododendron in the Ganesh Himal.

Buddhist prayer stone — Mani Stone — in the
Buri Gandaki valley.

below us the mighty river flowed — a great swollen ribbon of brown fury, carrying the Himalayas to the Bay of Bengal. Ahead of us one of the peaks of Ganesh thrust a snowy head to over 23,000 feet, into a sky that gave promise of another storm.

About 9 am we met a porter going in the other direction. The porter prattled a reply to our greeting.

'What did he say Tash?'

'He says you are nearly there.'

'Nearly there' inevitably meant at least two hours to go. This time it meant six hours. We flogged up and down, in and out of deep valleys — our depression growing each time we reached a ridge top only to find another to climb.

'Rumchet must be a big village,' said Tash.

'Yeah, let's have a feast,' enthused Pete and I. 'What about cooking up some of those lovely stuffed paranthas Tash?'

'Okay but I'll have to buy some flour.'

We got hungrier and hungrier as we thought of some tasty food and drew closer to Rumchet, then crossing a high ridge we could see the promised town laid out before us — drab, flat black-roofed boxes, crowded together on the terraced hillsides. The wheat had just been harvested and cattle and goats fed on the golden stubble — and from the village the sound of dozens of over-sexed roosters, all clamouring to get into our billy, drifted up to us. Famished and highspirited we entered Rumchet but found grotty little houses and dirty people — there was little joy waiting for us.

We tried in vain to buy some food and finally collapsed beside a house where we were promised some mokai (popcorn). The scorched grain soon arrived and we devoured it, watched by a toothless old man and a young man incongruously advertising "Singapore" across his grubby T-shirt.

Nearby a bosomy young lady squatted with a child hanging off one breast. The old lady of the house produced a small bottle of rakshi which cost only one rupee. It was true firewater — the best we had tasted. When a match was held near it, it burned with a blue flame like meths. The tactics may have been to soften us up; then to move in with the rubbish at a high price. The next bottle cost us five rupees and was about ninety percent water but the damage was done — we were well on the way.

When the second bottle was finished Pete peered into it — his face slowly taking on an expression of pain and disgust. 'Take a look in there.'

The walls of the bottle were generously stained by old dirt and lying at the bottom lay a fine menagerie of drowned spiders, flies and centipedes. Once the word about the strange sahibs got around people began arriving to see the side-show — mainly ugly women. Some brought eggs to flog to us at shockingly inflated prices and we amused ourselves by bargaining with them. No one would sell us a chicken and Tashi's promise of paranthas would have to wait. We ate boiled eggs and "dehy" again and made camp in an old hag's narrow porch. During the night the storm arrived and the porch leaked streams, so we sat in our sleeping bags, half propped against the wall under our umbrellas.

May 15 was an important day. We dropped down to the thundering river while cuckoos "cuckooed" their monotonous call, which we associated more with Swiss clocks than Himalayan forests. During my morning constitutional I was horrified to find my faeces covered in blood. I also noticed a swelling and tenderness in my groin. This swelling was in fact a rather nasty hernia. I was falling to pieces.

From the beginning, the valley of the Buri Gandaki or Bhote Ganga as the locals called it, was primeval. Between immense damp cliffs the turgid monsoonal waters rushed by. Monstrous bushes of stinging nettle and cannabis grew in profusion.

My poor old road shoes which had been almost new only two weeks before were now hanging in tatters from my feet. My toes were protruding through the side of my left shoe, surrounded by shredded sock. If I couldn't get any more boots of some kind in the valley I would be in trouble crossing the high snow-covered pass to the Manang valley. My hope was the next big town — a district headquarters called Jugat.

This town also possessed a potential problem in that it contained the first police check post that we had to get through in order to reach Manang. If we were turned back we would be forced to take a low-level route and this would probably mean that we would not get a close view of the next 8000-metre peak on our list, Manaslu. It would also cause further gloom in the party.

Below Jugat we passed the most depressed-looking Japanese expedition returning after a failure on Ganesh III. They all looked positively suicidal. About midday we reached the town and went direct to the shop. Pete was happy; they had biscuits.

'What about shoes?' I asked the keeper without much hope. From a dusty shelf he produced a box. 'Only one pair of shoes left — keep your fingers crossed,' I reminded everyone. Miracles! The one pair of shoes were robust Chinese basketball boots and they fitted perfectly. The old Dingle luck had done it again. We were in luck generally. The police weren't bothered about us and we managed to buy plenty of supplies to see us through the next week.

Loaded with rice, mokai, sugar and tea we continued up valley following a remarkable track which clung tenaciously to the almost vertical hillsides. In places it would have been possible to fall 3000 feet into the river. In one place Tash gave a jump and a startled cry: 'Snake.' Beside him a long black tail glided into the bamboo. I peered in where the snake had gone and found myself looking into the beady eyes of a horrible six-footer. My hair stood on end. I staggered away and hurried down the track with that cold chill sensation that only snakes can instil in me.

The day continued, a haze of steep green hillsides merging into vertical brown cliffs rising to eerie summits. Through these the narrow path zigzagged as if climbing to a giant castle.

'God knows where Nyak is,' said Pete peering upwards at the narrow ledge of a track disappearing up into vertical cliffs. In places it was built up with the aid of ingeniously placed slabs of rock. At times only the knowledge that

Graeme climbing onto the Larkya Banyang pass in
Central Nepal, at 17,000 ft.

these precarious tracks needed to support yaks and other loaded people gave us faith that the structure would hold. We passed a couple of happy Tibetan nuns labouring upwards with sacks of grain — the loads weighing at least 100 pounds apiece. They were really cheerful in their labour.

We were beginning to suspect that Nyak didn't exist when we climbed at last up to a saddle on which stood a huge chorten. A short way beyond lay the town gates and through them, Nyak: an amazing fairy-tale village framed by conifer forests and snowy mountains — a flourishing oasis surrounded by vertical hillsides. It looked quite Swiss with its solid wooden houses, ladders made from notched tree trunks, haystacks and neat heaps of split wood ready for the winter.

We immediately liked the town and its people. As usual our hopelessly weary bodies relaxed as we made ourselves at home in an old lady's house. We sipped rakshi and stared into the flames that cooked our chicken stew. The stew devoured, the rakshi bottle empty and the flames mere glowing embers, we lay back on the floor just like the old lady and slept. It was never difficult to sleep.

Before dawn Tash was blowing on the embers and the firelight soon licked about the blackened rafters. A brew, the most precious first brew of the day, was soon heralded by the call of 'bowls'. Reaching for the bowl became reflex — we became like good gunfighters. For some reason Pete had the slowest bowl in the west. It never ceased to make me wonder why he seemed reluctant to produce his bowl for food or drink. The next part of the ritual was food. It might be boiled eggs, or tsampa with daihi, or sometimes "dehy" — or even, occasionally, just a brew. Packing we could do with our eyes

Manangi village and their Buddhist Gompa above.

closed. First into the packs were our mattresses — the thin sheets of closed-cell foam. Folded into three this also made a kind of cosy back pad to our packs. Then our sleeping bags were stuffed in followed by any spare clothing, one-piece suits and the like. On top went the food and party gear, tent, primus and so on. Somehow my pack never looked as neat as Pete's but Tash was the worst — his would often hang over at the top like an old hobo's hat.

We planned to climb into the area at the head of the Buri Gandaki valley. From Nyak the valley continued its gorgey nature. A beautiful traverse through pines led us to an eerie descent down steep cliffs to the river where the sun hardly penetrated. We made quick progress up through sombre forest, the river's roar booming around the cliffs.

At the first habitation, a single poor house, we met some hardcase-looking Tibetan men who told us that they would escort us up valley. The man who was to lead us had himself been a policeman in the area but as we continued up valley we began to doubt the fellow's credibility. Pete was the first to voice his doubts, and was adamant about turning back. I was a bit annoyed about this change of heart. As usual Tash didn't care one way or the other — at least that's what he said.

We arrived back at Nyak first thing in the morning (having spent the night at the bottom of the hill), and began trying to get information about an alternative route across the mountain. It was hopeless — the locals knew of none and our maps were really vague. We were frustrated and dejected. Another chicken bit the dust for our dinner and in the evening I scoured the village for rakshi. While we sipped the terrible-tasting anaesthetic and waited for our chicken stew, an aristocratic man and his lady arrived at the house. He was the doctor from a check post village, Namdu. The doctor thought that we should return up valley and try again. So next morning — 19 May — we set off, this time full of optimism. At our previous turnback point, Gap, we ate some boiled potatoes and chapatis.

Beyond this we entered a new world. We crossed a wooden bridge, passed a huge mani wall, with some exquisitely carved stones, and entered a forest of giant firs. A group of happy Tibetan people playing in a clearing added to our feeling of well-being.

We crossed the river again, this time on planks suspended across a stupendous gap with the river rushing through the slit gorge it had sculptured for itself. One slip and your last couple of minutes would be a nightmare. We walked on through the enchanted forest where immense trees and boulders merged in perfect confusion.

'It feels like Gulliver's Travels,' said Pete.

At 4.30 pm we passed through the town gate. Tash went the wrong way around the mani wall but Pete and I felt we needed all the blessings we could get so went the correct way around the great heap of blessed stones, muttering 'O mane padme hum' reverently as we went.

Twenty metres ahead in the yard of the check post stood two policemen. We greeted them respectfully. One of them asked for our permits and passports and proceeded to read out aloud all the place names written on my permit by the officer in Kathmandu, who had perceptively noticed 'but this is many treks in one'. Once our particulars had been written into the book by Tash (the policemen could write), we were free to go. We bowed and, amidst copious thank-yous, departed on our way up valley.

Above Namdu the valley opened out considerably and became rich with crops. We felt we had never been in such a beautiful valley before.

As we passed through the delightfully Tibetan village of Lho some pretty girls took our hands and pulling us back gently said over and over 'Shim, shim!' Tash wouldn't tell us what it meant but the villagers laughed when we repeated the phrase as if it was rude. It made a pleasant fantasy anyway. We climbed toward Lho and caught fantastic views of Manaslu and Himal Chuli rising above the waving wheat, the golden crowned temple and beyond, the broad tumbling glaciers.

Somagaon was our objective for the day and, as we approached it the valley filled with towering cumulus clouds and big drops of rain fell. We entered the village across a grassy flat where badgers played, oblivious to man's presence. Somagaon was a little disappointing. The village itself was really interesting but the light which adds much to the atmosphere of the place was poor — Himal Chuli and Manaslu were smothered by cloud so we had no views and consequently took no good pictures. During the afternoon the nuns that we had passed down valley, carrying the huge loads, arrived. We drank tea together while they tried to sell us Tibetan boots. Unfortunately none were big enough for our splay feet. One of the ladies, Ang Phu, I found very attractive. She was a bouncy little thing with a shaven head and exquisite sparkling brown eyes. Pete laughed when I announced: 'I fancy this nun... Is it a sin to fancy nuns?'

Next day we seemed to enter Tibet itself — the valley walls were desolate, rising to jagged peaks. The only village, Samdu, looked like a disaster area. As had been normal with many Tibetan-type villages the roofs were flat but here the houses appeared half sunken into the hillsides. And there were no frills on the buildings at all, no pleasant crops to break the austere greyness — just rock walls, bare fields and mud houses with small windows, obviously made to withstand winds and storm and the austerity of the Himalaya at its most rugged. The main valley now turned to the west and after a short distance the river was devoured by the glacial ice. We climbed high above the shambles of ice and moraine heading for a hut which was supposed to be a couple of hours below the Lakya Banyan pass.

Early in the afternoon we reached a large and well-built hut. Tash reckoned that it had been built by the government for tourists but the cynical Hillary and Dingle team wondered why the government would build a tourist hut in such an area so close to the Tibetan border. While it snowed gently outside we settled down to a nice relaxing afternoon in the pit.

The cooking roster had been reinstated and it was Pete's turn to cook breakfast so he was up at 4 am. An hour later we shambled out to face the grey light of another Himalayan day.

As we climbed steadily through the heaps of moraine we were fascinated by the difference between the mountains on one side of the valley and the

Graeme divides the last of our meagre rations for
dinner under Tashi's watchful eye.

other. The valley seemed to be a fault dividing two rock types. To our right, the north, rounded glacier-free hills reminded us of Tibet while to the south side of the valley rose jagged ice-plastered spires. Somewhere up amongst them was Manaslu.

The Lakya Banyan was one of those frustrating summits that always seems to be just over the next rise — obviously designed to wear people out. One heap of moraine and glacier ice followed another until shortly after I thought we were doomed to the Lakya Banyan for eternity we reached the summit cairn with its cluster of tattered prayer flags.

On the west side the slope fell away more steeply. We plunged down, grateful for no more ascent but thick mist and thin-skinned snow made the descent a bit tiresome at times. After a little floundering around we picked up some clear yak prints in the snow and following these we were soon on to a good track.

'Like a Bombay highway,' said Tash happily.

While descending a long snow slope I tripped over and wrote off yet another brolly. I was glad to be rid of the bloody thing. Down below we wandered along a grassy moraine trough beside a large glacier as cold rain began to fall. Suddenly we were distracted by a human voice and on investigation discovered three Tibetans squatting beneath a rock — a woman with two shy little kids aged about ten and five. She asked Tash what the

Graeme and Tashi crossing the thin ice on Lake Tilicho.

pass was like and was understandably concerned about crossing over. I'm
sure that given good weather the unlikely trio would make it but even as
tough as they were a storm up there or a slight loss of route and they would
be snuffed out like candles in the wind.

As we continued down valley Pete said, 'I reckon that in New Zealand a
man would go to court for sending his wife over a pass like that.' Indeed,
how we have changed — modern man is so different from these people. They
need to take risks to survive but their empathy with the mountains makes
their margins of safety pretty good.

Below the glacier we descended into dense forest and following the milky
Dudh Khola we lost height quickly, wetted from time to time by heavy rain.
By evening we were over 10,000 feet below the Lakya Banyan and our long
day ended at the small Manangi village of Tilche.

Even before we had found somewhere to stay we were soothing our
battered feet and knees with a bottle of the local brew, internally
administered. It was so good that when we reached the house of a young
Manangi who agreed to put us up, we had another. While his pretty wife
finished her daily chores and tended to the needs of their young child our
host told us of his trading exploits to Bangkok.

The Manangis are crafty Tibetan traders from away back. They claim that
the land is too infertile to support them and have secured the permission of

the king to trade internationally. So each year groups of these canny Tibetans, some smelling like their yaks and dressed in traditional garb, head off on jumbo jets to Bangkok, Hong Kong and Singapore, their pockets stuffed with precious stones and so on. They then return to Kathmandu, trade off watches, radios and trappings of our technological world before returning to their unworldly wives and their simple stone and mud houses in the hills.

As the fire died Tash, Pete and I snuggled into our sleeping bags while our hosts lay under a common blanket nearby. Next morning after one hour's trek we reached the Manang valley at Thonje.

Here I set off to purchase eggs for breakfast and after a long search discovered three. 'Six rupees,' said the seller.

'But that's bloody extortion,' I squealed. 'We've never paid more than one rupee per egg.'

'This is Manang,' stated the seller, withdrawing his eggs from sale.

For fifteen kilometres above Thonje the Manang valley was much like most other forested and steep-walled valleys that we had been in. At Chame, the district headquarters, we had a good lunch. Pete even had a wash including his hair, so Tash and I suspected that he was expecting a lady friend at the next resupply. I definitely was, so washed my hair, my socks and my underpants — perhaps we were being a little keen — Jomoson was still at least four days away.

Above Chame the valley changed completely. The conifer forests became sparser. As Pete wrote: 'Whole mountainsides of bare rock slabs swept in huge geometric curves to the craggy summits far above; and to the south of the barren landscape rose one of the world's greatest ramparts, the Annapurna Himal, a string of huge mountains that fend off the monsoon, leaving Manang worlds apart from the green valleys on Annapurna's southern flanks.'

The women in this valley were really assertive. Unlike their Hindu sisters in other valleys, these Buddhist ladies were almost frighteningly forward — at least for us country boys! One happy group closed in one me, poking at my shorts with a stick and giggling 'derry ramro' (very nice).

We moved on to Manang, a pleasant cluster of flat-roofed Tibetan houses. Here we met some friendly American University students and so spent a happy, noisy day exchanging yarns and playing cards. The usual route from Manang to Jomoson lies north then west across the Thorong La to Muktinath, but we had decided to take the more interesting Mesanto La route, directly across to Jomoson.

May 25 began as a fine day with the sun shafting down into the barren valley. We climbed up to Khamsar hoping to hire someone to show us the way up to Tilicho lake. As elsewhere in the valley prices were exorbitant but after seeing a couple of hoods off with some carefully chosen Australasian words we discovered a thirteen-year-old boy who was keen to do the job for only twice the normal fee: fifty rupees for a day's work!

Little Mohan Bahadur proudly led us up the fascinating valley where big eroded sandstone towers stood as monuments to the time when the area was under water — perhaps the sea. As it happened we didn't need Mohan — the route up valley was quite straightforward. By mid-afternoon we were up among the glaciers again, climbing through the mist towards Tilicho lake. Pete and I were entertaining ourselves by trying to remember the names of all fifty American States. Weeks later we were still solving this problem.

About 4 pm as we fumbled about in the cold mist seaching for Tilicho lake we decided it was irresponsible to take Mohan any further. We paid him off and watched him bound away across the snowfield until he disappeared into the mist.

'My parents sure wouldn't have let me go off alone into the hills at thirteen,' said Pete, incredulous that any parent would.

Before long the mist began to break up so that we soon saw the ice-covered lake. On the far side, icefalls poured in from Tilicho Peak and Roc Noir. We found ourselves a snow-free patch of ground and settled down for the night. Dinner was cold rice and a little "dehy" — our last food apart from a few spoons of tsampa.

It was a freezing but clear night and in the morning we decided to stay in our pits until the sun reached us. On the other side of the valley — 10,000 feet above the lake — the main summit of Annapurna peeped over at us, a warm glow on her snows as the first sun slanted across at her. Breakfast was a little cold water and tsampa, then we began enthusiastically around the lake with the next-stop-Jomoson gait.

After a kilometre of good going, further progress was blocked by high cliffs and we had one of those dreaded choices — up over the top or take a risk across the frozen lake. After a short debate we chose the lake, the closest we would ever get to walking on water. The order in which we tied on to the rope probably indicated the level of each one's enthusiasm for the project. Me first, Tash second and Pete at the back with about forty-five feet of rope between each of us. I tippy-toed across with a feeling of impending disaster. In my imagination I could hear the boom as the ice broke, the freezing water racing up my body — sapping life... It was tempting to stay close to the edge but there the ice was thinner so I stayed well out, prodding the ice ahead as I went with my ice axe.

Once past the cliffs we moved directly back towards the lake edge and after crossing a nasty watery area we stepped happily on to terra firma and continued up towards Mesanto La.

From the top we were treated to a superb view. Back to the east beyond the lake rose Ganga Purna, Roc Noir and Annapurna. Above us rose the 23,000-footer Tilicho and away across the Kali Gandaki we could see the last 8000-metre peak in Nepal — Daulagiri, a hazy giant. And 10,000 knee-shattering feet below in the valley near Jomoson we could just make out the tiny forms of houses.

We began down, knowing that we'd soon be down with our friends. I think Pete had already taken the top off his first bottle of beer! A steep loose gully took us on to a very broken glacier. Suddenly we were in serious country — a steep icefall. For an hour we balanced along icy knife edges, climbed in and out of crevasses and down steep ice walls before finally exiting into a narrow gorge where we spent much of the time in cold rushing water. About midday we climbed up on to a ridge to the right and could see several thousand feet below us an army base. We thought that we could descend into the valley below the army base and continue on to Jomoson, but we were a little impetuous in making our decision — we descended quickly into "pooh country".

After much steep scree sliding, rock gymnastics and climbing through trackless scrub, we reached a good path down to the Kali Gandaki and by evening we had found our support party in the narrow streets of Jomoson.

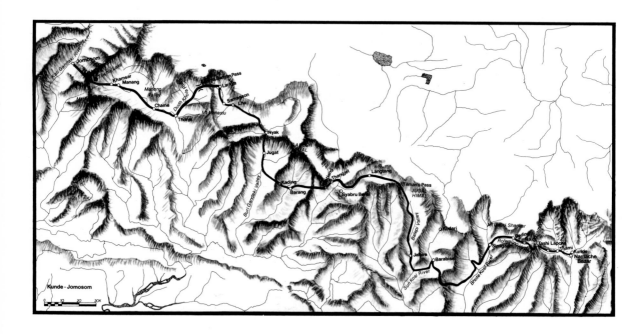

4

Time Warp

THE PATH FOLLOWED the arid banks of the river, dust floating up around
our feet with each step. Ahead loomed the Kali Kandaki gorge, a narrow
cleft between two 8000-metre-high giants, Daulagiri and Annapurna.
Mushrooming towers of white cumulus already billowed up the walls of the
gorge obliterating all but a glimpse of the green forests and hillsides that lay
there. Around us spread desolation. A barren, brown landscape ascending in
sweeping curves to the white peaks above.

Changing from our usual routine, we halted after just one hour at the
idyllic village of Marpha, a quaint and sleepy little trackside town. Nestled
below a vast rubble-strewn hillside the village sat among its green irrigated
fields, a picture of well-ordered whitewashed buildings. Narrow stone-paved
streets twisted through the village with low, wood-framed doorways leading
into small courtyards filled with tethered animals, fodder and straw. Groups
of the village gentlemen sat in sunny corners talking or playing cards and
there was the sound of horses' hooves — clip clop, clip clop — along the
street.

'Hello, Peter,' a voice called. I turned to see a stocky Nepali man whom I
had met briefly at the Jomoson airstrip the day before. He had been
expecting us. Large plates of Nepal's answer to "bangers and mash", dal bhat
(rice and lentils) were placed before us with some beer to wash it down. As
we sat in his tidy little hotel we talked with members of the Argentine
Daulagiri Expedition who had recently arrived after their tragic attempt on
Daulagiri's enormous north flank. They had stories of gale force winds and
extreme cold; of a leader's ruthless personal ambition and of his death high
on the mountain.

I followed Tashi and Graeme as we emerged from the hotel into the intense
midday sun and the strong southerly wind that rushed ceaselessly up the
valley. For countless kilometres we walked across the broad shingle flats on
the true left of the Kali Kandaki river, watching as we went the white puffy
clouds turn progressively a less amiable grey. The geography had changed
too. Gone was the sepia, rolling landscape of the Jomoson area. We were
hemmed in by huge walls and seemingly summitless hillsides, forests of pine
and green pastures latched on to precarious ledges amongst the towering
bluffs.

In the distance across the river flats one could discern tiny specks moving.
A stream of pilgrims walked up the valley; some limped, some staggered and
others strode out with a relaxed gait. They were draped in the thin cotton
saris and loin clothes of the plains of India, the material inscribed with Hindu
incantations. Their dark faces were anxious, almost fearful, as they looked
ahead. For many this would be their first time in the mountains: in the
deepest gorge in the world where the great rock walls magnified the roar of

the river, channelled the rush of the wind and captured the ever darkening and changing forms of the black clouds that masked the sky. They were destined for the shrine of Muktinath and the pilgrimage was a test of will, determination and nerve... a religious fervour kept them moving. The young and the old, the lame and the sick and the mysterious wandering men of Hinduism, the sadhus with their brass buckets and large knots of unkempt hair... their distant smiles. Men with no fixed abode and no set destination. Searching for truth, enlightenment, they roam India and Nepal drawn by the shrines and festivities of their faith.

In places the track was hewn into the rock walls, a slot cut horizontally leaving one side open to the river far below. Then came the hill country and the heat and humidity of the Himalayan foothills, as the path left the constricted gorge. I was amazed how tourist and pilgrim-orientated the area was. There were shabby little hotels everywhere, gaudy signs and remarkably comprehensive menus with amusing English spellings based on pigeon-English phonetics. At the village of Tatopani, we indulged "good and proper", finishing our disgustingly gluttonous repast with lemon pie topped with yoghurt before waddling awkwardly down to the river. There a grimy rectangular pool steamed on the bank. We lowered ourselves into the extreme heat of the sacred waters. Marginally cleaner but hardly refreshed we set off again in the mid-afternoon heat.

From Beni, the government's administrative centre for the district, we turned west again having come far enough south to circumvent the bulk of Daulagiri. Each day was something of a marathon as we strove to cover as much ground as we could. From ten to twelve hours a day we were on the move, packs on backs and perspiration streaming down our brows. Often we reached our destination as darkness came, feeling exhausted and dehydrated. From the banks of the Kali Kandaki we trekked west to the village of Dorban where the valley bifurcated. Here we followed the north-west branch back towards the Daulagiri Himal set magnificently at the head of the valley. The path followed the river for a short distance and then climbed steeply upward for 2000 feet through forests of breezy pines, their long needles scattered on the track. The refreshing scent of gum filled the air. As we climbed we peered up-valley through the trunks of the pines and the blur of salty perspiration that dribbled down our brows and noses. The brilliant white forms of mountains rose above us drawing us onward.

At a village along the way we halted for lunch. We sat on the shaded verandah of a villager's house, where there was also a small shop, enjoying the respite from the intense midday heat. At times like this we would write in our journals an expedition narrative, our thoughts and reflections and feelings. Groups of local people stood around watching our pens race across the paper.

With cloud hanging low overhead and the occasional crackle of thunder we reached the depressed village of Lungsum. Here we decided to spend the night. We paced up and down the stone-covered pathways that zigzagged the village from house to house, carefully avoiding homeward-bound cattle that filled the narrow track with their distended bellies, villagers carrying heavy loads of grain or firewood and the fleshy, green leaves of stinging nettles that leaned out over the tracks.

Eventually, time always being the chief factor in finding anything or getting anything done in the hills, our enquiries led us to a house where a group of the village' gents were playing cards, betting and drinking. Comfortably seated on grass mats on the balcony beside them, we ensconced ourselves for the evening. We sipped rakshi from sordid glasses and nibbled wild mushrooms and seasoned potato served on even grubbier enamel plates. All the while we vainly tried to fend off the household chickens and a pet dove who determinedly hopped all over us, our chattels and food. After our evening meal of dal bhat we had the pleasure of watching two dogs polish off the scraps from the plates. We knew we would be using them again in the morning after only a cursory rinse in cold river water... it was time for bed.

The man of the house, whose wife had died a year before, had two children by her, a daughter of about six or seven and a son of three years. The cute little girl came and sat by my bed and we grinned at each other. Before long I was showing her pictures in a magazine I had with me. She examined each page, her pretty dark eyes sparkling in the candlelight as she revolved the magazine in order to appreciate the illustrations inverted as well as upright. With a gorgeous smile she would hand me the magazine and wait in anticipation for me to select the next page of alien symbols, messages from an unknown world of press and newsgathering. Her little brother began to cry so, as duty called, she rose quickly and lifted him out of his bamboo basket-bed. He was very nearly as big as her and yet she cradled him in her tiny arms, trying to pacify him, showing him the magazine and talking to him patiently and lovingly. I tried to imagine a six-year-old in my own society taking the same responsibilities. No complaints, no school, long hard days and responsibilities, work, work, work... and still she could smile so prettily, so happily.

It was a "bloody rough night" as an assortment of undesired insects and scaly creatures had plummeted from the bamboo and mud ceiling through the darkness to land on me and my sleeping bag. They then proceeded to go exploring in my sleeping bag and crawl all over me. I arose to greet the clear morning feeling like a thunderstorm.

We walked in silence, climbing rapidly above the river into the forests until we reached the rhododendron belt. Looking north-east the huge walls of the Gurja Himal paraded along the horizon. Daulagiri's bold form stood further to the east, rising abruptly from the hazy valleys at its feet, monolithic in the blue sky. Beyond still the shimmering massif of Annapurna. Annapurna was the first of the 8000-metre peaks ever to be climbed. An extraordinarily strong team of French mountaineers led by Maurice Herzog walked from the Indian border into the kingdom of Nepal. They reached the summit and made history but some of them got frostbite in the process. As the modern aid of helicopters for fast evacuation was then not available, gruesome tales of tossing dead and blackened fingers and toes out of train windows accompanied their return to New Delhi, India's capital.

It was a wonderful day as we climbed on, leaving the prickly heat below and finding the fresh, clear air of the mountains once again. Elated by the splendid views and the rhododendron forests with their twisted, moss-covered limbs we moved quickly, reaching 12,000 feet and the pass that would lead to the village of Dorpatan. Nearby we saw a simple straw hut with a wisp of smoke rising from its roof. The two men there were cow-herders and they had fresh milk and curd to sell us. From heavy wooden vessels that lined one wall inside the shelter, they ladled the dairy food into our bowls.

We left the pass and the views of Daulagiri and Annapurna to their fates with the billowing clouds that rose around them. Crossing broad, green pastures we passed herds of cattle and dozens of horses grazing peacefully in the warm sun. Further on there were large flocks of sheep, with shepherds preparing their shelters for three months of high-country shepherding during the coming monsoon. We crossed clear streams bubbling over large white boulders, entered mysterious rhododendron forests with canopies so thick that even the midday sun was reduced to a gloom. I admired pale rhododendron blooms, the colours so delicate and fresh and strangely incongruous with the hot, dry wind that funnelled up the valley. There were stands of tall scented firs and forests of juniper with the tinkling bells of cattle and horses feeding in the grassy glades. The further we went the vaster the valley became, the more gentle the curves of the rolling hills on either side and the more enormous the scale. The geography had changed so suddenly leaving the great snowclad summits behind us. I chatted with Tashi, as we trekked across the now wide open pastures of the valley, about his family and how we all missed the people we had left at our homes.

'One good thing about this type of trip,' said I, 'is you really appreciate your family and friends when you get home.'

'No,' replied Tashi emphatically, 'they appreciate you.'

The broad valley conjured up thoughts of the American West. I looked out across the almost infinite green flats into the haze that masked all fine definition, towards the scrub-covered hills far to the west. In my day-dream, I would not have been surprised to see Adam, Hoss and Little Joe along with Big Daddy, of "High Chaparral", galloping across the plain towards us, demanding an explanation for our trespass. It was then that I remembered a story I had heard while we were in Kathmandu. A peace corps volunteer working in the Dorpatan region had decided to take a couple of Nepali porters and travel into the hills north of the valley. Near the top of a pass he stopped to rest; his porters crept up behind him and crushed his skull with a rock. They made off with the loot — a cheap watch and about 800 rupees ($70). Some very tough interrogations by the Nepalese police led to the apprehension of the porters and the discovery of the volunteer's corpse. It made me feel apprehensive as I drove my footsore, dehydrated and wind-buffeted body on towards Dorpatan.

Dorpatan was immense. There was no high-density village nucleus; it spread out across the valley floor. The people were Tibetan Kampas, tall, proud people, who arrived in Nepal seventeen years before as refugees from

Tibet and were now, quite obviously, doing very well. Near where we were told there was once an airstrip, we stopped at a house for the night, kicked off our shoes, washed our pungent socks and relaxed... it had been a long day. Tashi, particularly, enjoyed our brief time in Dorpatan for he could speak his mother tongue with the locals, share a common ancestry. Our host and hostess were tall, fine-looking people, clearly successful. The house was not palatial, but it was comfortable and warm and with plenty of space. We sipped Tibetan tea (a strong Chinese tea with butter and rock salt) as we talked and listened to the wind blowing over the shingled roof. Outside, a whinny... horses... and again I thought of "High Chaparral", Tibetan style. A young fellow sauntered in, looking around at us as he entered. He muttered something to the big man, our host: the horses were home from grazing in the valley.

I stood outside in front of the house. It was nearly dark; a uniform pale grey sky reigned above, broken only in the west where a group of motionless, wind-sculptured clouds, like saucers, hung above the hills. The wind rustled the firs behind the house and flapped the tall Buddhist prayer flags and I looked across the broad plain before me. What a transition from the morning's views of 8000-metre Daulagiri and Annapurna.

Over the next five days we covered a lot of country seldom visited by foreigners. We had enjoyed the night at Dorpatan and it was with some regret that we stepped out on to the frosted plain and hastened down valley. The valley narrowed and the path traversed steep hillsides, covered in pasture and magnificent forests. We asked locals who we passed along the way how far to the next village. They would eye us up and down before replying: 'Two to three hours.' An hour later it seemed reasonable enough to make enquiries again as to how far to the next village and again the same reply: 'Two to three hours.' When we were actually less than half an hour from Shera, the village about which we had been enquiring, we again quizzed a passerby carrying a large load of wood on his back. 'How far to Shera?' Tashi asked him in Nepali.

'Two to three hours,' he answered without a moment's hesitation. Sometimes the errors or misinformation seemed extraordinary for people supposedly so closely in touch with their immediate environment. The answer was probably quite simple. Here in the hills, time goes slowly, nobody has a watch and if someone did it would be more a status symbol than a device for time-keeping. Instead of distances and times local porters would talk about the number of rests required to reach a destination.

'But what if you don't rest?' Graeme and I asked Tashi.

'Then you don't know how long it will take, but if you keep going you will get there.'

That's the way the villagers approached the problem, and to them it wasn't a problem because they had all the time in the world and what's more, their time was free. "Time is money" would be received with incredulity by the village elders. In a way, their approach made fools of us. Providing you had an inkling of where you were going and you kept moving, you would most assuredly get there.

From Shera we crossed the river and proceeded on till we reached Thak, a host of flat-roofed houses crammed together in the chaotic and cluttered form of Nepalese high-density housing. Typical evening noises were rising from the village: the voices of children back from the fields and hills, the bells of goats and cows returning along the stony paths, the raucous barking of the enormous dog population and the occasional raised voice making a brief penetration above the racket.

We located "the shop" and looking inside found that everything was out of stock. The lethargic shopkeeper managed with some difficulty to find sufficient energy to show us where we could sleep — on the flat roof — and where the heavy brass water urn was. While Tashi went to collect water at a little stream near the village, Graeme went with the shopkeeper in search of some rice and vegetables and a "spot" of rakshi. I remained with our three packs to ensure their safety and mended some torn clothing we had with a needle and thread. Tashi arrived back first, huffing and puffing beneath the heavy load of water he carried; then Graeme with little to show for his efforts other than stories of 'dogs everywhere.' The constant barking of dozens of dogs gave ample support to his story. He had seen a child dragging a tiny puppy on a rope. The child seemed oblivious to the fact that he was strangling it. As Graeme had looked down on the vanquished creature he watched it breathe its last.

It was a full moon that rose that evening and with it rose the raucous din from Thak. Sleeping on the flat roof of the shop beneath the star-studded heavens, we struggled to sleep with the constant barrage of barking, howling, fighting and yelping of the mobs of undisciplined mastiffs that roamed the moonlit village. With few regrets we paid the shopkeeper, once we succeeded in locating him, and started up the hillside.

At the village of Padmi, situated on top of a knoll that extended out into the main valley, we stopped briefly. There was a superb view of Mt Kanjiroba to the north-west, but we were still uncertain of the exact route ahead. Tashi queried some villagers who gave a fairly broad selection of answers although agreeing that at some stage we should go via Juphal. That they told us was the most direct way to Jumla. Our ex-U.S. army map didn't enlighten us much so we decided to take their advice. Through pine forests, stippled on the grassy flanks of the valley that plummeted into the gorge below, we followed the track northwards. The glorious scent of pine; and a row of peaks filed along the horizon with the billowing dark shapes of thunderclouds forming above provided a suitable setting for retrospection. I thought of my family, the past and the happiness and time's impartial movement even in the face of tragedies. And as grey clouds swelled overhead with shafts of warm light penetrating the diminishing blue interstices, I wept for those I had lost and the ones I missed.

From the village of Maikot we descended to the river expecting to find at the end of the path a wooden bridge spanning the swift-flowing waters. Just short of the river the main track petered out into a maze of indecipherable animal tracks. Before long we were clambering along the boulder-strewn banks of the river searching for a crossing point. There were no bridges, so we sought a suitable series of boulders spaced evenly across the river that might enable us to jump across in a succession of daring bounds. No such luck. There was a shout from further up stream. Graeme had found something and waved to Tashi and me to come and join him. A large log had become jammed across the river just above a plunging tongue of water that surged beneath the greasy and inclined log. One end of the log was in the water, which flowed swiftly enough to cause our proposed means of crossing to twitch. Especially for Tashi, who cannot swim, this form of river crossing was nothing short of traumatic.

Having inspected the log, we all stepped aside for a quick round of nervous urination. We *had* to cross; so with eyes bulging with apprehension and arms and legs flailing and groping on the greasy trunk we wriggled across on our bellies, our packs making balance much more difficult and the consequences of a slip more dire. One by one we traversed above the raging torrent of white water and the deep pool of aerated water till we scrambled on to the large white boulder on the far side. There we sat soaking up the sun's warmth and soothing our taut nerves.

In the sweltering midday heat we climbed to the village of Ramgoan. We engaged a smiling local called Manjit to guide us along the ill-defined bush trails that would lead us to a high pass and thence to the town of Juphal. With luck and by reckoning of the villagers we could then be in Jumla, the main centre for West Nepal where we hoped to be met by S.P. with provisions and mail, in four days' time.

Manjit led us at a strong pace into the pine forests behind his village and up a superficial path that switchbacked abruptly up to a rhododendron-clad ridgeline. The frustratingly undulating ridge became tedious as we checked our watches and the sinking sun with still no signs of water nor a place to camp for the night. As darkness loomed, we reached a clearing on the forested flank of the ridge and there beside a wood tiled shanty was a cool spring.

I sat in the early morning sun repairing my rapidly failing gymshoes with some contact adhesive I had been carrying while the others set off up the track. With my footwear slightly better off for my efforts, I wandered through rhododendrons and tall, stout firs after the others, the track sidling down into the valley below. At a clearing where several dilapidated buildings stood, with roofs of loose planks and fragile dry stone walls, I came across a stone cairn. A piece of note paper was planted between the two uppermost stones: 'Pete, follow the cairns, blazes and arrows across the clearing,' signed "Anonymous Dogooders".

Again into the forest following the well-blazed trail of the anonymous dogooders through the thick forests. After half an hour, I came across an anonymous dogooder cutting a blaze on a tree with his ice axe. Reunited, we crossed streams, climbed a precarious ladder system up a precipitous shortcut route, and scrambled along notched logs that bypassed steep, blank sections of rock. We finally emerged on to a large meadow marked with many signs of man's presence. The charred trunks of tall firs stood like sad, symbolic epitaphs to the forest glory that once had been. At the bottom of

From Jomoson we descended the Kali Gandaki
gorge passing through Marpha, an idyllic village
on the upper side of the gorge.

Tashi and Graeme west of Daulagiri en route to Dorpatan.

the wide clearing was an old man and a flock of sheep and goats. He was scantily clad, a rather wizened but merry old fellow with a toothless grin. He sold us some ghastly goats-milk curd pale green in colour with goats' hairs floating through it. He then began to prepare his own meal. Half of his thick tsampa paste food (barley flower and water) he consumed himself and the other half he served in his own plates to his two sizeable and ferocious mastiffs. He had no shelter nor possessions to speak of, other than a very crude lean-to. He and his sheep and goats and mastiffs lived together in the forest and appeared to enjoy a similar standard of living.

Above the forests we climbed on to alpine meadows of azalea, juniper and tall frondy shrubs topped by heads of lemon-yellow bloom, tiny purple violets, red daisies and yellow buttercups. The sky was choked with pastel-grey cloud as we crossed a chuckling, clear-water stream and hiked up the mountainside towards the pass, the Kulta Banyang. The slopes had been burned off and with the spring growth they were now a bright green and ablaze with bloom. A group of local porters moved slowly above, straining beneath the weight of their leather headbands and puffing in the thin air. Engulfed by cloud we reached the crest of the Kulta Banyang at 16,500 feet.

Peering through a clearing to the far north we gazed at a vast valley. Visibility ceased beyond the hazy impressions of barren ridges diving into the indistinct grey of a gorge. Down the wet snow slopes to the north of the pass we glissaded. Shrieking with delight we sped down the slopes and on to rolling green pastures, feeling exhilarated. To the west lay massive tablelands, their surfaces buckled with gigantic geological corrugations, perched above the cliffs and gorges that flanked them. We could discern the miniature shapes of horses and squat wooden huts scattered across their extensive surfaces. I was astounded by the potential for livestock up there and amazed by the diversity of the country through which we were travelling.

At a knee and ankle shattering rate we descended into the valley below. Our descent was made more excruciating by a hailstorm that greased the steep clay path sending us for some boisterous, bottom-bashing spills as we went. At 13,000 feet we collected wild spring onions and rhubarb for our evening meal as we passed through a forest of birch with peeling golden bark. A village of shabby, flat-topped houses appeared through the pines and we homed in on it like pilgrims to Mecca. Taligaon was the least salubrious and most distinctly un-Mecca-like village I can remember visiting. We were ushered into a tiny dark room where layers of dust and seed husks covered the wooden casks and simple bed that took up most of the space. Outside on the verandah (or rooftop for the next house down) we unpacked and began to prepare our evening meal. All was performed under the supervision of a crowd of villagers decked out in tattered and sordid rags. They spun wool on their simple spindles as they stared unflinchingly through dark, mystified eyes at the curious fair-complexioned people before them.

For people in Asia dark brown eyes and black hair and at least olive to black skins is not only the norm but the rule; and along came Graeme and I, a couple of very odd humanoid types with funny coloured hair and skin and eyes. We had a host of extraordinary equipment made of silky smooth, garish nylons... and spoke in a strange, slow monotone. The people of Taligaon were an enigma; their poverty, general inactivity and the restrictive confines of the Hindu caste structure defined their lot. Yet all around them lay magnificent pasture lands, crystal clear rivers and brooks and thick green forests. There was infinite scope here, yet their apparent inability to recognise this potential thwarted any improvements in their standard of living. It reminded me of an old Sherpa in the village of Kumjung, now far behind us, who asked my father to help the Sherpa people. 'We need schools,' he said, 'our children have eyes, and yet they cannot see.' The level and quality of housing, hygiene, diet and agriculture in Taligaon was that of the destitute, the "have-nots". Even to non-agriculturalists such as Tashi, Graeme and me the possibilities here were considerable.

A clear sky spread above, the peaks around us emblazoned against its brightening expanse. Far above we could see the pass over which we had climbed the previous day, a snowclad nick in the ridgeline set above the grand alpine meadows and the fir forests. I turned my back on the splendour of the hills and followed Tashi and Graeme down the dry dusty track across terraced fields, descending into the deep valley below. We sweated our way across fields of golden wheat and through a little village that sweltered in the midday sun. I was engrossed in a daydream of enjoying R. & R. on the beautiful beaches of home, crystal clear water lapping on the shore, cool and inviting, when I was jolted back to reality. At first I thought it was a swarm of inquisitive flies that had engulfed me. The marauding bees hastily upset that notion when the first attacked my bare legs and top. Like a madman I sprinted off along the track swatting frantically at the enemy squadron that circled in rapid tactical orbits.

After 100 feet they were apparently satisfied that they had escorted me beyond their jurisdiction — they had certainly given me sufficient painful incentive not to return. I hobbled on, trying to ignore the several painful stings I had received. We began a descending traverse through a forest till we reached the outskirts of Juphal, 1000 feet above the Thulu Beri river that flowed along the base of the very barren valley. We followed the stony paths that crisscrossed the village, passing fields and houses and local people toiling with hoes and sickles and single-furrow, bullock-drawn ploughs. We searched for accommodation. At an official-looking building we met a man who introduced himself in halting English as the representative for Royal Nepal Airlines (R.N.A.C.) in Juphal. Enjoying the opportunity to demonstrate his multilingual prowess, he proceeded to enlighten us on a number of things. He told us, in the first breath, that the shops had very little to offer. The hotels, there were only two, served only dahl bhat. There was an airfield nearby where twin engine aircraft periodically landed, and Juphal was in a 'restricted area'.

'This is a restricted area?' quizzed Graeme.

'Oh, yes,' confirmed our Royal Nepal Airlines information man. 'This town is in the District of Dolpa. This is very restricted area.'

'Gor blimey. And I wanted a rest day.'

We decided the risk could not be too great as we had not seen any uniformed authorities and, besides, we did need a rest day. Time to eat large meals, wash, and rest and write our ever-lagging journals. At the hotel beside the airstrip, we took a spartan room and consumed an equally simple meal of dahl bhat while attempting to communicate with Manjit, our very humble guide, over glasses of innocuous rakshi. Manjit was a Karmi, a very low Hindu caste, and as such was not supposed to touch the food, utensils, and abode of those of higher caste. He should stay outside of the hotel, refuse to eat with us and certainly refrain from eating off the hotel's enamel plates. He should tolerate being called 'bai' or younger brother instead of the more respectful 'dai' (older brother) and be subjected to the mistreatment reserved for those of the lowest castes. We told him to lie. 'Tell them you are a gurung (a middling caste),' we commanded. We watched him enjoying the greater respect, attention and treatment — normal treatment — that he received from the hotel proprietor.

Tashi told Graeme and me of the consequences should our seemingly harmless deception be exposed. Caste was not taken lightly. The villagers, Tashi said, would beat him cruelly and we would be ejected from the hotel for association with such a person. The hotel proprietor and his employees did ask him what caste he was and he proffered the lie, but I noted the eye contact between them. There was clearly doubt in their minds. Manjit was so conditioned to his lot of inferiority that he could never hope to carry it off for too long.

It was late afternoon and the sun was heading west towards the rough, barren hills and craggy snow-glazed summits of Dolpa; a high and desolate wilderness on the Nepali-Tibetan border. A gentleman with a black Nepali cap, who had formerly introduced himself as an R.N.A.C. official reappeared under the title of local policeman. Tashi was nervous. He talked with the policeman for a while, speaking softly and intently. He was asked to procure our permits. Reluctantly Graeme and I handed them over. The policeman scrutinized them at length showing them to other hotel guests who had gathered to observe our trials and tribulations. Many of the guests, we later discovered, were also policemen, waiting for a plane to take them out of Dolpa so they could go on leave... just what we needed.

After considerable deliberation the policeman informed us that we were not supposed to be in the district of Dolpa and that he would have to take us to Dunai, the district headquarters, in the morning. 'We leave at 5 am tomorrow,' he commanded in Nepali. There we could put our case to the chief district officer. We were aghast, horrified at the prospect and what it could mean to our bid to traverse the Himalayas. We had followed the advice of local people on the route to Jumla west of Dolpa, and had never intended breaking any regulations or restrictions. Ignorant of what lay ahead, we had inadvertently hiked into the prohibited border district of Nepal.

Explain though we did, the policeman was adamant, much to the entertainment and amusement of the audience that had gathered. When some of them saw fit to contribute their views on the matter Graeme reacted ferociously. He roared at them and chased them away from the room where we were discussing our situation with the policeman. The policeman refused to consider our predicament or the unintentional nature of our visit to Dolpa. He was nervous. He was torn between his duties and the responsibility we placed upon him. He wanted to confide in his superior officer.

Some time later, Tashi and the policeman returned with the officer, a short, bald-headed man wearing a pretentious toothy grin and a decidedly more ebullient mien than his lugubrious offsider. He seemed ready to consider releasing us. However, he now felt the matter to be far too public. We would have to visit the C.D.O. in Dunai as the policeman had originally decided... The day had not gone well. My ankles were swollen from the bee stings and were quite painful and our looked-forward-to rest day had turned into a pain in the neck!

A glass of rakshi was in order so together with the friendly R.N.A.C. man we sat in front of the squalid hotel and discussed at length our predicament and the mysterious forbidden district of Dolpa. It appeared that the authorities had some compelling reasons for closing the district. There had recently been the ghastly murder of a German couple who, according to the story, had been mutilated with knives. There was the American Peace Corps volunteer whom we already knew about and there were tales of local people returning home after working in lowland Nepal being attacked, robbed and murdered. Then there were stories of bands of wild Tibetan warriors being armed by Indian and CIA sources. They apparently made frequent sorties across the high and desolate border into Tibet to attack Chinese border patrols... If only a tenth of the bloodcurdling stories were bona fide that would be sufficient to justify all of our apprehensions. There was a prison in Dunai and inside it were some 'very bad men' including the murderers of the German couple. But the R.N.A.C. man assured us: 'The C.D.O. will only send you to the border of the district under a police escort to ensure your safety... no more. You will soon be able to leave,' he added positively.

At the crack of dawn we sent Marjit hurrying back home, concerned that he might become involved and used as a scapegoat.

At 5 am the senior policeman was in the dusty square outside the hotel rooms, wearing his uniform. Just Tashi and Graeme would accompany him to Dunai while I remained in Juphal with my uncomfortable bee stings and all our equipment... and to act as a possible "safety" should anything go wrong at Dunai.

The day ticked by tediously and I did my utmost to keep myself busy, distracted. Reading, writing, mending some of our gear, cups of tea and walks upon the deserted airstrip. I began to understand a little, the lot of those who remain behind when soldiers go off to war. The anguish of speculation. By evening, I was sure there must have been complications and I resigned myself to not seeing them until the following day. I would have to make a number of decisions based on my assumption that their absence meant there was trouble in Dunai... at the Dunai jail.

At 6.30 pm our R.N.A.C. friend came into my room. 'There are four

Cedar forest above Juphal in western Nepal.

*Graeme among the dry hills of western Nepal,
with Mt Kanjiroba in the distance.*

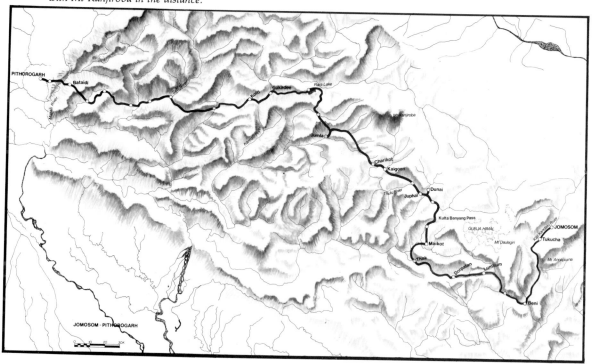

JOMOSOM - PITHOROGARH

125

people coming. They could be your friends.'

I rushed outside and, looking past the barbed-wire fence that ran between the yard and the airfield, I saw a lone figure; half walking, half running in the evening gloom. It was Graeme, and as he approached I could see he held a letter in his hand. He appeared tired; his drawn face reflected the tensions that he must have endured.

'What's the situation?'

'It's O.K.,' he answered with reserve.

'Can we go?' I pressed impatiently.

'Yes. We'll leave tomorrow.' He seemed strangely reluctant to impart what had happened and what lay before us. 'Here, read this, and tell me what you would have done.' It was a note Graeme had sent to me by the police officer who had set out from Dunai to return to Juphal in early afternoon. Graeme and Tashi, who had been allowed to leave later in the day with another policeman, had caught up with him as he made leisurely progress. I opened the envelope and read.

Dunai 10.6.81 (1.30 pm)

Dear Peter,

The CDO has asked us to stay in Dunai tonight while he considers his verdict. He is a very astute man and is trying to be fair — he feels that he is in a difficult situation. He will probably give us his decision in the morning. I told him about your altitude sickness on the pass and about your sore ankle, but he did say that if you felt well enough he would like to see you. It has to be over to you to consider whether or not you are well enough to come up. If you do could you please bring:

1. Our sleeping mats.
2. Our pile jackets.
3. My diary.
4. Any spare beautiful woman for Tash.

If you do come, I'm sure you'll put a lock on the room. Just thought of No. 5 — bring the blue trekking map.

I'll restate, we don't need you but if you feel well enough that's fine. If you don't see us tomorrow, we'll send another message.

No. 6. Tash has just said bring his watch.

Love Tash and Ding.

Putting the letter down I turned to Graeme who stood watching me intently. 'I would have remained here. If things had gone badly, our best chances would have been my staying away from Dunai... and the Dunai jail. Anyway tell me what happened.'

This is Graeme's story:

We had walked the ten kilometres to Dunai by 7 am and were taken to the police barracks. Here I was seated in a chair and watched over by a guard armed with a vintage Lee Enfield, while Tash was marched off for the first of the interrogation sessions with the Chief District Officer — the highest

126

authority this side of Kathmandu!

He was back within 15 minutes, his brow lined with concern. 'What's he like?' I asked eagerly.

'He's a karmi,' replied Tash with a little grin.

'What did he ask you?'

'Where I came from... how much I am being paid.'

'How did you answer that one?'

'Oh, I said I was getting 25 rupees a day!'

We sat there for about five hours discussing tactics, reflecting on our possible fate, or just nattering — we felt very close, very confident in each other — it was a good feeling. The grey walls of the Dunai jail looked on without emotion — beyond stretched endless mountains. A jail here seemed incongruous.

About midday we were summoned by the CDO. We climbed steep wooden steps and were shown through a curtain in a pleasant office. Behind a large desk sat the CDO, a good-looking, middle-aged man. The second-in-command sat opposite him, and next to him stood another officer with bulging eyes. An ADC with a side arm stood at the door, and beyond him a guard with a rifle.

I introduced myself confidently and shook the CDO's hand. Tashi bowed slightly and "namasted" with his hands. Then the interrogation began.

'What are you doing in Dolpa? How did you get here? How many days did it take?'

I explained that we had asked the locals the best way to Jumla and they had told us that this was the only way. I apologised for the inconvenience we had caused and said we had no intention of breaking any law.

This brought a firm reply: 'Maybe you did not mean to, but you have and you should be in jail. The minimum punishment for this violation is two months in prison... and for the guide,' he added, looking at Tashi, 'four months in prison.'

With this Tashi fell to his knees. If it was an act, he did it very well.

'But Tashi is a good man,' I protested firmly.

'To you he may be a good man, but to me he is the culprit,' replied the CDO. 'He should be in jail.' With that he looked out the window to begin the first of many silences.

I decided to make use of them to ask him about his family, to tell him he spoke excellent English — I was sickeningly charming. Finally he looked back at me and asked, 'What am I to do with you — everyone knows about you — I am forced to punish you. What do you think I should do?'

'Well sir,' I began, trying not to sound too eager, 'I suggest that you have us escorted out of the area and that you ask us to reimburse the Nepalese Government for its trouble.'

'This is nothing to do with the government, I am the law here... where are your permits?'

He began scrutinizing our permits, reading out all the names on my crazy one.

'Why is your friend not here?'

127

Rara lake in western Nepal, a magnificent sweep of water at 10,000 ft.

'He has very bad altitude sickness and has been stung by bees.' This sounded a bit much.

'Why has he got an official trekking permit?'

'Because he does some work with the Himalayan Trust.'

'What is this Himalayan Trust?'

I told him about the trust and about Ed Hillary.

'Is this Sir Hillary from New Zealand?' He didn't click to the relationship between Pete and Ed and I decided not to tell him unless it became necessary, in case this whole business went bad.

The CDO threw a command at the door and the ADC escorted Tash out of the room. We were to be questioned separately.

Suddenly he blurted out, 'How do you like dahl bhat?'

'I don't mind it too much, but I get sick of it every day... it's so different from what we normally eat in New Zealand.'

'What do you eat?'

'Lots of meat,' I said, feeling on difficult ground as the CDO was probably a strict vegetarian.

'Do you speak Nepali?' he asked, changing the subject.

'Ali cutti,' I said uncertainly.

'What do you speak?'

'I studied French and Latin at school and later learned a little Spanish, but I find Nepali very difficult.'

'How much Nepali do you speak?'

'Just enough to ask for necessities.'

'How much English does your guide speak?'

'Perfect English.' He looked surprised — I didn't tell him that Tash also spoke two Tibetan languages as well as Sherpa, Hindi, Bengali, and Garhwali. He had been speaking to him in Nepali, which was Tashi's first language.

'Where was he educated?'

'At a government school in Darjeeling.'

There was another long silence while the CDO stared out the window.

'Is this area restricted because of the murders?' I asked innocently, and immediately regretted this question, as it touched a nerve and the CDO became instantly alert.

'What do you know about the murders?'

'I know that two Germans were murdered near here during November.'

'When did you first hear about these?'

'About two months ago when I spoke to some Germans at Makalu basecamp.'

'Yes, the two murderers are in the prison now — have you seen our prison?'

'Yes, I had noticed,' I gulped.

Eventually the CDO said, 'I am going to keep you here for the night, and give you my verdict in the morning.'

I was then led back to my chair in the courtyard where the ADC told the guard with the ancient Lee Enfield to keep an eye on me.

Twenty minutes later Tashi was led back, looking worn.

Another hard day in the interrogation room, eh?

About 2.30 our police escort from Juphal set off for home, so I gave him a note for Pete. The note was written to be read by the CDO so I was exceptionally careful. At about 4 pm we were once again led to the CDO.

'How do you feel?' he asked, searching my face.

'Nervous,' I answered with deliberate cold understatement.

'Where did you meet Tashi?'

I decided it was time to tell him that the Indian Government was involved in our trip.

'Tashi is a top Indian mountaineer working for the Indian Mountaineering Foundation.'

'Why are you in a hurry to reach Jumla?'

'Because we need to meet our Indian leader there in a few days.'

'What is his name?'

'S.P. Chamoli.'

'What is his profession?'

'Indo-Tibetan border policeman,' I said boldly.

'Are you writing a book?'

'Yes.'

'I am not allowing you to go on to Jumla. How would you like to be sent back the way you came?'

'I am afraid that my friend is too sick to go back over that pass.'

'What am I to do then?' asked the CDO.

'Send us down the valley,' I suggested, as this was roughly the direction we wanted to go.

The CDO conferred with his aides. 'Okay, you will be escorted down valley — you will pay the escort 500 rupees.'

With our permits restored, Tashi and I left Dunai quickly, hurrying down the path to Juphal like a couple of naughty boys running home from school. The experiences of the day had cemented the bond of trust and friendship between us. We nattered vigorously as the sun dipped behind the high hills and the valley became instantly cool.

As we sipped from grubby glasses of rough rakshi I could feel the easing tensions in Tashi and Graeme... The fading image of Dunai's austere prison set amongst those barren, brown hills near the Tibetan border, the despotic CDO, our trans-Himalayan adventure in the balance. I began to realise just how much I would have had to have done should the CDO have decided not to be so reasonable. The onus would have been on me to communicate with the outside world intimating our whereabouts and our predicament.

The night passed uncomfortably slowly as we lay restlessly in our sleeping bags eager to get moving in the morning and leave the restrictive boundaries of the forbidden district of Dolpa.

We paid the bill at the Juphal hotel and without regret followed our policeman escort down the rubble-strewn track. With my thoughts on possible repercussions from the incident we crossed the river to a village on the north side and climbed up a side valley to a forested pass. Our policeman was getting very tired. Not even loud bursts of ethnic music from his constant companion, a transistor tuned into All Nepal Radio, seemed to help him as we hiked up through stands of tall firs below the pass. Graeme and Tashi stopped at a yak breeding farm to get him a cup of tea. Apparently the government stud farm was not progressing as well as was expected and there was little milk available. There were ten animals on the farm; nine male yaks and one female nak.

At the pass a group of friendly local people who gave us chapaties to nibble on, told us that a police inspector was on his way. We set off down the far side, rounded the first bend in the track and there, beside his horse, stood a large gentleman reeking with importance and authority. With visions of being re-arrested and again interrogated, Graeme and I greeted the inspector with self-conscious toothy grins and a polite 'Namaste' and continued down the track at a good pace. Tashi and our escort soon caught up with us having delivered an explanation to the suspicious inspector, and on we went towards the border. At the village of Kaigoan a local policeman took over as escort. He set out to rectify any wrong impressions we might have had about the fitness of Nepali policemen. However, the policeman's rapid pace and lack of a pack on his back failed to grind us into the dust as all three of us were in a "bloody-minded" state. At a scorching pace we followed the track across the hillside opposite Kaigoan, climbing higher and higher. We passed through small villages of flat-topped houses, their entrances protected by simple wood carvings, not unlike Polynesian traditional carvings. The inhabitants were clad in rags, a reticent and shy people. The policeman was treated with excessive respect, not for what he was but for the all-powerful force he represented. We were the subjects of their innocent awe; perhaps to them we were humanoids no more closely related to them than man is to chimpanzees or orang-outangs.

Graeme hypothesised a connection between the Polynesian-style carvings that we found in this area of West Nepal (and saw at no other point during the entire Himalayan traverse) and those of the Polynesian people. He contended that the Maori people of New Zealand migrated through this part of the world, paddling their canoes from island to island over hundreds of years. Down the Indonesian archipelagoes and finally to the atolls and islands of the Pacific basin. It was great stuff, however tenuous, and it passed the time of day as we plodded along the track behind our harried escort. At the village of Charikot we purchased some popped corn and some tea. We continued on without our police escort to a 14,000-foot pass, the boundary line of the district of Dolpa. I turned to take a last glimpse of Dolpa and raised my hand into the cool mountain air that breezed from the west. The other side of Churchill's victory sign, delivered with a degree of passion, accompanied my parting glance before turning and stepping into another world.

For two days we converged on Jumla, the largest town in Western Nepal, passing trains of heavily-laden horses and porters. Whereas yaks and bullocks are the load-carriers in the eastern Himalayas horses are in the west. At one stage the track climbed up a side-stream to avoid a gorge in the main valley. This was clear, swift water, its white boiling turbulence highlighted by the shafts of sunlight that penetrated the jade-green canopy. Tiny birds flitted, alighting briefly on the moss-covered stones to catch insects. As the stream's gradient eased the countryside was transformed. Before us spread a vast plain of green, fertile pastures, a slow meandering stream, pine forests that reached high toward the weathered tops; summits contoured to gentle curves by time. The peaceful beauty around us sent me off into a pleasant little world of daydreams and anticipation of the letters and replenishments that we hoped to find awaiting us in Jumla along with S.P.

From the comparative cool of the pasturelands we descended a dusty track to the heat of the main valley: dense conglomerations of brown, mud-walled houses; fields and paddies being prepared for the monsoon growing season; cud-chewing cows; the tinkling of bells on horses laden with bamboo baskets of grain or goods; the crying of babies perched on their mothers' hips; the strange uncomprehending gaze of the village people. The people of Western Nepal are darker skinned than elsewhere in the country and their features are more typically Indian. Change has been particularly slow here. Lifestyles dictated by caste and serfdom are still strong, with a man's lot predestined from birth to death. Down the broad valley we went, its tilled surface a mosaic of greens and browns. We marched on in the early afternoon heat till the fields gave way to the rambling rural metropolis of Jumla.

Along the stone-paved mainstreet of the town we sauntered, nibbling sticky, sweet jilebies, and peering into the gloomy shops, like a trio of country lads come for a night on the town. It was as if we had stepped backward in time and were visiting a medieval township of long ago. There were groups of district headquarters civil servants loitering in the street, some gathered in groups and chatting. I wondered how we would ever locate S.P. with so many people around.

A familiar voice: 'Hey, up here!' Behind us and leaning out from a street-side balcony, was S.P. Chamoli. He was looking very well and was obviously pleased to see us. He ushered us into the dingy hotel where he was staying, cautioning us to watch our heads as we stooped to enter the dark and narrow stairwell. As we groped in the near darkness he muttered something about how 'completely useless the hotelkeeper was,' and how 'you cannot get even one cup of tea in the morning.'

S.P. had brought letters, food and another pair of shoes to replace my dilapidated pair. A hush settled over us as we became engrossed in our letters, with occasional breaks to imbibe the food treats sent with S.P. by Michael Okkerse, from New Zealand. It was always easy to please us as food represented one of the chief problems on our journey and edible treats were always received with much enthusiasm! Then there was a letter for me from Mountain Travel Ltd in Kathmandu; I had official permission from His Majesty's Government of Nepal to attempt the West Ridge of Mt Everest in 1984. I was delighted as my plans for several years of intensive Himalayan activities were shaping up well. We were nearly halfway to completing the first traverse of the world's mightiest mountain chain and already I was receiving permission to attempt some of the world's highest mountains for the years to follow.

S.P. was in good form, very enthusiastic and obviously looking forward to travelling with us across far western Nepal to the border with India. His presence and company would cheer Tashi and bring the traverse team up to four, the number originally intended. When we departed for Rara lake the next morning, S.P. was well prepared. He was kitted out in long blue socks, a pair of baggy "room for two" running shorts, a blue paisley shirt, a red cotton headband and some movie-director-style dark glasses. With beads of perspiration on his brow he pounded along the path at a brisk pace, swinging his bamboo stick and smiling happily. The sun blazed down on us as we hiked upward above the haze-filled valley of Jumla and the gently-rolling pine-covered hills; so different from the wild mountains and gorges of Eastern Nepal. We crossed over a pasture-clad pass from where we could peer through the morning haze at the Kanjiroba massif, a convoluted mass streaked with fingers of white snow. We descended the far side of the pass into the forest, passing a succession of groups of Nepali people on their way to Jumla. Some sang as they went, some chatted and laughed while others walked in silence. Then there was that new breed of Nepalese track-users, folk who go nowhere without their transistors blaring out music from All Nepal Radio. Occasionally, we stopped for tea at trackside teashops —

dilapidated shacks built of whatever was available in the area — and confirmed the local love for spice. Even the tea was liberally spiced with pepper or chilli so we returned to the hot, dusty paths... hot!

From a stream where two water wheels drove large grindstones that whirred smoothly, with the smell of freshly-ground flour seeping from the doorways, we climbed several hundred feet. A tiny settlement of two flat-topped teahouses nestled beneath a great cliff-face that yawned out over the buildings, sheltering them from the elements. We laid out our sleeping bags on the roof of one of the buildings. While sipping copious quantities of tea, I looked out from our niche in the hillside at the landscape around us, a classical Japanese painting. Towers of golden rock and cliff-faces that rose from a sea of pines, with the gnarled shapes of older trees standing above them. The sun splashed a rich glaze on the scene until it left us in a cooling pool of grey.

Over another pass and down through thick forests, our feet making a crunching sound as they hit the pine needle carpet; we marched in silence, each of us lost in his own thoughts. Progressively during the expedition I had noticed a reduction in verbal communication, as if all that could be said had been said, perhaps because there remained little to discover about our companions. We had congregated as a group of friends, fellow mountaineers and adventurers to undertake an extraordinary challenge. Now, much as partners in a business venture, our interactions were largely restricted to the business of the traverse, social interaction frequently becoming unrewarding. I found myself often siding with S.P. while poor Tashi continually endeavoured to maintain a neutral stance between us all. Perhaps the reduction in our communication was a good thing although it meant more time for introspection and dwelling upon our problems. Again and again I had confirmed that the greatest challenge in crossing the Himalayas from Kanchenjunga to K2, daunting in itself, was the ten months that Tashi, Graeme and I (periodically accompanied by S.P. and others) had to be together. Walking and climbing together, eating and camping together, assisting one another whether sick or just homesick, the "trans-Himalaya or bust" resolution wavering.

I stopped by a stream of crystal clear water that drained a narrow valley above the track. I wanted to be by myself. I washed my face and hands in the cool water and brushed my teeth, enjoying the simple rituals involved in basic hygiene. Tiny flowers floated on the surface of the stream. Looking up I found a spray of lavender and white jasmine hanging down over the flowing water, exuding its gorgeous scent. Hmm. *We* could all do with a little jasmine, thought I, as I heaved my pack on my back and continued on along the winding path.

Reunited, we hiked up the hill at a brisk pace. We reached an alpine meadow that swept before us towards a distant hill clad in dark firs. I was certain that Lake Rara was not far ahead so I walked more quickly in anticipation. The green sword swept downward and a vast plain of blue appeared before me. Rara, Nepal's largest lake. Fringed by dark green forests and clearings of pale green, the great lake nestled amongst the hills. The dark rolling forms stood against the hazy sky and, in the distance, the sepia images of the Kanjiroba massif loomed indistinctly. Across the lake, its surface flecked by light catching the backs of tiny waves, I could see some buildings. I knew they would be the newly-formed Rara Lake National Park Headquarters and that there we would find an old friend, Lhakpa Norbu. Lhakpa is a Sherpa from the Everest area of Nepal who spent four years in New Zealand studying national parks and park administration. He was administering the park.

With Tashi, I followed the path as it wound its way around the lake's shoreline — waterweed, rushes and here and there, stretches of rounded pebbles. At the western end of the lake, we crossed a wooden footbridge that spanned the lake's sole outlet stream, a structure liberally ornamented and protected by Polynesian-style carvings. Around the emerald clear waters by the shore we continued to the buildings that comprised the Park HQ. Playing volleyball with the members of the army patrol was a stocky and very agile character. On hearing us approach he swung around with a smile on his face and in a strong New Zealand accent greeted us: 'Gidday Peter. What a surprise! What brings you to Rara?'

It was already late in the day as Lhakpa led us across a field of alpine flowers to his abode, a spacious log cabin on the fringe of the forest. Soon we were all ensconced in the cosy building, seated around a table, our exuberant faces lit by the light of a flickering kerosene wick. We talked into the night of mutual friends, New Zealand, Nepal, our bid to traverse the Himalayas; the frivolity of, as S.P. terms it, just chitchat. Lhakpa told us of his work at Lake Rara and his problems with enforcing the rules of the National Park here in the hills at 10,000 feet. Two villages had been moved out to make way for the birds and trees and wildlife. There was still trouble with people grazing animals on the lush meadows and fishing in the lake so most of his time had been spent enforcing the National Park ethic and trying to explain to the local people the reasons for doing so. The two deserted villages stood above the lake, eerie and silent, quite uncharacteristically still for a land of vibrant villages, their stoic wood carvings overseeing the desertion. I wanted to climb up to one and wander along its vacated pathways, but something prevented me.

After a day of rest in the peaceful surrounds of Lake Rara we headed west following the little outlet stream from the lake, into the forests of huge poplars and flowering chestnuts. All day we followed the gradually descending river tracing the sun's arc, from east to west, towards the Karnali river. We had exchanged the cool of Rara and its pine forests for the heat and the barren hillsides of a dry and parched Western Nepal, awaiting the alleviation of a monsoon dousing. By the river, small villages sprouted from the hillsides with banana palms and green paddies filled with water connected by small hand-dug irrigation canals. Footsore and tired we turned south into the Karnali valley and stared down at the great body of water that surged below. At the village of Sukadee we halted for the night, finding lodgings at the local police station. In fact we moved in before the policeman had returned from somewhere in the village on the advice of a local resident. When he did return there was no problem.

Tashi and I cooked dinner and collected water from the village water collection point-cum-irrigation ditch-cum-animal watering spot. Graeme rested as he had become feverish and S.P. chatted to the policeman, asking about the route ahead to the Indo-Nepal border. Large black clouds loomed down valley, crackling with lightning and filling the hot and humid sky with foreboding.

The clouds had cleared with the dawning of the new day and our suspicions that the monsoon might have finally caught up with us dispersed. We descended through paddy fields to the Karnali river. Here we found people queuing for a ride on a precarious flying fox across the river's broad expanse of rushing water. A new bridge was approaching completion alongside so we balanced across the swaying wire cables, saving ourselves a lengthy wait for the flying fox and giving ourselves a little heart-racing excitement. We balanced, groped, almost pirouetting upon the quivering cables fifty feet above the surging torrent. The bridge-building team to my surprise, seemed quite happy at our unconventional crossing of their uncompleted bridge, and plied us with tea as we stepped on to the western bank.

Down the true right bank we scrambled, following a path that wound its way across bare rock bluffs, boulder-strewn river flats, stands of tall spiny tree cacti and through pools of desert heat. A strong dry wind blew up valley over the parched land, the sun blazed relentlessly down on our perspiring brows. Large lizards, reminiscent of a bygone era, scuttled across the smooth river-worn boulders, halting on top and pumping the scorched air into their bodies in a series of rhythmic pressups. We walked single file along a thread of the web of tracks that crisscrossed the valley floor. You followed the heels of the one in front and, if you were the one in front, then you followed your nose. At one rest stop, I noticed a tiny scaly creature crawling down the side of the rock I was sitting upon. It looked strangely familiar. On closer examination I could see front pincers and a curled tail... a juvenile scorpion.

Ten kilometres of this strange stony desert and we again turned west — up a side stream towards the village of Kolti leaving the Karnali to flow southward without us. We staggered on for several hours in the almost intolerable afternoon heat till we reached the village. Sitting on the steps of the local shop the four of us awaited the food and rakshi that the shopkeeper had unenthusiastically agreed to supply us. I took off my shoes and aired my sore, pink feet and looked across the grass-covered quadrangle before me. A tall pipal tree stood in the middle offering its shade to a flock of goats that were chewing their cud with obvious contentment. Beyond was a row of houses, their stone walls plastered with white clay. Some were roofed with a thick thatching, others with slabs of rock that passed for tiles. Men sat in groups around the open doorways, chatting, looking our way. No one seemed to be doing anything. The food was taking a long time; the shopkeeper had changed his mind about our staying the night at his house... Both he and his wife were drinking heavily and were becoming quite drunk and belligerent.

The crowd around us parted and a lone European walked up to us. He was

135

an American Peace Corps volunteer who had spent nearly two years in the village. He described the people as an extraordinary group; the most inhospitable, unfriendly and selfish lot he had ever come across. He thought it remarkable that they had agreed to give us food at all; for that we had to thank S.P. who had pressured them into cooperation after a long argument in Nepali and Hindi. The American told us that they stole from one another and that disputes and squabbles involved them in incessant conflict. The rumpus that ensued over payment after we had finished our meal was all the incentive we needed to farewell the progressively more and more hostile inhabitants of the village. We marched on in the falling rain to the next village where we were received by an aristocratic gentleman of the highest Hindu caste who agreed happily to provide us with food and shelter. The kindness with which we were received by this man's family was in spectacular contrast to the reception in Kolti. Being devout Hindus there would be no meat, no eggs, no alcohol and none of Kolti's unpleasantness; they plied us with delicious vegetarian food. As a family they seemed blessed with smiles and a happy, gracious disposition. Tashi and I slept outside on the stone-paved courtyard beneath makeshift shelters we constructed with our ponchos. It rained lightly during the night, cooling the air; and I slept soundly.

It was early. I looked out from beneath my poncho shelter towards the east where layers of slate-grey cloud lingered about the hills and beams of the rising sun filtered through the gaps. Our smiling host appeared before me with tea and biscuits and we exchanged cheerful greetings. As I drank I looked up at his large house behind him. The dazzling whitewashed walls, three storeys high, the sky-blue window sashes, a wooden grill for one window, a figure-8 opening in an ornately carved frame for another, shutters and a flower box for the next. Above the stone slates of the roof, the forested hillside climbed steeply to the grey sky.

For six days we forged on, westward, a little closer to Mt K2, and our journey's end still over 2500 kilometres away to the north-west. Half-way point for the traverse would be the Indo-Nepalese border. A succession of low passes, green pastures and gnarled stands of holly and oak unfolded before us. Small shanty villages were scattered across the landscape. At the end of the first of the six days before the border, we climbed to the village of Nawakot and there halted to have our evening meal. The village had a very clear demarcation between the homes of the high castes and those of lower castes. A gap of several fields separated the two groups of houses — one above and one below. Western Nepal is so removed from the influences of the outside world that it resembles a journey backward in time — a quick journey in Dr Who's flying phone-booth. Whereas the caste system is being modified in India and Central Nepal, it clearly had not changed one iota in the west of the country. The villagers were intrigued by our European hairy legs and white skin and the strange paraphernalia that accompanied us — all things that Nepalese in central and eastern Nepal on the main tourist routes are quite familiar with. Here men and women have very definite roles and places. The women are meek and softly spoken, hovering in the background,

*Tashi with Polynesian-style wood carvings in
western Nepal.*

even secreted away upstairs or cooking the food that periodically appears.
Unheard of is the self-made man. You are what your father begat in station,
aspiration and expectation.

I remember a small boy from the lower tier of houses in the village coming
to the shop where we were having our food. He held a tiny brass vessel in his
hands and stood with resigned patience just beyond where we sat eating. The
shopkeeper was ignoring him until we gestured that, perhaps, he should
serve him. The boy, wearing a tattered cotton vest and short pants, placed
the brass container he clasped on the ground and stood respectfully
backwards. The shopkeeper, who was of high caste, stepped forward and
uplifted the vessel, once the low-caste boy was well clear. Thus he could not
be polluted by his close proximity. The shopkeeper filled it with the kerosene
the boy wanted. The process was repeated in reverse with the container
being replaced on the ground and a rupee note the boy had left there being
taken in payment. The shopkeeper returned to where the boy stood.
Without as much as a word of acknowledgement or thanks, he dropped the
change, from a safe distance into the boy's cupped hands.

A day later we witnessed another equally poignant but far sadder incident.
We had stopped at a track-side teahouse near a hilltop to rehydrate with cups
of syrupy, sweet tea. There we saw one of the most unfortunate and yet
valiant people I have met. A porter came trudging up the track, the deep

valley dropping away below him, and feeling hot and thirsty, as we were, he decided to stop for a cup of tea. He was an untouchable, a man of no caste at all and considered in Hindu society as very lowly. Special, rather grubby, glasses were kept outside the teashop for such people. As he approached the building in which we sat sheltering from the sun we noticed he was injured. His left hand and wrist were bandaged in grimy dressings that covered a weeping wound and a grossly swollen hand. The other arm had been broken just above the elbow in the humerus so that the whole forearm could move independently of the upper arm. Remarkably, his hand was still quite useful as apparently the arm's musculature had adapted to the total breakage and separation of the bone. It was fortunate, too, as his other bandaged hand was almost useless and obviously very painful. We bought him tea which the teashop walla poured into one of the glasses for untouchables. The disabled porter drank his tea, keeping well clear of the teashop. When he had finished, he washed the glass himself and replaced it outside the building for the next untouchable to use. Tashi queried him about medical treatment for his arms but he replied that he had been to a hospital down on the plains several times and they had given him some pills and sent him away. The pills had not helped. No wonder, I thought; this man needs the attentions of an orthopedic surgeon. Alas... he will never receive that help. I watched him replace his headband, and lift his bamboo basket of goods, then plod slowly off up the hill.

The grey sky hung ominously low over the rolling hills as we walked on in the humid heat, passing fields of cultivated wheat and corn. The humidity began to take its toll with S.P. who developed the dreaded prickly-heat crutch — one of the more uncomfortable afflictions one can acquire while walking in the Himalayas. Poor fellow, he walked like a Texan who had lived his life in the saddle and for whom walking was an unusual experience. As a distraction from the heat and humidity and the overcast, dull days Tashi told us folk stories of the Himalaya. He always related them with a grin on his face as if he could be pulling our legs.

'In the very beginning all yaks and buffaloes were brothers. They had short hair like cows and lived down in the low country and on the sweltering plains. One day one of the brothers decided he had to go and visit the great snow mountains, the Himalaya, that were clear in the early mornings along the northern horizon. He wanted to visit these great places, go to the snow and escape the heat. His brother urged him to take his coat of hair as well, warning him of the cold in the high mountains. So the brother took both coats of hair and, looking remarkably hairy, like a yak, he took leave of his now hairless brother, requesting him to look after his family while he was away.

'The hairy brother climbed through the hills until he reached the snows of the Himalaya. He liked it there and never returned as the double length coat of hair kept him amply warm in the cool mountain air. Meanwhile, his brother, the now hairless water buffalo, his neck outstretched and eyes peering forward — as buffaloes do to this day — kept looking towards the Himalaya awaiting his brother's return. Never did he come, nor did he send back his additional coat!'

Just then a torrential downpour pelted from the heavens, turning the track into a waterway of rushing brown water. With umbrellas erected and shoes filled with water we navigated our way to the next teahouse. We crammed inside with a large number of local people who were also seeking shelter and waited for the rains to abate.

Further west we reached the Seti river, a large grey braid flowing south towards the Gangetic plains. We followed the banks of the river through small villages and paddy fields where the people were preparing their paddies for the monsoon crops. Men were ploughing the soil with single-furrowed ploughs drawn by brahman bulls; others worked on the walls of the paddies with short-handled hoes, or redirected channels of water. The women followed, bent almost double as they laboriously planted the delicate rice seedlings in the murky, foot-deep water. Singing together they moved slowly forward across the paddy.

Branching off the Seti valley, we followed the Kalanka river, stopping occasionally for a much-needed swim in the refreshing waters. The month before the monsoon is always the hottest period in Asia as the land swelters until the cooling rains fall giving life to the parched land. At one village we ate at a house where the mother had recently died. It was the thirteenth day since her death and they were holding the final ceremony. All her sons had shaven their heads and were dressed in white. Down by the river they had set up an altar, stepping stones on which her spirit would ascend to the next life, offerings of food and flowers and a calf adorned with a tikka, a splash of ochre on its brow. A holy man chanted incantations throughout the ceremony. They made the offerings and prepared the body for cremation and the spirit for its journey to the next life.

In intermittent rain we followed a major track that traversed the hillsides and crossed passes on its way towards Bataidi, the main centre for the western border district of Nepal. With shirts off, umbrellas up and the track a slick, muddy surface, we descended from the passes into the valleys. The descent required good skiing postures and quick footwork or you reaped the consequences of a miscalculation — a resounding thump on the steep, almost frictionless surface. Down in the valley, I pondered the contrasts between our lives and those of the people we passed on our journey. On one hand westerners, who must appear to the hillpeople as technological vagrants, and on the other hand a vast population of dark-skinned people wearing tatty clothes and living in very simple conditions, miles from technological civilisation. Our every move was observed by these people across whose land we were travelling; entering their lives briefly and then departing for somewhere else. Almost an analogy in itself of our two different lives. Although we travelled the paths of their country in the same way as they did, we possessed an alternative. The potential given us through education and the good fortune to be born in a land where the population pressures didn't hamper development were enormous. It was seldom that we had experienced any resentment from the local people who regularly greeted us with friendly grins and kindness — no room for truculent jealousies.

The track descended the ridgeline to Bataidi, the hilltop headquarters

139

perched above the Makali river, the natural borderline between India and Nepal. We skirted the forbidding stone-walled jail to the east of the town and marched down the main street through the busy bazaar. The path descended abruptly to Jolaghat, the border crossing-point where a footbridge spanned the river. Beyond the river loomed the dark hills of India beneath a layer of grey strato-cumulus cloud. The monsoon was about to break. We needed to keep moving west to minimise the inevitable delays that it would pour upon us.

We followed the steep switchback track down to the river and marched into Jolaghat. Through the vibrant bazaar we strode triumphantly. We descended to the footbridge passing groups of smiling officials wearing traditional Nepali dress and soldiers on duty near the bridge entrance. We stumbled on to the bridge feeling like an over-zealous herd of elephants and stamped our way across above the foaming Makali river. We had traversed Nepal.

On the Indian side of the bridge a policeman with an old Lee Enfield rifle, bayonet in place, halted us. Visions of being turned back raced through my mind. S.P. confronted him, producing our documents and letters of permission. He appeared bewildered. A few minutes later S.P. had the matter sorted out. Much to our relief, we were admitted on to Indian soil.

S.P. was jubilant at returning to his homeland. It was like another world; there were cars and buses, motor roads, electricity and in the shops was a wide range of foods (our preoccupation) and merchandise. We had reached an outpost of the technological world leaving the mysterious valleys of Western Nepal behind in just a few minutes. We had been transported into a different age, like falling into a celestial time warp. What made me particularly happy was that we were now over half way across the Himalaya. Our journey from Kanchenjunga to K2 had frequently seemed a daunting, almost impossible task. It was slowly becoming a reality.

'Congratulations, mate!' croaked Graeme, his chest infection again relapsing. 'We've done the first traverse of Nepal.' We shook hands and smiled at each other. It had been a long way, a long time, a hard time — physically, psychologically and for compatibility. I almost thought I saw his bright blue eyes pale a little... ready for some R. & R.

'Let's have a decent rest in Pithorogarh, I think we've earned it.' I wrung S.P. and Tashi by the hand — it was a great moment. A homecoming for S.P. and Tashi, and for us all, a triumph.

The dilapidated junk-heap flippantly referred to as a bus, grumbled and groaned as it rolled out of Jolaghat with the four of us squeezed on board like sardines in an economy-sized tin. We were travelling south to the town of Pithorogarh where we would rendezvous with our support team. There we would rest before returning to the high Himal and continuing westwards towards Kashmir and Pakistan. The bus climbed slowly above the river on the thirty-five-kilometre, two-hour scheduled journey.

Suddenly, a crashing sound accompanied by the ticket collector's shrill whistle brought us to a grinding halt. Two leaves of the front suspension had broken so the bus's own travelling mechanic set to work to repair what should never be repaired. Eventually we continued onward until we reached a wayside teashop where we stopped. The mechanic set to work again, attending to the wheelnuts of which there were only a few. He was attempting to cross-thread them in order to keep them in place. Filled with an apprehensive horror we climbed back on board. With a wild crashing of gears we started up the hill following the long switchbacks. A whistle blew again and the bus stopped. The rear wheel was in danger of falling off! So while the travelling mechanic worked on yet another problem that called for a discard rather than repair, we bathed our sweaty bodies in a roadside stream.

Graeme went hunting in the stream and succeeded in finding two Himalayan freshwater crabs before a commotion above drew us back to the road. Another overcrowded bus appeared around the bend. It stopped beside our vehicle and in a frenzied state we, along with the other passengers, crowded inside and on to the roof of the other bus. With much yelling and screaming and the occasional round of rowdy trumpeting on the horn by our new driver we chugged slowly up the hill. Near a road sign that told us it was only four kilometres to Pithorogarh, we stopped for a tea break. Exasperated, we waited impatiently for departure. We reached Pithorogarh more than four hours after our departure from Jolaghat, a mere thirty-five kilometres away.

We walked through the bazaar looking out for any sign of the support team. A man came up to me and asked if I was a New Zealander. He knew there was another "Kiwi" in town who was waiting for some friends. A little later, we were reunited with Doug who had come on ahead of the others.

We spent two weeks in Pithorogarh attending to complications with our onward permission and resting and eating. We changed travellers' cheques at the local bank which took a whole morning, went to the Pithorogarh body-building competitions and spent some time with the town's leaders. The district magistrate, Mr Joshi, was a very impressive gentleman and extended to us considerable hospitality. He organised a volleyball game for us — we were soundly beaten — and a number of engagements where we spoke to the town's dignitaries and educational groups.

'I have great pleasure in asking the esteemed Peter Hillary,' said Mr Joshi, 'the son of the illustrious Sir Hillary, on this august occasion, to tell us of his wonderful experiences.'

And then we had an evening of playing "housie" at the officers' club. Everyone, other than ourselves, was dressed impeccably, the ladies in fabulous silk saris. I remembered noticing, as did the other members of the expedition, an extraordinarily beautiful lass with dazzling, dark eyes, a Mona Lisa smile, and diamonds on her fingers and suspended from her ears. She was adorned in a magnificent silk sari with a gilt brocade on the loose ends that she draped over her head. We all smiled at her and she smiled prettily back. Perhaps we could speak with her later, while we had tea? All seemed set for a scene out of one of the passionate love stories for which Hindi movies are famous.

'I'm her mother-in-law,' announced a large matriarchal woman sitting

141

beside the petite figure. A valiant effort to engage the madame in conversation ensued, but she remained severe and we contrite... and then it was back to "housie".

However, our lengthy sojourn in Pithorogarh was not all "beer and skittles". Tension ran high. The traverse was running well behind schedule and the monsoon was irrefutably upon us. It was Shubash Roy who helped lighten the atmosphere. Shubash joined the expedition in Pithorogarh to be the third Indian member and to accompany the support team. His light-hearted and pragmatic approach helped us all. He was just what our five-month-old expedition needed.

We had to get moving again despite the monsoon rains, to recapture the momentum that had carried us across Sikkim and Nepal. We were half way there. And yet K2 was still a long way off. Over 2000 kilometres. We had to get moving.

5

Sacred Temples

OUR NEW COMPANION, S.K. Roy was a good-looking, aristocratic young man from Calcutta. He worked with the border security organisation known as the S.S.B.; we were ignorant of what this organisation did, or why our journey deserved the services of one of its officials. However, we found him a totally charming and good-natured character with the ability to make fun of the most serious situation — in fact, it called for a concerted effort to get S.K. to hold a serious conversation.

S.P. took advantage of our enforced overstay in Pithorogarh to go home. When he didn't arrive back as planned on 11 July, we decided to get under way again. I had planned a personal pilgrimage up to the place on the Milam glacier where Jill Tremain and Vicki Thompson had died, but sadly this was not possible because of our permit problems. Instead we decided to cross over to the Maiktoli valley and from the head of that valley we would try to cross the apparently never-before-crossed Sundarhunga Khal. However, Tilman may have crossed this pass in the early 1930s.

The monsoon was by now well and truly under way. We reached the road end at Barali in one of those unbelievable monsoonal deluges. The skies simply opened up and emptied water on to the earth. The hillsides flowed, the water hosed off the roofs and the rivers turned into raging mires of brown sludge. Whenever these rains came landslides blocked roads and wiped away people's fields and houses. During this Barali deluge a small stream turned into a brown raging monster — building up against a large concrete bridge which we were sure would soon be taken away. The population turned out as if to watch a football game — under brollies or just standing there getting soaked, waiting for the bridge to be destroyed — but the rain eased to a normal downpour and the flow soon stabilised. Amazingly the bridge remained intact.

Next morning, the 13th, we began up the winding road to Loharket. Every few hundred yards the road was destroyed by washouts and landslides. We were carrying very heavy packs containing full climbing and camping gear again and were soon hoping for a short day as our bodies began to tell us about it. About 1 pm we passed through Loharket without knowing it. We had actually asked a woman there where that town was. She had looked at us and pointed quickly up the hill. Questioning Hindu women was rarely successful — they were just too shy and would answer anything just to get rid of us quickly. We trogged on for a couple of kilometres before realising our mistake and returning to a well-appointed resthouse at Loharket.

Once we had established ourselves in this grand house some very wet soldiers arrived and made an abortive attempt to kick us out. They didn't count, however, on a very stubborn pair of Kiwis. With Tashi's support I reckoned we could easily hold three times our number at bay. Sadly perhaps the troops didn't put us to the test and when their officers arrived we actually enjoyed their company. They had attempted to go up to the Pindar glacier but had failed because of flooded rivers. Tashi told them that we could cross any river and so we were seconded into the Indian army for an hour to teach river crossing. We had the advantage over these guys in that we knew that if things went very wrong at least we could swim. Few of these people swim well and rivers to them are places to be avoided.

As we began up the hill above Loharket in the early morning the air was already heavy with moisture. We felt that our biggest problem during the next few weeks could be the rivers. Tash spoke of the Rishi Ganga with great respect. We would need to descend this river out of the Nanda Devi sanctuary if we succeeded in crossing Sundarhunga Khal. This worried us because by then we would be low on food with no chance of getting any in the sanctuary — we might have a hungry time if we were stopped by an uncrossable river, and it was a long time to the end of the monsoon.

We had hired two useless porters in Loharket to help with our huge loads, bulging with the extra food we had purchased there. Unlike most other Himalayan people who used headbands to carry loads these Garhwalis often used thin rope shoulder straps which must be thoroughly uncomfortable. It was odd that they were so slow and hopeless at carrying loads.

A good path took us upwards through misty rhododendron forests to Dakuri — renowned for its superb mountain view. But heavy cloud robbed us of this bonus. At Dakuri we waited impatiently for our porters. 'Useless bastards,' breathed Pete, as they came down the hill two hours behind us.

A sign in India.

*We walk through forests in cloud and rain during
the monsoon in Garhwal.*

After lunch we walked for only an hour before the porters claimed a fair day's work. We had walked a total of only three hours and what was worse, we had no aid to ward off the boredom. So while the rain poured down on to the leaky roof of our schoolhouse-hotel we crawled into our sleeping bags and dozed away the rest of the afternoon. Thankfully, we met some shepherds on their way to the high grazing at Maiktoli. These guys were hard men and delighted in terrifying our porters with stories about flooded rivers, landslides and difficult climbing. The eldest of our porters pysched out completely and by morning developed some strange illnesses. While he went back to Loharket we continued with the shepherds up the Pindar, then when it forked, up the Sundarhanga towards the high grazing area at Maiktoli. All morning we flogged along behind the shepherds through drab, leech-infested jungle.

I have a particular enthusiasm for mushrooms and in one place I picked some from a tree trunk and carried them to the next resting place. Tashi and the shepherds insisted that I throw them away — they were adamant that they would pick me many more higher up in the valley. Later in the day, having passed up many delectable fungi I asked when we were going to get to the profuse area.

'Oh, there are no mushrooms up here,' the shepherds chorused. I was furious.

The trek up the valley was quite difficult and dangerous in places. It was a very spectacular valley but we were so keen to get to the higher reaches that we scarcely appreciated it. The shepherds were mainly barefooted and wearing heavy coarse-spun woollen coats and pants — even though a steady drizzle fell they appeared to remain quite dry. As they moved steadily over the slippery ground littered with logs and rocks they would spin wool — deftly twisting the fibres with the fingers of one hand and spinning it on to a spool with the other.

About mid-afternoon we came to a particularly tricky bit. A smooth, steep slab of rock plunged into the raging river. The shepherds were confidently familiar with the problem and negotiated it quickly. But when it was Tashi's turn he recognised that one slip would be his last, so he asked me to go in front. A painfully enthusiastic shepherd noticed the trouble and dropping his spinning he hurried back to the rescue — his prehensile toes gripping the greasy rigosities as he clambered towards me.

I made a feeble attempt to fight him off but he grasped my wrist and swung me to safer ground, then set about rescuing "India's top mountaineer". He took Tashi's wrist and began to swing him but began to lose purchase and reached for me. My right hand gripped a good hold vigorously as swinging from it was a human pendulum nearly sixteen feet long — and stretching steadily longer. But we were rescued and our hero returned humbly to his spinning. Late in the afternoon we emerged from the forest and entered mist-shrouded Sundarhunga — a junction of the Sundarhunga and Maiktoli rivers where a few damp shepherds' huts were our shelter. After a night dodging raindrops which fell through the thatched roof we climbed up to Maiktoli. My diary entry for the 18th gives no great enthusiasm for the place:

'The green, beflowered alpine paradise called Maiktoli is for us a wet hell. We pitched camp on the river flats below some shepherds' huts and the first night all crowded into our little two-man tent. We got pretty wet so Tashi moved into the kitchen — a rather embellished adjective for a stone wall with a nylon poncho stretched over it and an umbrella pitched underneath. For three days we have mucked around this wet hole looking less at home than the floppy-eared goats and sheep which stand despondently dripping on the wet grass, unenthusiastically growing footrot and arthritis.

'Sundarhunga Khal looks like the most interesting yet. Pete and I have been twice to 14,500 feet but have seen nothing but vertical buttresses rising into the mist and ghostly white icefalls plunging down — apparently no reasonable route anywhere. A few days ago Pete called me a "devious bastard" over some trivial matter. This really pissed me off at the time. I know the shit will hit the fan at Joshimath when Doug, Ann and Corrina want to join us for the next section — I can't help becoming tense in anticipation of it — horrible.'

On the 19th we made our move although the weather showed no sign of improvement. Our task was a simple matter of climbing to 18,000 feet, descending into the Nanda Devi sanctuary, and proceeding down stream to Joshimath — five or six days would do it, if all went well. We carried our sodden possessions up the glacier then up the misty cliffs to a camp at about 15,500 feet.

As if in appreciation of our efforts the Almighty caused a remarkable clearance — the first since we arrived in the valley. Away below, the Maiktoli river flowed like threads of silver through a carpet of green. And all around us were magnificent ice-sheathed mountains. Directly behind our little tent a steep glacier rose at a horrific angle towards an area of broken seracs. Beyond we figured was Sundarhunga Khal.

It did not pay to dwell on the possibility of one of these seracs collapsing. In all probability it would sweep us back to the valley bottom. A few large rocks came down, crashing alarmingly close to the tent, but our sleep was largely undisturbed. Horrors, the morning was fine and we had a decision to make — never a happy event with this trio. Pete was keen on making a dash for the pass but both Tash and I felt that a reconnaissance was a much wiser move. After all we were still only guessing as to the whereabouts of the pass and the going above looked dangerous enough for lightly-laden people, let alone heavy lumbering, unacclimatised bodies.

We began climbing up the bluffs beside the icefall, then traversed across on to the steep ice and cramponed uncertainly up this. Pete went on ahead while I waited for Tash; then we went on together into the most dangerous part where tottering seracs hung precariously at odd angles. After a short time we met a very tired Hillary and together we climbed on through the maze of giant ice blocks. An hour later we reached the base of the gully — an obvious chute for any debris. Up this we began, the danger lending strength to our leaden limbs. Finally we climbed out on to a safe neve, to the left of the gully, and collapsed into the snow. On the other side of a gentle neve, a symmetrically curved dip in the ridge, was Sundarhunga Khal — we had done it, but sadly our gear was still down at the tent.

I had decided 500 feet lower down that this route was unjustifiably dangerous for us to take with our packs and was not looking forward to giving Pete my decision about it. Happily, he had come to the same decision. Tash as usual, didn't mind what we did. There then followed the most amazing situation that highlighted the problems in our decision-making process. I was keen to get down before debris loosened by the warmth of the day began falling down the gullies, but suddenly Tash said: 'Let's go to the pass.' I think I was moved because Tash rarely made demands but after going for a time I realised that we were being stupid in putting the pass before our own safety.

It wasn't a particularly attractive pass, certainly not a coveted dream worth much of a risk. As warning bells began to sound I called to the others ahead: 'I'm going back, I think we should get down before things start warming up too much.'

Tashi looked unhappy but without much ado we turned and began down again. We hadn't gone far when Pete's tired voice came back: 'A continuation of the mediocre eh?'

It took a while for the words to sink in and as if he was having a go at me I retorted: 'If that's the way you feel about your successes I feel sorry for you... damn it... let's go up... I'm not having you blaming me for a failure!' And I began back up our steps with Pete struggling behind. Tash was

Peter and Tashi at our tent in the Sundarhunga
valley during the monsoon in Garhwal.

Graeme at 15,000 ft above the Sundarhunga valley
during our attempt to cross into the Nanda Devi
Sanctuary during the monsoon.

Trisul rises above the monsoon clouds in Garwhal.　　　　　　　　Doug Wilson

understandably confused and sat down. Cloud now covered the pass and so our about-turn looked more futile than ever.

We hadn't gone more than 100 metres when Pete said: 'We aren't going to get a view... let's go down.' With this I let forth the most fantastic tirade of abuse at him. Back at the top of the dangerous gully I apologised to both Pete and Tash and this relieved a lot of tension. We reached camp just as the rain set in again.

Later in the afternoon Tash told me what a difficult position he found himself in. I felt so sad for him and so grateful for such a good friend that I burst into tears. The relief for me was instantaneous. In the evening I suggested to Pete that we try to relax a bit about the trip and not take it so seriously. He agreed and we all felt better for it.

It was another fine evening. The scene down valley was a kaleidoscope of purples and greens. Great hammerhead clouds rose to 50,000 feet.

'That one's probably just drowned 10,000 people,' chuckled Pete. Like three strange people eating TV dinners we watched the sunset and ate our meagre soupy stew, then crawled into the tent for another scintillating night in the Garhwal.

Tonight I had been given the dubious privilege of being in the middle. This meant that I was sandwiched neatly between the other two with my head down the sharp end of the tent. It was certainly warmer there and it meant that I wouldn't get the wetness of being against the outside of the tent. The middle person did, however, get knees from both sides — the old knee in the groin treatment or the heel in the nose. The real advantage was probably that this person never had to get up to make the early morning brew.

Dawn revealed another clear morning — at least for a few hours. Tash wasn't feeling too enthusiastic so Pete and I set off in pursuit of a safer route. We soon found what we thought to be one and returned quickly to the tent to pack up. While Pete stayed at the campsite to write his diary I went on ahead to cairn the route. I scrambled along a series of gently rising ledges to some large avalanche fans. Here I waited for the others as the mist streamed in again. Before long Tash arrived and we continued on, chatting as we climbed. 'Peter is obsessed with the idea that you and I are friends and he is left out,' Tash confided.

Because of poor visibility we were soon forced to look for a campsite. Avalanche debris scattered about indicated to me the need for a sheltered spot and although Tash was keen on a small flat in the open I was adamant about the need for protection and began digging a ledge in the lee of a large boulder. Nearby a small stream of melt water trickled down over the cliffs. Rain fell all afternoon and we went to sleep to its gentle drumming on the tent fabric. About 9 pm I awoke with a dreadful start — it was pitch black, the rain was now thundering down on the tent and Tash had just called out: 'Graeme we must move from here!'

I was fighting desperately for my senses. Shutting out the din of the rain, wind and avalanches falling down the gully only 10 feet from the tent, I played for time. 'Why, Tash?'

'Because rocks and ice will come down with this heavy rain!'

I was now wide awake and staring blankly into the blackness. I figured that although Tash was correct, we would be in greater danger moving in the darkness than staying put — at least our sheltering rock would deflect the worst of any avalanches. The bit that worried me was that the top of the tent could be caught and we would get flung over the cliff below — this worry we simply had to live with.

With his head at the sharp end of the tent and above the din of the storm, Pete couldn't hear what we were saying. He was also concerned that he would not be able to make a fast exit from the tent if it became necessary, so he turned around — which was a bit like putting all the sardines in a tin thick ends together.

Each of us lay silently engrossed in his own thoughts and fears. I forced out the fear and endeavoured to sleep. When I awoke a watery light radiated into the tent. Tash was making a brew on the stove. Pete stuck his head out the door: 'There's two rows of ice cliffs above us!'

We drank our Sustagen breakfast and automatically began to pack, not knowing whether we were going up or down. Tash was very unhappy about continuing on but despite this some force was pushing us upwards almost against our better judgement. I took Pete aside and told him that I thought we should abide by Tashi's decision. 'If he wants to go up, well and good but if he says "down", we go down without question.' After all, Tash had done exactly what we wanted for a long time.

Back at the tent Tash made it clear that he wished to go down, arguing that if we had clear weather it would be a different matter. Despite this we were still hanging on to what hope was left. Somehow we reached the decision that we should climb up and if we found a safe camp spot and the weather tomorrow was fine, we would go for the pass. If the weather was bad we would go down without question.

By now the mist had rolled in obscuring the route above. As we were about to start up, Pete asked Tash once more: 'Are you sure you want to go up Tash?'

'No,' said Tash emphatically. 'Let's go down.'

Thank God — the decision was made and we began down. Sod's law of course determined that the weather should show a definite turn to the better. But this clearance for me simply confirmed the wisdom of our decision. Two thousand feet above, I could see the dome we had been heading for guarded by the most evil-looking ice cliffs! As we descended I grappled with the question: Lack of courage or sound mountaineering judgement? My conclusion was, a bit of both! But our decision was the decision of survivors. We knew that the game of wandering blindly under seracs and ice cliffs is a game similar to Russian roulette.

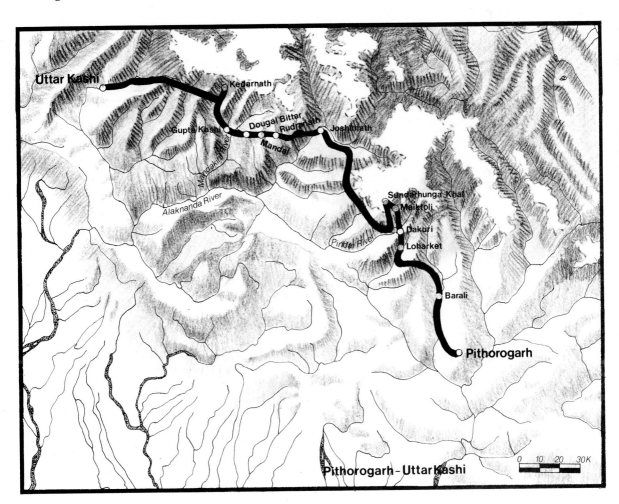

*Kedarnath temple at 12,000 ft, with Hindu
pilgrims from the plains of India.*

Graeme with his dislocated shoulder at the scene of the accident in Joshimath, Garhwal.

Doug Wilson

Survivors play this game with the utmost judgement — the successful person must balance the risk against the potential gain. For us Sundarhunga Khal was not worth the risk — the traverse could survive without it. Within two hours we were in another world — the lush green world of the Maiktoli shepherds. We ate their chapatis and listened to their "sideline advice" about crossing Sundarhunga Khal. They had no idea what that icy world was like. For the next three days we tramped down the Pindar valley. A neverending mire of ups and downs through wet forests and ten-feet-high jungles of cannabis. Leeches and inaccurate information from the locals nearly drove us insane and our packs hurt our bodies. In three days we had walked more than 100 kilometres and climbed and descended 50,000 feet.

At Dupal we turned right and headed north-west again, skirting the Nanda Devi sanctuary towards Joshimath. Rain, mist and leeches were our lot. Each day we crossed passes between 11,000 and 12,000 feet high but there were no views of the mountains we longed to see — Nanda Devi, Trisul, Dunagiri, Kalanka and Changabang — that exquisite spire which Tashi had made the first ascent of with Bonington, Haston, Scott, Boysen and Balwant Sandu — what a team!

My diary reading of 28-29 July gives little inspiration: 'Onward via Ramni over another 11,000 feet pass, across the Bircehi Ganga. Rain, leeches — nearly trod on a big brown snake! Across Kuanri Khal, which Frank Smythe described as being the best vantage point in the Himalaya, but for us, nothing but mist and cold rain or as my old man would say, "Wet bums and no fish". Pete and I are now getting on well and having lots of long talks, often fairly intimate discussions about his family.'

Sick to death of the bloody monsoon but pleased with progress, we reached the humming military town of Joshimath on the evening of 29 July. Corrina, Doug, Ann and S.K. had also had a wet time on a side-trip into the Valley of Flowers where the bad weather had thwarted their attempt to climb a peak. Meanwhile S.P. had dashed into the Nanda Devi sanctuary to meet us if we made it over. When there was no sign of us he hurried back to Joshimath.

S.P. had been given specific orders not to take us to any 'military or para-military installations'. But when the officers of the Indo-Tibetan Border Police invited us to dinner at the mess S.P. couldn't refuse. Before dinner he called a meeting in his room of the mess. In an atmosphere full of tension we sat around a polished table waiting for S.P. to deliver the inevitable speech. He began by welcoming us to India and apologising for the lateness of the welcome. (We had now been in India for two months and this was his third welcome speech.) He then went on to request us not to ask any more embarrassing questions relating to Indian security. We sat there looking at the ceiling in pained silence. We respected the fact that India had sensitive borders but it annoyed us that after six months together it was apparent that he still did not trust us. We had explained over and over that if anyone wanted to spy on India they wouldn't send white-faced Europeans who didn't speak any of the languages, they would simply employ some locals. Besides, most surveillance of these sensitive borders could be done by satellite.

The easy part of the meeting out of the way, S.P. asked who was going on the next stage to Uttar Kashi. This would be a technically easy section as unfortunately we had not been permitted to take the logical high route from Badrinath across to the Gangotri glacier. Instead we were being forced to take the old pilgrims' trail to the south of the big mountains — a confusion of jungle-clad ridges and monsoon-swollen rivers. Doug and Ann said that they were no longer interested in joining the traverse group — they would be content with their own private side-trips.

S.K. didn't care and both S.P. and Corrina wanted to join us. I was still keen that others joined in with the traverse when it was possible and practical but said I would abide by a majority decision of the three traversees. I felt that neither Tash nor Pete wanted the party's size increased. In defiance of the trio's wishes S.P. then became adamant that another Indian should join the traverse and although he clearly wanted to be that person S.K. somehow got the job.

Doug, Ann and Corrina now launched a fairly persuasive argument that if S.K. or S.P. were to get the opportunity to join then so too should Corrina. Suddenly Pete's "no comment" changed to a personal attack on Corrina and it was all on.

S.P., having won a partial battle and now satisfied that he had diverted any attack on himself, opened a bottle of whisky and was desperately trying to restore peace as we were now one hour late for dinner. Only fifty feet away in the mess hall all the dignitaries of Joshimath had gathered — all soberly waiting for the celebrities. In the event, a couple of whiskies seemed a fair thing, even though Joshimath was in the dry state of Uttar Kashi and alcohol was prohibited.

Unfortunately the whisky I drank did little to cheer up those that didn't drink it and I decided that it was clearly time for a funny act — one that would help dissolve the black cloud now hanging dismally over the team. There was no question of entering the mess under such a cloud. Peter's dark glasses and a brolly gave me an idea. I would pretend to be a blind man stumbling over a cliff. In a moment I had put on the dark glasses and was tapping my way out of the room and into the night. I tapped down the steps and across a pavement towards a fence which bounded the mess on that western side — a fence designed to assist in stopping blind men from falling down the cliff beyond. Way below the lights of Joshimath flickered in a sea of inky blackness.

My plan was to stumble over the fence with a scream but to keep hold of the top rail, thus cunningly avoiding a painful flight down the cliff. Of course my plan relied heavily on a strong fence which in retrospect was a foolish expectation. As my brolly and outstretched hand struck the fence there was an awful sound of smashing wood and a moment later I was flying — a graceful downward parabola into the blackness. For the moment my eyes were still masked ridiculously in dark glasses, my right hand clutching the brolly, and my left firmly fixed on to a piece of fence.

One's instincts for self-preservation are rather remarkable. As I was not particularly keen on using my nose, teeth and jaw as landing gear, an

A pilgrim makes an offering at Kedarnath.

unconscious power in me had thrown my legs over my head. They say that it is not the falling that hurts, just the stopping, but nobody mentioned the bouncing. As my somersault was about completed, my left shoulder followed closely by the back of my head struck solid rock but I continued accelerating down the wall feet first. Finally, I bounced over two or three low terraces before coming to rest some twenty feet below the hole in the fence through which several heads now peered into the darkness.

I was aware of injuries — left arm dislocated at the shoulder, one or two cracked or broken ribs, right hand sprained and a crack on the back of the head for good measure. The head wound dripped blood gently and of all my injuries this worried me the most as I knew I had hit it hard and felt half senseless. I could hear voices above me and in a moment my friends were with me — Tashi, Pete, Corrina, Doug and Ann Louise. Doug took control quickly and I was carried back to the mess.

As I lay on a bed in the mess, occasionally laughing insanely as the funny side of the incident struck home, and waiting for the doctor, S.P. approached, his face a picture of concern. He bent over me and began to berate me for my stupidity. 'Oh my god... you have really got me in the thick soup now,' he moaned at least twice before I interrupted: 'S.P.... why don't you push off?'

He reeled from the room, his eyes wide with wonderment that a wounded man could be so aggressive. It was a long wait for medical help — fifteen hours and five minutes to be precise. At midday the next day I saw the army surgeon. He was furious that no one had contacted him sooner because the reduction of the dislocated arm and shoulder would have been easier soon after the accident, but his words immediately inspired a renewal of my flagging confidence.

'I am sorry we have no anaesthetic but if you can stand a few more minutes of pain I'll have it back.'

I lay there determined not to utter a sound as he struggled to reduce the dislocation. After only two tries the arm was once again attached to the shoulder, more or less as it should have been. Unfortunately there was nothing that could be done for the collarbone which stuck out of my shoulder like a foot under a blanket. I was soon bound up and told to leave the arm like that for one month. Once the sling was removed I was to do only minimal arm movement for another month. Although I still couldn't believe that for me the traverse was over, I had to agree that things looked pretty grim.

Back at our rooms Pete asked me what should be done. I answered that they had better prepare to go. I really wanted him to say: 'Why don't we wait for two weeks until you have been repaired?' but it didn't happen and this made me feel rather embittered and neglected. Doug had now decided to join the group.

On 3 August they left for Uttar Kashi. It was all I could do to hold back my tears as I said 'goodbye and goodluck.' As they walked slowly through the crowded market and down to the Alaknanda river it began to rain again. My depression made my injuries more painful as I lay down and closed my eyes.

A moment later I sat up with renewed enthusiasm. 'Bugger it, why can't I walk?' Even if I had to walk along a road it would be better than catching a bus to Uttar Kashi.

'I'll carry all the gear... I'll show Hillary,' enthused Corrina. Ann agreed to make sure that all the resupply stuff got to Uttar Kashi.

On 4 August Corrina and I set out for Uttar Kashi. A strange pair — one brown with long black hair, wearing a long skirt and carrying a big pack and the other looking like a white Mahatma Gandhi after being run over by a Calcutta bus.

We tramped down the wet road to the little village of Helong where our choice of accommodation was the concrete floor of the local jail — an impressive unused monolith surrounded by a jungle of six-feet-high cannabis — or the mud floor of the local chai shop. We chose the latter in the hope of an early morning brew. Unfortunately the deal also included a leaking roof and fleas. First thing next morning we left the road and crossed the raging Alakananda on a graceful suspension bridge; then around a ledge of a track as rain set in again. A theme ran through my head like a cracked record: 'I mustn't fall over... I mustn't fall over.' The very thought of more pain was repugnant, but the consequences of a fall could be disastrous. So I watched the ground with previously unknown concentration — so intently, in fact, that over the next few weeks I cracked my head several times on overhanging branches and rocks.

We turned up a side valley and soon came to the first real obstacle for a one-armed man — a greasy step where the track had fallen away into the river far below. Corrina climbed up, uncertain in her newfound position of responsibility. She then extended her brolly and using this as a handhold I scrambled up. We continued up through pine forest that slowly turned to rhododendron and Himalayan oak, then firs as we gained height.

We passed many local people laden with animal fodder and food for the market and I was fascinated by the number of people who stopped to speak with Corrina, particularly women (inevitably they thought she was Indian). Only then did I realise how little real contact we had had with the hill women on this journey. Usually after speaking to the locals, Corrina would continue carrying a small gift of food, usually apples — she was proving more useful than I could ever have anticipated. Almost everyone that we passed asked me what was wrong with my arm, and after a time the stories became pretty wild: 'Oh, it was near the summit of Nanda Devi — five men on the rope. Dislocated my arm holding them you know.' Doug later added that I dislocated it going for a knife with which to cut the rope.

It was a long way for us both. We crossed a pass and descended to Dumak. As we approached the village in the evening, Corrina suddenly stopped (I was too bushed to do anything suddenly). 'That's Doug and Pete,' she said, pointing. Sure enough in the courtyard of a house sat the "A team". We approached casually.

'What the hell are you doing here?' they asked.

'Oh just out for a walk.'

Pete had a fever and they were waiting for him to improve. Tash was the least surprised to see us. The night before he had had a dream and on waking had said: 'I think Graeme will come today!'

We passed a pleasant evening together and next morning Pete was still sick so "Team B" forged on into the lead. Tash and Doug accompanied us for two kilometres to help me across a flooded river, where the options were singularly unattractive. Doug solved the problem by crawling across a tree felled over the river and fixing a rope for me to use as a handrail.

Once across we began on a long climb to an open ridge nearly 12,000 feet high and along this we continued to the holy temple of Rudranath. Our map for this stage was worse than ever before — it was a tourist guide to the religious shrines of the Garhwal — and Corrina and I were horrified to find that no path existed that would take us further westward. Our options were to continue blindly through trackless jungle and river gorge or return along the high ridge and to drop off this to the west. Considering my condition this was all we could do. On the way back along the ridge we met "Team A" going towards Rudranath — they were hoping to do the high-level route to Uttar Kashi but were so far being frustrated by bad weather. After a short chat we said farewell and headed in opposite directions. 'Bugger,' I said after they'd gone. 'I meant to wish Tash a happy birthday for the 14th.'

A few moments later I turned around to see them descending towards us. Pete went past like a rocket followed closely by Tash and several lengths back came S.K. and Doug.

As Doug went by he said, 'I don't know what's got into Pete. It's quite obvious that you guys are going just as quickly — I don't know why we don't go on together.'

We descended 5000 feet down that slippery hill and just before dark reached a road. Along this we walked happily through the night towards Mandal, eleven kilometres away. Corrina and I were having a great time — away from the pressures and politics of the main team, it was like being on holiday. Nights were the worst. Sometimes I'd lie awake letting out involuntary groans of pain. I couldn't lie on the injured side and for some reason my back hurt like hell when I lay on it so I had only one choice, my right side. After a while my hips also began to hurt — I was a mess all right. One night as I lay there I heard Corrina groaning in a very similar way in her sleep — sympathy pains!

At Mandal we met "Team A" again and over a dinner of omelette and chips we discovered that they had somehow lost S.K. Pete wasn't very sympathetic. In the morning a search party was sent out but S.K. was found in the room next to us. He had taken a wrong turning and had reached Mandal at 11.30 pm after a cross-country jaunt.

8 August was a cool overcast day. The forest echoed to hundreds of different birdcalls as we climbed steadily up a well-graded mule track. After 4000 feet we emerged on to a ridgetop and a most welcome chai shop where we found the "A team" drinking tea and eating biscuits. We continued together to a village called Chopta Chatti where we ate a huge amount of pukoras. Pete was keen to reach the Mandakini river that day so after lunch they took off with a rush. Corrina and I were happy to saunter on slowly towards Dougal Bittar where there was supposed to be a pretty good resthouse.

At about 4 pm as we approached Dougal Bittar we could see the others standing on the road apparently arguing. Suddenly Pete marched off alone. 'What's wrong Tash?' I asked from a distance. Tash was fuming. Pete felt that the group wasn't covering enough ground and when Tash wanted to stay in the resthouse he had become furious.

Once Tash had cooled off he became concerned that something might happen to Pete and that if it did he would get blamed. 'He might get attacked by a wild animal or some people and then I'll be in trouble,' said Tash.

Next day we walked to Gupta Kashi, in the Mandakini valley, and there the team still minus Pete had a discussion that climaxed with the unanimous decision that I was to be sole leader of the traverse group.

From Gupta Kashi the road wound tortuously to the fetid pilgrim staging post, Sonprayag — the following day we walked up a pilgrim-crowded mule track to Kedarnath temple at 12,000 feet. Here we met Pete and in a fairly nervewracking session the ultimatum was delivered by Doug. Pete was very unhappy but accepted the situation, rather like a cornered lion.

If this section had a highlight it was the brief clearance in the weather while

Sadhu — a holy man of Hinduism in Garhwal.

we were there at Kedarnath. In the morning we were able to see the southern walls of the Kedarnath mountain glowing in the early sun.

At the temple thousands of pilgrims, mostly aged, mostly reeling from the altitude, lined up in frenzied queues to conclude their amazing pilgrimage from the plains. Inside the ancient temple they would file slowly around a stone phallus symbolising the mountain and they would pay for a blessing from the old pujaris — 50 to 5000 rupees depending on their means and their keenness to be one of the chosen ones. The route to the temple was lined with half-naked sadhus with matted hair — their emaciated bodies covered in ash.

But apart from the view from Kedarnath there was little to delight the heart of the mountaineer on our route to Uttar Kashi. Although mist-laced forests, flooded rivers and rest at the end of a hard day can give great pleasure, we were now thoroughly sick of nearly two months of continuous rain. Our constantly wet feet were beginning to fall to pieces and had become raw and painful. Snakes slithered across our paths and the leeches never gave up their desperate purge; as if trying desperately to suck their last blood before the monsoon ended (leaving them dehydrated for a year) they seemed to become worse than ever.

On 14 August, Tash turned forty-three. In a makeshift buffalo-herders' shelter we presented him with a Swiss Army pocket knife. Later in the day as we crested our daily pass in rain Tash said: 'What a horrible birthday.' The truth of it made us laugh.

By way of the temples of Trijugi Narayan and Buda Kedar we tramped towards Uttar Kashi. Twelve long days after leaving Joshimath we descended through pine forest towards the Nehru Institute of Mountaineering where my old friends Balwant Sandhu and Prem Chand were respectively principal and chief instructor. For Pete, Doug, Tash and S.K. it was simply the end of a tiresome stage but for Corrina and me it was a great victory.

On 19 August we celebrated Corrina's birthday at the institute. It was a double celebration — we had just learned from Prem Chand that the Indian Army expedition were so far behind us that they were as good as out of the race. They had recently reached the Everest area and were expected in Kathmandu at the end of August. They were at least four months behind and at this rate it looked unlikely that they would be able to finish before winter.

Our own tally to date was 3,500 kilometres covered and one million feet of ascent and descent. We deserved a party.

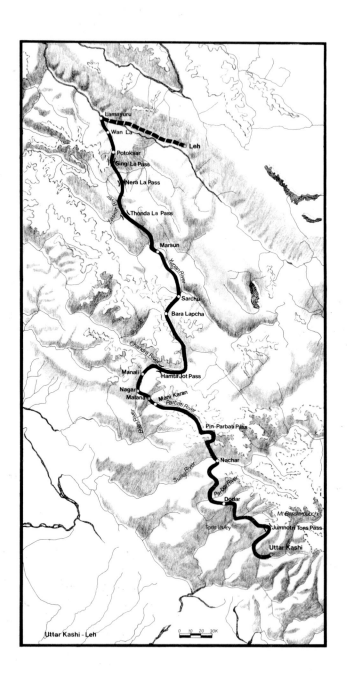

Lamayuru

Wan La

Leh

Potoksar

Singi La Pass

Nera La Pass

Thonda La Pass

Beazer River

Marsun

Yugan River

Sarchu

Bara Lapcha

Chandra River

Manali

Hamta Jot Pass

Nagar

Mani Karan

Malana

Parbati River

Beas River

Pin-Parbati Pass

Sutlej River

Nachar

Parbal River

Dodar

Mt Bandarpuuch

Tons Valley

Jumnotn Tons Pass

Uttar Kashi

0 10 20 30K

Uttar Kashi - Leh

6

Across Himachal Pradesh

IT WAS STILL dark as S.P., Tashi, Graeme and I marched down Uttar Kashi's main street looking as if we really meant business — our packs strapped to our backs and striding out with renewed vigour. We headed west following a track that the villagers told us would lead to the ridgetop and over to the Jumuna river. A switchback track ascended steep pastures and hiked through the forests to the ridge where heavy cloud cover restricted our vision to the immediate vicinity. A crackle of thunder and it began to rain, big drops falling from the tall firs that stood around us and smacking on the surface of our nylon ponchos. We descended a slippery track through the trees to a large and silent clearing, where we had glimpsed some huts. The dark, vaguely rectangular shapes appeared through the mist and rain, beseiged in a sea of dock, ragwort and flowering hemlock. They were squalid open-sided shacks which had sheltered both man and beast, but without alternatives they were, in S.P.'s words, our Hotel Intercontinental. We bent low and hobbled inside.

It fascinates me how a little food, a hot drink and a relatively dry spot in which to nestle in one's sleeping bag transforms even the most unpleasant circumstances into cosy ones. I lay in my sleeping bag, grasping my bowl filled with hot tea, and gazed out at the pelting rain, the sea of mud and animal droppings and the lush green dock leaves.

During the night the veil of pale grey stratus had been swept from above us, and the route that the previous day had baffled us, lay clear. A trail followed the ridgeline through the rhododendrons and firs till it rose out of the forest into the alpine scrub where it traversed beneath the hilltop before descending to a grass-covered clearing. A hip-roofed, thatch building stood there surrounded by a herd of black bony water buffaloes that two strongly built Guja men (Kashmiri descent) with jutting beards were milking.

'Ah, just what I need,' I said. S.P., who felt the same, engaged the Guja men in a conversation of rapid Garhwali, asking them to sell us about two litres of the thick creamy milk. We dropped our packs on the grass and while some milk was boiled for us in a brass urn — we were very particular about such precautions to minimise the risk of TB, hepatitis, dysentery and God knows what else — we watched the men milking. Nearby one of the Guja woman and her two children drank milk directly from the udder by squirting a jet of the creamy liquid into opened mouths. They were beautiful women with strong Aryan features, pale olive skin and dark flashing eyes. They wore strings of silver jewellery from their ears and noses, pinstriped bloomers that tapered to a close fit at the ankle and richly embroidered smocks.

The milk was soon ready and we slurped it down in our typically hurried "Himalayan Traverse Expedition" fashion with an accompaniment of grunts

Tashi, Graeme and S.P. in the Tons valley, Garhwal.

Peter, Tashi and S.P. in the Tons valley.

Guja herdsman milks his buffalo to give us some milk.

and remarks of approval. Replete, we continued downward through the forests till we reached the main path that led upstream by the banks of the revered Jumuna river, a pale jade thread of flowing water. We followed this pilgrim trail up valley for the rest of the day. I pushed on ahead of the others in the afternoon as I felt a need for some time out from the confines of our small nomadic group. As I approached the head of the valley, freezing rain poured down from the grey ceiling that hung low within the valley walls and although I donned my poncho I was soon chilled and wet. Rounding a bend in the track I peered ahead through the veil of falling rain and there stood Jumnotri temple, a clutter of ancient stone and dilapidated corrugated-iron buildings with a wisp of steam rising above the rooftops. Steep green flanks ascended abruptly to a maze of rocky crags far above. There I could discern the white broken shapes of two glacier snouts protruding from the mountain-side. I rushed along the rubble-strewn track till I reached a cluster of teashops, where groups of people sheltered from the rain, and large "dharam salas" where pilgrims can find shelter and accommodation. The track led on to a rickety wooden bridge that spanned the river, now running brown with the afternoon's rain, and up a broad flight of stone steps to the temple which stood below a tier of vertical rock bluffs. Here hot, sulphurous water hissed and bubbled from a vent at the base of the bluff; below was a deep pool of hot water.

'Just what a cold, rainsoaked bloke needs,' thought I, removing most of my clothes and slipping into the tepid waters to await the arrival of the others. While I luxuriated in the warmth a distinguished-looking sadhu (Hindu holy man), draped in thin white loincloths and with a great knot of unkempt hair on his head, appeared by the pool. He smiled and introduced himself as Bengali Baba and stepped down into the water. We talked a little, he with his halting English, and I with my almost halted Hindi, our heads only above water level like a couple of beach balls floating on the steaming surface. He ran the tiny ashram beside the pool where he told me he had lived for ten years throughout the monsoons and the snowbound winters. When the others arrived and we were all together in the hot pool, smiling at each other through the clouds of steam, he invited us to dinner at his poolside abode and ashram — a humble tin roof with sacking slung between the uprights to divide off his room and private temple from the open air.

It was a magical evening, for Baba had us all singing and beating drums and cymbals as he gracefully performed Hindu rituals blessing both us and our food. He was completely unconcerned by the variety of philosophies that the four of us embraced. We were people, that was enough. For me it was a wonderful experience, as if something was uplifting me, making me feel fresh and at peace. Perhaps it was the admiration I have for the true devotee of any faith, inspirational not so much because of his particular belief, but because he *does* believe.

Baba served us food, piling rice and dahl and spiced potato on to our plates. We ate ravenously while he worked over the bright flames of his fire — adjusting the firewood, stirring and transferring pots to and from direct heat. The light from the fire lit up his face in golden hues: strong features, intent dark eyes and a smooth brow, a nose like a prow and his cheeks, shallow recesses. It was clear he gained a special pleasure in serving, helping, extending kindness.

The flickering light of two single-wick lamps cast shadows that dodged around on the walls of the small room. They proffered shards of pale light to the bronze images and florid pictures of Baba's gods that were arranged above us on his altar. Steam and warmth wafted from the warm rockface that composed one of the walls and a cosy atmosphere of conviviality and the exotic scent of incense pervaded the dimly-lit guru's menage.

Baba embraced each of us, wishing us good-night. We descended the stone steps to the river and crossed to one of the dharam salas where we spent the night. We rose early, stuffed our gear into our packs — a procedure that had become like clockwork and distinctly personalised — and proceeded in the indecisive lighting that precedes dawn to Bengali Baba's ashram for tea and rotis (unleaven bread). He had prepared a considerable stack of rotis and a mound of curried potatoes for us. We ate a light breakfast and the remainder of the food we packed away into our loads for the long hike up to the Jumnotri-Tons pass, 6000 feet above. Again, Baba hugged us with the saintly fondness of a man who loves mankind and we departed, reluctantly, from the peace and sanctity of Jumnotri.

We climbed straight up the valley side opposite the temple, thrashing our way through thick rhododendron, bamboo and wiry bushes bristling with thorns.

'Do we really need a guide for this?' I quipped, studying the sinewy character who we had hired to guide us through the bush.

'Do we pay him or does he pay us?' added Graeme. It really did seem a ludicrous route and Graeme found the thick, entangled bush difficult with his bad shoulder. Eventually, the bush line was reached and we waded up the ridge through thick, green pastures to just below an expansive basin where our dubious guide turned back. We plodded on over the settled moraines of some bygone glacier, everlasting daisies and eidelweiss protruding amongst the rocks. Above us soared craggy rock summits in an overcast sky.

At the head of the basin was what we understood to be the pass — judging by the vague lines on our antiquated, tiny-scale, black and white map. When I reached the crest of the pass I looked over the far side, it dropped away vertically for hundreds of feet and the valley on that side drained in a direction that did not tally with what we considered it should. I saw cairns and evidence of a route further to the north-east and shouted down to Graeme, Tashi and S.P. accordingly. We retraced our steps down the basin and across to the entrance of another glacial valley, this one filled with unsettled moraines. The going was slow in the thin cold air at 17,000 feet. We scrambled up the loose slope to the second pass where we found the descent on the far side to be far from straightforward. However, 'it would go'. The valley below us drained north into a large green vale that corresponded well with what was marked on our map as the Tons, noted for its beauty, magnificent forests and spectacular peaks, its white, crevassed glaciers. With some difficulty we descended the steep scree slopes and fractured rock slabs till we reached a bergschrund that divided glacial ice from terra firma. An ice bridge provided the necessary link and we were soon on the glacier crossing the rock-strewn, glistening surface towards the Tons.

We marched in silent single file down the glacier, across loose moraines and on to a vegetated lateral moraine whose undulating spine we followed down to a grass flat. Cloud drifted in masking the rock spires and walls of ice across the valley and in the cloud-locked gloom of evening we descended to the meadows of the beautiful Tons valley. There was a serenity about the place that hinted at minimal impact by man... But there were men here. A tiny hut with smoke rising through the rough-hewn shingles on its roof drew us across the meadow, shouting and whistling — and Tashi has a very piercing whistle!

The commotion caused three figures to emerge from the hut, one of whom came across to us. He indicated for us to cross a fast flowing brook by a log that wobbled precariously as we balanced along it — arms extended to each side and eyes focused upon the narrow circumference of the log directly ahead. Once safely across, the shepherd pointed down valley, directing us to a green platform scattered with giant boulders. There, he told us, we would find a very good bivouac rock, dry wood for our fire, water, a place to spend the night... It was cold and the heavy dew already on the grass chilled our

lightly-shod feet as we wandered among the boulders in search of the bivvy. A narrow entrance led beneath a monstrous boulder, crawling inside we discovered a low-roofed haven. With straw covering the floor and a blackened ceiling, charred by countless fires, overhead we laid out our sleeping bags and set about preparing dinner.

Emerging from our cosy, rock den — feeling distinctly prehistoric — we travelled from the head of the Tons valley beneath Bandarpunch's snowclad bulk across the crisp, frosted pastures and in and out of stands of silver birch. The upper pastures of the valley gave way to fir forests, broadleafs and sundrenched glades. Occasionally there was a clearing, a herdsman's hut and the smell of burning fir, with animals and the unflinching gaze of the herdsman's family.

The afternoon was a painful one for me as my bad ankle became particularly sore, my slow limp leaving me far behind the others. I was glad when I rejoined them in the early evening so that I could roll out my sleeping bag and take the weight off my ankle. We departed early the following morning. Curiously, my ankle seemed much better, which relieved me. In the growing light of dawn as we traversed a hillside, I looked eastwards across a gully of tall trees. The rising sun reflected from a billion waxy leaf-cuticles, a plain of floral gilt. I decided it was a good omen for the day and marched on reassured. I would complete the traverse.

At Naitwar we turned off into the Rupin valley, a beautiful valley of scented pines scattered upon grassy hillsides with a river of clear water rushing down amongst giant white boulders. It was oppressively hot and when S.P. suggested a swim there was no hesitation from members of the team. We plunged into the cool waters to wash, refresh ourselves and then swim across the strong, swirling current. The track left the riverside and climbed steeply; for a while we thought we were off route but as we were about to retrace our steps we came upon a house whose inhabitants confirmed the way. We asked them for some water as we were all thirsty. They hesitated. One of them spoke softly to S.P., 'We are of low caste, will you drink our water?'

The track wound its way up valley passing through forests, crossing terraced fields with the valley floor far below until it reached the village of Dodar, a village of exceptional architectural beauty. Lanes and courtyards paved in stone separated the houses, magnificent rectangular towers of wood and stonework. Constructed from interlocking cedar logs with impeccable stone masonry filling the space between the smooth planed logs, the buildings rose vertically for twenty to thirty feet. Extending out above the walls were verandahs, the living area of the house, from where groups of smiling faces looked down at us over the superbly carved filigree of the railings. Ornately carved doorways with large brass padlocks and attachments opened on to the yards. Aloft, stone-shingled roofs arched elegantly to a high ridgeline. The attention to detail was exhaustive and the general orderliness and cleanliness of the village was far in excess of any I had ever seen before. These people were houseproud and with good reason. I looked out over the valley, at the sprinkling of compact communities on the valley flanks around me, the river now several thousand feet below, and pondered the enigmatic quality of Dodar. We were in the middle of nowhere, there was no tenable explanation. Enterprising folk with skill and time... plenty of time.

From Dodar we climbed to an 11,000-foot pass with Graeme and Tashi suffering from what could be described as stultiloquent flatulence. So much so that it was as if they were attempting an alternative form of communication. S.P. and I quickly moved in front leaving our near hysterical comrades to trail behind. At the pass we looked down to the Parbar river and the Indian state of Himachal Pradesh. It was a fine moment... we really were making progress. Beyond Himachal Pradesh, we would turn north into Kashmir and Ladakh and finally the Karakorams of Pakistan... and K2. The dream of traversing the Himalayas was no longer preposterous. As if to celebrate, Graeme bugled a flatulent note: it was chorused by schoolboy laughter.

A short distance down the Parbar valley we again branched off, heading up the Ageri Gad stream and hiking north towards Shatall pass and the Sutlej river. The track ascended across a hillside of terraced fields, through the forests above the cultivated land and on to steep pastures. A semblance of a track traversed for several kilometres around precipitous spurs and into and out of gullies till we reached a lone, canvas tent. Incongruous in its locality it was pitched on what was unquestionably the "most level" piece of sloping ground available. Here, surrounded by a flock of sheep and the kindness of the four shepherds who invited us to share their tent, we unrolled our sleeping bags. We set about preparing dinner... with a difference: seasoned sheep's intestines, chapatis and two of our dehydrated stew sachets all to be washed down by a couple of slugs from a bottle of very rough spirits we had bought in a village earlier in the day. This soon had us all reeling in an exceedingly good frame of mind with no thoughts on going on... until the old shepherd let his two mastiffs off their chains to patrol the flock during the hours of darkness, to protect them against bears and snow leopards and wolves. The night passed with spasmodic bouts of barking and the old shepherd bounding from beneath his blankets already dressed to call the dogs and check his flock. It was an uncomfortable night — slipping downhill and being sandwiched firmly together with the others in the little tent. I was ready to move on as the stars faded into the pale blue of a clear sky.

We strode through long grass, till we reached the track which we followed for an hour to where the pastures stretched upward to the screes and above to the passes. A shepherd who had come with us pointed adamantly to a niche in the skyline at the left side of the valley despite a col on the right side where Tashi and I had noticed a line of rock cairns.

'Well, he should know.' We resigned ourselves and set off for the pass on the left side while the shepherd returned to his tent down valley. We meandered through several boulder gardens and hiked up narrow fingers of vegetation that extended up the talus slopes until a rock rib led to the west of the pass. I descended off the stratified rib on to the sloping slabs below the pass and scrambled up to the lip. No cairns or any sign of man's passage. The

*Dodar village temple of immaculate stone masonry
and woodwork.*

other side dropped away vertically for 500 feet to a small glacier, itself surrounded by precipices. This was certainly not the route. Muttering character assessments of the shepherd who had directed us to this pass, I descended to the others. Considerable deliberation and pouring over the map tended to confirm the obvious, that the other pass was the one. We descended to the upper limits of the alpine vegetation and there spent the night in the open with only a meagre quantity of dehydrated stew to sustain us.

At first light we ascended boulder screes, then shattered rock ribs to the pass. I enjoyed the physical effort, steady deep breathing, the rhythmic flexing of working muscles... the cool morning air. Such times were ideal for meditation and pondering the problems of our journey. No rush; plenty of time to think things through... an opportunity, I realised, that might never offer itself as abundantly to me again. A clump of blue alpine poppies bloomed on top of the pass where we stopped to rest. To the north a satisfactory descent route down a side valley lay between us and what was obviously the massive Sutlej gorge. 'Arizona-like' peaks, to quote Tashi, lay to the west and directly below us a shrinking glacier peppered with rockfall debris and a bergschrund. It was the resting place, according to the old shepherds, of two men who had perished during an early winter storm just

A satisfied and happy Dodar village resident.

Grandmother and grandson in Himachal Pradesh hill village.

eight or nine months before. They had been carrying a holy devta (a Hindu deity or idol) across the 16,500-foot pass when snow had begun to fall and the wind to blow. They almost certainly had insufficient clothing and bad conditions at these altitudes would not have taken long to induce hypothermia.

The valley was as straight as a die, broad and green once we had made our way down the glacier and over the plentiful moraines. For several hours we marched briskly across the pastures, keeping a keen eye open for any sign of shepherds or foragers... but the occasional cattle beast was all we passed. We were tired, hungry and very thirsty. Yet we were determined to reach Nachar, the semblance of civilisation we knew existed far ahead in the bowels of the Sutlej gorge. The day was hot and a dry wind blew gently from the sheer rock walls that barred the Sutlej's northern flank. An almost mesmerised condition kept one foot following the lead of the other as the thought of tea and rice and lentils... and perhaps even a beer... hung like a carrot on a stick tantalisingly before us.

After over twelve hours on the march the track, which had progressively increased in size and reliability, sidled into the Sutlej gorge. Still 2000 feet below us the huge silty, grey torrent of the Sutlej river flowed westward from its source high on the Tibetan Plateau. Latched precariously on to the steep flanks above it were stands of trees, pastures and villages interspersed with bluffs. As darkness fell we rounded a bend in the path and there, amid groves of apple trees, was the higgledy-piggledy shambles of the town of Nachar. We all began running, forgetting our fatigue and our packs and the long day. 'Last one shouts!'

Among the shacks that served as shops on the roadside we found a restaurant — a tiny room in which to sit and imbibe a few glasses of pleasantly rehydrating and intoxicating beer. Not even the local policeman's compelling stories of snow leopards in the area were sufficient to keep me awake. I slept like a log.

Making a leisurely departure from Nachar we followed the spectacular motor road a short distance down valley. Near the secluded entrance of the Shurong valley we descended to the banks of the Sutlej river where a flying-fox cable spanned the rushing water. Graeme and I climbed into the steel case that was suspended from the wire cable. Sitting there, white knuckled, S.P. gave us a push. We careered out over the surging waters of the river. The cage came to a halt halfway across so we pulled on a hemp rope that was attached to the cage and dragged ourselves across to the far side. Once we were all there on solid ground we set off up the steep flank of the gorge. A narrow, dusty track switchbacked up towards a line of sheer bluffs where it made a delicate traverse into a gully that climbed abruptly through the tiers of cliffs. A short distance up the gully we stopped briefly to chew some sweets that S.P. gave us and to brush away the sweat from our eyes. It was a dry, hot mountain face, the Sutlej river directly below and the opposite wall of the gorge rising steeply before us. As we stood to leave a small, golden scorpion scuttled from where Graeme had been sitting across the sunbaked stones on the track to a shaded cranny.

174

'Nothing like a little incentive to keep moving up this bloody hill, eh?'

I felt impatient, so I pushed on ahead of the others into the blinding heat of the day, sweat streaming into my eyes as I climbed. Just below the crest at the top of the gully, I came upon a small flock of sheep and a lone shepherd. He smiled at me, pointing over to my left when I quizzed him about the village of Kamba where we intended to spend the night. From the crest I looked down and could see the others far below, labouring up the track. Turning, I descended the other side into the village. There was wild, tribal music ringing in the air; drums and some kind of horn. I strolled along the track past stone houses and terraced gardens to the village water tap. Two elderly villagers with little caps with a felt trim and thick wool jackets and pants came ambling along. Pointing up valley they told me there was no route leading over to the Parbati valley. Our map indicated that there was and S.P. told us that there was 'No doubt about it'. I decided to change the topic.

'Apples?' One of the old men shouted to a woman who worked in front of the house nearby. She gave me two red apples. Sitting on a rock by the large, brass tap that composed the village water-point, I munched enthusiastically on the crisp apples. I had been there for less than a minute when half a dozen men came along the path. I called 'Namascar'. No reply. They stopped before me, all of them looking down on me... and my apple.

'Where are you going?'

'Where have you come from?'

'What do you want here?' they demanded in fierce Hindi strongly laced with the unpleasant odour of distilled home-brew. I wasn't enjoying the confrontation as they were beginning to look aggressive. I didn't like the odds. Suddenly one of the more obnoxious members of the group stepped right up to me, passing his hat and coat to a friend. He stood defiantly before me with his hands on his hips. My Hindi is hardly commendable but it became patently obvious what they were shouting: 'Go back... Get out of here!'

I had heard some rather grisly stories about lone trekkers being molested, even killed, and I wasn't keen to join the statistics. I tried to explain my friends were coming; that some of them were Indians. They either could not understand me or didn't care. They became more belligerent and a great deal more voluble.

'O.K., O.K. I'm going.' I heaved my still open pack on my back, intending to retrace my steps and rejoin the others. Just below the crest of the ridge, from where I would be able to descend the track to where I had last seen Tashi, Graeme and S.P., the rowdy group began shouting again. They started to run along the track towards me. That was enough; I kicked up my heels and ran. It was only a short distance to where the track went over the ridge, but with my pack I was too slow. The clamour of shouting, running and heavy breathing was right behind me.

I realised one of them was getting very close and as I looked behind he lunged forward, grabbing the back of my pack and dragging me down. The two of us rolled down a rock slab that inclined below the track on to a level

175

S.P., Tashi and Graeme lost in deteriorating
weather in the Pin/Parbati region.

Eastern Kashmir sunset. Graeme is silhouetted
against the sky.

patch of dirt where our tumble was halted. Looking up the slab, I could see that the contents of my pack had spilled everywhere. The mob descended towards me, scrambling down the rock slab. I decided one of two things would happen. They would go for me or for my possessions. Fortunately a few more reasonable and less intoxicated types had been attracted by the commotion and to my surprise the mob stood around me glaring as I endeavoured to recover my chattels. The pause was only momentary. Two of the mob grabbed me, dragging me towards a muddy path that descended into the valley below. It was clear that now they simply wanted me "out"! I felt like unwanted garbage, I was distraught.

Again I tried to communicate with them when I saw the shepherd I had met before reaching the village. I called to him. He tried to calm the two men who still clung to me. He spoke rapidly to them. It was no reprimand; more likely an informatory speil on the imminent arrival of my three companions whom he must have seen. They relinquished their holds on me. I cautiously climbed back on to the track and returned over the crest. A short distance below, Tashi came pacing along the track followed by Graeme and S.P. I descended towards them feeling shocked and emotional... Immediately S.P. and Tashi climbed on to the crest and gazed down at the village. There was no one in sight.

It was the festival of the harvest. The whole village was participating in the three-day mala. There was dancing and music, the villagers in their best traditional clothes of fine woollen weave with bands of bright coloured embroidery; there were parties and plenty of home-brew. Despite invitations to stay in Kamba and enjoy the mala by the village leaders I was not enthusiastic. In the dimming light of dusk we set off for the little village of Shurong, a short distance up valley.

The track faded. We had no idea where Shurong was but in the darkness we could conceivably have passed it. Resigning ourselves to a night out we groped through the tangled undergrowth below the track to the Shurong river. Beneath a wild plum tree we erected our tent fly and crawled into our sleeping bags.

After an abortive attempt to find the route up valley we climbed above our overnight spot. Meandering through fields of crops bowing gently in the early morning breeze we reached the village of Shurong. At a group of houses we found some people... friendly people and hospitality. The bush telegraph had been at work and my plight of the previous day was common knowledge. A tall man with a flourishing moustache urged us to spend the day at his house which after brief deliberation we agreed to do. He and his delightful family made us feel at home, seating us on the verandah in front of the house with the Shurong valley dropping away below us. We were served tea, apples, nuts, baked grain, subji (fried vegetables) and roti by his four beautiful daughters. When we asked for a bottle of apple wine, the mother looked uncertain. After a pause she cautiously asked S.P., 'But will it make them go crazy?' We assured her we would remain well behaved and that we were really very decent chaps. She brought us some apple wine.

In the early afternoon the family descended to Kamba to attend the second day of the mala. They left one of the daughters to look after us. She was a beautiful girl, with a wide smile and dark flashing eyes. She had been educated, unlike her sisters, and had been trained as a stenographer which seemed mildly paradoxical considering where she was living and the work she was doing. S.P. and I sat on the verandah in the sun and chatted with her. I asked her through S.P. how she found working in the village after her education and training. She replied she enjoyed her work in the village, the menial tasks. She had no complaints although she wanted to get a job sometime. I quizzed her on male and female roles in her society.

'It is my duty to serve men. My brothers also, regardless of their age. They should sit in the house and enjoy themselves. I will prepare food and bring them drinks. It is my duty and my pleasure.'

I told her of the more egalitarian situation existing in western society. She dismissed it with a shrug. 'I'm happy.' She was aware of the past British rules. 'They neglected the mountain people,' she said, 'as for them there was no financial reward in the hills. The roads and amenities came with Indian governments.'

She was conscious of the pros and cons of the roads. When asked what a road up the Shurong valley to her village would do for her she replied: 'We would no longer need to carry heavy loads of food and necessary commodities to the village. It would bring greater affluence with the ease of trade, availability of goods and electricity. But there would be many more people, there would be litter... and there would be dacoits.'

I was immensely impressed by this girl; she was positive and sure and she had plenty of ideas.

The day drifted by lazily, writing and chatting, just watching the sun track from the eastern ridge of the Shurong valley across to the craggy western skyline. With the valley yawning beneath us and in the distance the Sutlej gorge it was a grand location for daydreaming or merely gazing out at the magnificent contours.

As rain pitter-pattered on the shingled roof I lay in my sleeping bag on the verandah. Listening, I could hear people on the path below the house. It was the family returning from the mala. Shaking the rain from their coats at the entrance they filed through the darkness into the house.

With a shepherd dressed like Robinson Crusoe in an intensely patched and darned wool suit we left our kind hosts. They had stuffed our packs with fresh apples, dried apricots, walnuts and baked grain so our food reserves were temporarily replenished. We marched along behind our guide following a vague route that meandered through the forests till it reached the high pastures at the head of the valley. The shepherd was going to assist a group who were bringing the flock down to the village, away from the threat of lower levels of snow. About mid-afternoon, we reached the flock grazing in a grassy meadow. In the middle there was a bivvy rock from where smoke rose into the air. A group of rugged-looking shepherds sat around it watching over the flock. Ahead rose steep grass-covered flanks, topped by rock crags, tiny snowfields and plummeting snow-choked gullies. A dense, grey cloud spread a gloomy ceiling over the valley. The shepherds pointed straight up into the gloom when they described the route to the Pin valley; but when we inquired about a route from Pin to the Parbati valley they were not so positive.

'People say there is a way. We have not gone that way.'

We asked whether these people had taken sheep over the Pin-Parbati pass.

'No,' they replied emphatically.

This could prove to be a difficult crossing, we agreed, as we walked up valley to a higher bivouac rock. What with the unstable weather, our vague wartime map, one ice axe among all of us and little fuel and food we would need to gamble as we crossed the high passes ahead. Winter was fast approaching — we couldn't afford too many hitches.

The closeness and warmth of the bivvy rock, its blackened ceiling gleaming with the flickering of the fire's flames soon eased any apprehensions we had. A hot meal with a cup of sweet coffee to wash it down, along with a cheerful barrage of gossip and joking had us all in a happy frame of mind. S.P. and Graeme engaged in a jocular discussion over route-finding which kept us well entertained until about 7 pm — bedtime.

Before crawling into my sleeping bag for the night, I went outside the bivvy and looked up at the sky. Clear patches and a horde of tiny lights, twinkling, changing... drifting. Infinite dimensions, so much more than anything I could ever know or understand. It shrunk even our journey across the Himalaya to insignificance. The heavens above are as elusive to questing man as are our own lives. As we learn each lesson its application is lost as we change, others change, our environment changes. I thought of the inter-personal relationships within the expedition, always changing and never easy, perhaps the most difficult part of this yearlong challenge... Imagine a "Himalayan" traverse of that celestial sword, the Milky Way! The problems that lay before us suddenly diminished in stature. I lowered my gaze, and wandered back to the bivvy rock. The peaceful, slow breathing of sleep, the pale glow of the embers drew me within.

It was bitterly cold. A heavy dew lay upon the meadow as we silently crossed it. We hopped from boulder to boulder across an entwined braid of streams that cascaded from the peaks above until we reached a sketchy track that appeared and disappeared. We climbed into a shallow valley filled with moraine and on to a receding glacier, scattered with boulders and riddled with moulins and melted troughs. The glacier divided, leading to two neves encircled by the remnants of mountains; gendarmes and brittle rock towers. On the eastern side lay a break in the serrated ridgeline but we could see none of the cairns the shepherds had indicated there would be. Here we had two alternatives; cross the 16,000-foot pass and proceed to the Pin valley or continue up the glacier in the hope that we would be able to find a way through the glaciated wilderness to the Parbati valley. The map gave little indication of what the route would be like — there was next to no details — so we reluctantly decided it would be most prudent to follow the longer shepherds' route via the Pin valley. After all, 'people say there is a pass'.

Without further deliberation we climbed on to the pass beneath an ominously grey sky. We descended the moraines on the east side with an icefall of tumbling, white ice on one side. I heard a rock falling over to our left. A flock of burrel (blue sheep) danced nimbly across a broken bluff face, disturbed by our intrusion into their seclusion. The valley veered to the north, and we followed a lateral moraine trough to a lovely dell wedged between huge mounds of morainic debris. This was Nestol, like the eye of a hurricane. A meadow amidst the clutter of vast moraines. We halted by a brook and boiled the billy, sitting on smooth glacial boulders surrounded by clumps of alpine flora. The withered remnants of flowers lingered on their stems. The sky darkened and descended upon the peaks around us; light snow drifted down, tickling my nose, melting instantly.

Skirting the tall moraines before us we entered on a sparse river flat, its surface imprinted with the hooves of a large flock of sheep. Domestic or wild? There was no evidence of man's presence. They must have gone down valley leaving the broad meadows of Wangchuk Leng to the oncoming winter. Consulting the only reference we had, our very vague map, we concluded we were on course. A 2000-foot climb should have us looking into the Pin where, according to the shepherds, we could descend easily to the valley floor. There, we decided, we would spend the night.

Sleet poured from the laden clouds that now enshrouded the mountains. We climbed, breathing deeply and methodically in the rarified air up to the pass with the sleet beating down on the screes around us. We reached the line of old cairns that stood as sole sign of the passage of man and gazed expectantly over the pass. Perhaps I should describe what I expected to see before I describe what I did, in fact, see. We had been led to understand by the shepherds and our map that a broad and probably grassy Pin valley would spread before us — an ample reward for the day's exertions. However, the scene was far from that. It was wild, rugged and inhospitable. A glacier swept before us plunging into a valley to the north where a succession of icefalls tumbled in uncompromising chaos to a valley somewhere in the mist below. To the east, above a mountainside of boulders and ice was a dip in the ridgeline, promise of a possible passage. It was now 4 pm and a further climb in the wind and sleet and the uncertainty of the route would be a gamble.

We dropped down to the scalloped and rutted surface of the surprise glacier and searched for somewhere to bivouac. A large boulder about fifteen feet across lay perched upon a two-foot pillar of glacial ice — it would have to do. As the wind lashed us with flurries of sleet we worked on a shelter. Two hours of chipping ice with the ice axe and building rock walls followed until we were able to drape our tent fly over the big boulder, fixing one edge to the glacier. Just on darkness we scrambled inside our 16,000-foot-high "shelter from the storm" — recess where a stove roared producing hot brews and where only a little of the chilling wind and sleet penetrated. Sporadic gusts pierced the flimsy barrier we had erected, showering spindrift on our sleeping bags but we weren't uncomfortable or unthankful. I had the dubious convenience of being the one near the entrance, a complex series of parkas and ponchos draped across the opening. To this the occupants of the shelter made frequent migrations to answer the eternal call of nature, trampling

Graeme climbs by a Buddhist prayer inscribed in the rock in Kashmir.

over me in the process. The freezing wind rushing in off the glacier as the doorway of parkas and ponchos was removed. We retreated into the depths of our sleeping bags, noses only protruding, in classic cold conditions posture, and dozed.

The sun shone across the ridge causing the frosted rocks to glitter as we climbed towards the dip in the ridge that we hoped would lead us to the Pin. If not, we had a serious dilemma... where were we? Plugging in snow six to ten inches deep we approached the pass and reaching the crest looked down the other side. What a relief! A broad valley descended gradually to the north-east; by description and orientation it tallied with the Pin. To the east rose a skyline of mountains, their faces crossed by the massive striations of tilted strata — a forgotten seabed reincarnated. Graeme pulled the map out from the top flap of his pack and we passed it around, each of us attempting to interpret its dotted contour lines, wishing that the reliability diagram in the margin didn't indicate "poor". We decided, after weighing up the possibilities, to move north across the head of the Pin valley, ascend to a ridgeline and there, hopefully, intersect a route marked on the map as leading west to the Pin-Parbati pass.

Leaving the 16,500-foot Pin pass we dropped down into the valley a short distance, cutting across to the left and on to a snow-covered glacier. This led to a 17,000-foot pass, a glacial interworld, between the Pin and one of its side-valleys that lay on the other side of the pass. What we saw was in line with what we expected. We continued.

I was concerned about my feet as they were very cold in the dilapidated Indian gym shoes I was wearing. The many miles of plugging in deep, cold snow that we had already completed were not ideal for such footwear... and the glacier swept for miles ahead of us. A freezing wind blew across the mountain wilderness and mare's tails above were being rapidly undercut by layers of cloud. We felt very ill-equipped for our plight. Crevasses crisscrossed the glacier's surface and we had no rope; we had only minimal clothing and footwear, food and fuel and still only calculated guesses as to our whereabouts. For several hours we plodded in the heavy snow down the glacier, winding around crevasses, jumping those we couldn't circle. Our horizon hardly built up our optimism; snowcapped summits and shattered glaciers that plummeted into bottomless gorges spread as far as the eye could see. A lassitude drifted upon us but our trained limbs continued mechanically, carrying our weary psyches. From the glacier we scrambled on to its rubble-strewn flank and hiked up towards yet another dip in the ridgeline. According to the map and our calculations — it *had* to be the Pin-Parbati pass... and freedom from the clutches of the mountains and the elements.

It was with a strange mixture of disbelief and resigned hilarity that we looked over the presumed Pin-Parbati pass. The scene that met our eyes was all wrong. The valley below flowed into the one we had just descended which flowed, eventually back into the Pin. Where, then was the Parbati valley, or more accurately, where were we? We sat down on the ridge and from our 15,500-foot vantage point scanned the country that lay around us, feeling smaller and less significant by the minute. We were all very tired and the weather was looking bad. S.P. suggested we returned to the Pin valley, a suggestion that met with unanimous disapproval.

'We've got enough food,' someone said optimistically. And then we listened to one of those 'it could be worse' stories. Graeme related a tale of a solo yachtsman's unenviable lot after being demasted in a storm. There was a common denominator however... food. Apparently he had run out of food so being an enterprising fellow he chewed his way through a pair of leather boots and swallowed a pint of engine oil... I eyed a piece of brittle schist near my foot with distaste.

On the far side of the valley to the west we spied a possibility — a gently rising flank with a depression at its crest. There were some tiny shapes on the skyline, too, that could be cairns. A quick reference to the map, and we decided that with some imagination, and ignoring the fact that there was at least one valley unaccounted for, we could perceive a resemblance between this next possible pass and the map's sketchy indications. There were no other feasible routes.

We descended 2000 feet of extremely steep screes, the slope interspersed with small bluffs, into the valley. Again there were the tracks of some cloven-hoofed creatures by the stream on the narrow valley floor, but no signs of man. We hiked up the almost completely denuded hillside towards the zebra stripes of a partially melted layer of snow that covered the slope beneath the pass. The country looked as if it had been chronically over-grazed or burned too often — a delicate environment from which man had taken and taken until it could give no more. Now man no longer visited this high valley.

I tried to warm my chilled fingers in my pockets as the wind tore through the meagre shelter afforded by my flapping poncho. The slope eased, rolling forward till it exposed a line of rock cairns. Could this be it? Below, the long white slope of a glacier appeared through the wind-blown clouds. It flowed north, which vaguely concurred with what the map indicated the Parbati valley should do. It didn't really matter. We were going down to that glacier to find some shelter anyway. We were exhausted, having crossed four passes in one day and covered a lot of difficult ground.

Leaving the 16,500-foot Pin-Parbati pass we dropped down to the whiteness of the glacier. Beneath an angry grey sky, we marched down the glacier's rutted surface with an air of jubilation. We didn't definitely know we had reached the Parbati valley, but we had escaped, that's what mattered. We strode over the perfect, white curves of the glacial snout and on to a riverbed beyond it. There we searched for shelter among the giant boulders scattered beside the river.

Out of the flurries of snow we stooped forward and peered into the dimness. Conveniently propped up by three boulders, a huge morainic slab formed a spacious bivouac. There was room for a dozen. We bent double and stepped beneath its substantial shelter. We moved small rocks from the ground to create a smooth platform, rolled out our mats and wriggled into our sleeping bags.

Corrina in the desolation of eastern Kashmir.

A cup of tea and an apple to sustain me, I emerged into the day from our overnight lair. Avoiding the verglassed rocks near the river we set off downstream into the dawning day. Ahead of us were the imposing pyramidal features of a peak, its faces splashed with the budding day's kaleidescope of colours, an optical light show of gliding fluidity.

The river cascaded down a sculptured groove, to rows of moraines 500 feet below in the main valley. After some scouting about we found a route down the true left side of the river, climbing down precipitous fingers of rubble stacked against the smooth rock bluff. We wound our way through the piles of moraine till we reached the river flats beyond. On top of a boulder below the moraines we found a red cotton scarf inscribed with prayers, wrapped about a stone. Perhaps an offering left by a sadhu after a period of solitary meditation in the upper reaches of the valley. Men had been here, so there must be a way down the broad valley. In the hazy distance, the valley swept around to the west which coincided with our map... at long last. It was definitely the Parbati valley.

We marched down valley exclaiming at the magnificent buttresses and massive flanking walls. It was a climber's paradise for rock, ice and snow. The meadows were speckled with edelweiss and daisies, blue alpine poppies and buttercups of every hue and colour.

At the end of the first of the two days it took us to descend the valley the

*In light snow we climbed up valley towards the
Bara Lapcha pass.*

long hours we had trekked seemed to have made little impression on its size. We started early on the second day. We had forty kilometres of rugged terrain to cover in order to reach Mani Karan so we moved relentlessly. We crossed a huge natural bridge below which the swirling waters tumbled through a series of hollowed basins and smooth, voluptuous curves and entered a narrow gorge. The path wound its way across grassy platforms flanked by cliffs and sidled along tiny ledges with the river hundreds of feet below. At a waterfall that liberally doused the track on its way to the river we stopped for a drink. While we sat there resting on the ledge a white goat came wandering around the corner. On seeing us it stopped, cocking its head on one side and surveying the obstruction that we represented.

'I think I would have killed that goat had we met it yesterday,' declared Graeme, referring to the starvation rations of the past few days. The goat, wisely, ran before us along the narrow ledges. By the time we reached easier ground we were highly impressed by its nimbleness.

Eventually we reached villages, people and food. There were occasional groups of dishevelled-looking foreigners wearing eccentric costumes amid the calls of village children, 'Hippy, hippy.' We were obviously not far from Mani Karan as this area of Himachal Pradesh is well known for tourists and young, hippy-type people. At 7.30 pm in near darkness, we reached the electric lights of Mani Karan, its steaming hot pools and temples. We searched for a room to spend the night.

185

We slogged, in the hot, dry air, up the gorge that led to Malana, a village renowned for having the oldest democracy in the world. On reaching the village we concluded something had gone terribly wrong and that if the slovenly state of the village and uncooperative nature of the shopkeeper were anything to go on then the oldest democracy was no recommendation for matured democratic process. Above Malana we crossed a pass from where we could look into the Kulu valley where the Beas river flowed. Not far up the valley lay Manali, our next rendezvous point with the support team. It was already late as we strode along a track that traversed a broad hillside above the treeline and descended a spur into the forests. As we entered the gloom of the forest canopy we passed a shepherd's hut, chatting noisily as we went. The noise attracted the attention of the occupants. A tall European girl emerged. 'Where are ya from?' she drawled in a heavy New Zealand accent. She was from Hamilton, Graeme's home town. Into the spooky darkness of the forest we descended, groping in the minimal light as we floundered along the track. S.P. led the way, establishing himself as a nimble and canny mover in the dark.

'We vegetarians see very well in the dark,' he nonchalantly declared as we stumbled along behind him.

We spent the night in the village of Nagar and continued the next morning through magnificent apple orchards to the valley floor. Following the banks of the Beas river we walked along the road towards Manali. It was a beautiful valley, broad and green, with an atmosphere of prosperity. Fields of grain spread before us and there were extensive orchards. Magnificent pine forests descended the mountainsides to just above the valley floor. Far above were the peaks of the Himalaya.

In mid-afternoon we arrived in Manali and were reunited with the support group at the Western Himalayan Mountaineering Institute. In no time at all we were deep in the things we had gone without for three weeks — music, letters, a wide variety of foods, fresh clothes and a good wash with soap. I deemed it time for a change and took a razor to my tatty beard. Doug gave me a red felt cap to wear, the Himachal Pradesh State hat; feeling unaccustomedly dapper, I joined the others for a dinner on the town.

Manali was quite different from other towns in India. It was alive with narrow bazaars and colourful hawkers. Freaky-looking Europeans thronged the streets and there were busy restaurants where pop music blared out and beer flowed. So easily, we had slipped into another world, a far cry from the serenity of the mountains.

Sadly, during the five days we spent in Manali, the smooth and happy rapport that had existed between S.P., Tashi, Graeme and myself deteriorated radically. The atmosphere was no longer light and enjoyable. One evening Graeme told Tashi and me that Corrina wished to go on the last Indian section of the journey to Leh. He said that, as far as he was concerned, there were two alternatives. Either Tashi, Corrina, he and I proceeded as a foursome or we went as two separate groups of two. If Tashi and I wished to complete this section with the same threesome that set out from Sikkim then there was no choice. I opposed Corrina joining the traverse party for what I considered extremely good reasons. I felt she was very demanding on Graeme. In an expedition of this kind, if each member was self-reliant then his own personal wellbeing strengthened the party as a whole. To me, Graeme had not always been able to differentiate between his personal commitments and those to the expedition.

As if to ease our problems we were very fortunate to be present at a meeting with the Dalai Lama, the spiritual leader of the Tibetan Buddhists. He is a magnificent person, exemplary in both his acts and his words. We all warmed to him immediately. When asked whether he hoped to return to Tibet and its old ways he replied, 'No way can we go backwards and no use... but I think I will return there sometime.'

We talked of Tibet and of climbing in the Himalaya, scaling the world's highest mountains using oxygen bottles and the relationship between India and Tibet.

'Buddhism came from India. Our script came from India. We are very close. Indians consider Tibet a holy land and they like to pilgrimage there. They undergo great difficulties crossing the mountains... and without oxygen too... ha, ha, ha.' He talked of happiness, the importance of striving to be happy, working at it.

One serious character with bushy eyebrows asked him: 'How do you see God... and spiritual matters?' He apparently anticipated a revelation.

The Dalai Lama gave a high-pitched chuckle and smiled. 'There are many philosophies and they are all similar. Love and kindness; that's what is important.'

S.P. returned to his home in Mussourie to attend an important religious ceremony marking one year since his father's death. I was sorry to see him go. However, he would rejoin us in Leh at the end of the next section. There was still no word from Shubash Roy who had returned to Calcutta as his father was seriously ill, but we expected to see him in Leh also. Doug and Ann Louise would transport our supplies by road through Kashmir to Ladakh and meet us in Leh in two and a half weeks' time.

The quartet moved north. Graeme and Corrina, Tashi and I climbed through fields of grain and into the pine forests above the Hampta Nal valley. We were on our way again.

Till now the major component of our heading across the Himalaya had been west. From Manali in Himachal Pradesh we would move north, traversing Eastern Kashmir till we reached Ladakh, "Little Tibet", and the Indo-Pakistani ceasefire line. We would then proceed to Leh, capital of Ladakh, where we would rendezvous with S.P., Doug, Ann Louise and Shubash. From there the five New Zealanders would go on to Pakistan to complete the journey to the foot of Mt K2. The Indian members of the expedition would trek north of Leh across northern Ladakh to Karakoram pass.

Together we tramped slowly through the whispering trees on to a high meadow. There ran a bubbling brook and above rose massive granite walls marked with cracks and chimneys, proud buttresses and defiant prows, huge arches and fine, smooth slabs that extended a thousand feet above the valley floor, unbroken.

Tashi looks down on the first habitation we had
seen in a week in eastern Kashmir.

'If this place was at home there would be dozens of climbers all over it,'
enthused Graeme.

We passed shepherds descending with their flocks and climbed on to the
alpine meadows already exhibiting signs of the imminent winter season: tips
of leaves and blades of grass burned by frosts and cold, dry winds. At the
terminal moraine of a small glacier we halted. Far above a great rock tower
protruded from a snow-white neve and as the sun sank it turned a bloody
red. Below the clouds receded like sinking ships into the gloomy valleys as
we erected our tent fly beside a large boulder to spend the night. Graeme was
ill and had become very weak towards the end of the day which concerned
me. This was the first day of the journey and it did not bode well for the
almost three-week section to Ladakh.

We climbed the short distance to the Hamta Jot pass (14,500 feet) and
scrambled down the far side following a winding track through bluffs and
across long scree slopes till we reached the meadows on the valley floor. The
track sidled across the narrow entrance to the valley and we looked out over
another world.

Below, a tiny cluster of tents lay beside the silty waters of the Chandra
river. Gone were the breezy pine forests and scented alpine meadows of the
Kulu valley. What lay before us, spreading all around the groups of tents

*Across the roof-tops of a Ladakhi village towards
the moonscape of the desolate Ladakhi mountains.*

below was desolation, a land barren and dry. A harsh world of rigorous climate; broad flats where the wind lifted swirls of dust as it blew across them, razor-edged mountains of bare rock crumbling into sweeping talus slopes, a host of pastel shades and hues. All lay stark and devoid of real vegetation beneath an unrelenting azure sky.

It was in a state of shock that we descended to the river as the geographical transition had been so sudden. It manifested itself at Chattru, the group of tents where we purchased extra food in a panic-stricken shopping spree. The teashop proprietor told us that there were no more shops after Chattru till we reached Ladakh and Leh. What is more, he said, the route over the Bara Lapcha pass, which we intended to cross, was a very long one. If this was our last shopping spree then we would make good use of it. We enjoyed a large lunch of spiced lentils and roti and copious cups of tea. This kept the proprietor tremendously amused, as most patrons order only one cup of tea. We consumed over thirty!

All afternoon we walked along the dust and rubble-covered road watching the granite walls and peaks around us dissolve progressively into the smooth, eroded contours of a Tibetan landscape. Ruby-red screes and pure white glaciers oozed between the residual domes of once great mountains. We stopped briefly at a magnificent slab where we climbed some finger-sized cracks that ran up its glacier-sculptured surface. Along the road in the unceasing wind we plodded through the brilliant reds and golds of a fiery sunset. Mare's tails and foreboding alto-stratus edged over the southern ramparts of the valley; a meteorological frown.

In darkness we reached a bridge referred to on our sketchy map as Batal where we decided to stop for the night. It was pitch black as we groped about erecting the tent fly to shield us from the wind and began cooking our dinner, coaxing the stove to bear the chilling blast of the wind and produce our sustenance.

We left the dusty road and followed a lattice of sidling tracks that traversed the screes flanking the Chandra valley. Where there was any vegetation it had been burned dry and crisp by the relentless wind from the south. Tashi assured us the scenery was typically Tibetan: rounded contours and eroded gullies, a harsh climate where only the very tough survive. I wondered if we would. Illness and the slowness of the party could be a problem.

In the early afternoon, I sat by the shores of Chandra Tal, a large glacial lake of translucent green with maroon talus slopes rising to a jagged ridge-line. Golden towers of brittle rock, lightly dusted with snow lay above, giving an impression of great separation from where I sat. It was a long wait, for Graeme and Corrina had fallen far behind. We hadn't seen them since we met a group of Ladakhis, a Tibetan people clothed in tattered, maroon, wool bakus and with cosy Tibetan boots on their feet. They were on their way down valley with mules and yaks. Winter was in the air and the hardy people of this parched land were descending to their villages in the lower valleys.

Graeme flopped down beside me. He looked old and grey and his face was drawn and gaunt. 'Can you give me some aspirin?'

'You've finished the others already?'

'Yeh.'

I rummaged in my pack and produced the expedition medical kit and handed him a strip of the foil-wrapped tablets.

We continued on for another two hours passing high snowclad peaks and glaciers that peered at us through the gathering high cloud and banks of windborne dust. At a primitive shelter we stopped. It was a stone igloo, dug into the ground a short distance with rock walls built up and cantilevered inward until only a four to five-foot gap remained overhead. We slung our tent fly over the top and retreated inside from the blast of the wind and the ominous weather. It was a terrible night. Snow fell in sporadic flurries and the wind never abated. Graeme suffered frightful fevers that left him shaking and perspiring.

We moved on in the morning, plodding steadily in the few inches of snow that had fallen. Both Tashi and I were concerned about the strength of our party and the low grey ceiling that lingered about the mountain tops, casting a chilling gloom on the brown valley. It was after twelve when we sat eating our lunch in the falling sleet. I watched Graeme playing with his food; he looked like a wax figure escaped from Madame Tussaud's. Only his determination was keeping him going. I asked him what he wanted to do for the rest of the day.

'Plod on, I guess.'

'I think we should stop at the first shelter,' I countered.

'Well, I couldn't fight you over that,' he conceded, his voice weak.

Across a series of dry streambeds we found the stone walls of what was once a crude shelter. We draped our tent fly over the top, enclosing it, and secured it with rocks. Graeme crawled inside and slipped into his sleeping bag.

'It's so good to be lying down,' he moaned.

'How do you feel now?'

'Terrible.'

Later, I asked him what he wanted to do in the morning if he was still unwell. Both Tashi and I thought that returning to Chattru could prove prudent.

'Wander on,' he replied. 'I didn't want to stop early today. I would have gone on. You decided we should stop.'

I sank back into my down bag and stared at the tent fly flapping above me. Is our going on sensible, I wondered, or is it simply further into trouble? In flurries of light snow we headed on up the valley towards the Bara Lapcha pass (16,500 feet). Tashi and I had taken some of Graeme's gear from his pack and we hoped it would help him. He refused to consider anything other than continuing towards the pass.

The sky cleared as the valley broadened and we trekked across wide meadows, now golden brown. Around us lay the mountains, like giant shingle mounds, their surfaces smooth but broken here and there by stubborn pinnacles of rock or teetering tors capped with large stones. We strode across the almost infinite plain of pebbly ground that inclined gradually upwards to the Bara Lapcha. Never have I seen, let alone crossed, such a pass. We walked and walked yet the ground never seemed quite flat enough nor elevated sufficiently for it to be the crest of the pass. Eventually we reached a pile of stones with sticks and Buddhist prayer flags protruding from it. Tashi placed several stones on the pile in traditional Tibetan style and we consoled ourselves that this was the elusive pass. Huddling in the lee of the stone chorten I handed out a special treat; small squares of cheese carried all the way from Manali.

In single file we followed a vague track that continued along the stubbornly ill-inclined-to-descend ground. It was another half hour before we reached the watershed at 16,500 feet. From there we marched for an hour over barren, rubble-strewn tundra, making an almost imperceptible descent to another pass. A narrow motor road crossed over it joining Lahul and Spiti districts — the meeting place of three great valleys. However, the road was deserted and it remained that way over the ensuing two days that we followed it. While Tashi and I awaited the others, sitting by the roadside in the cold air at 16,000 feet, we looked out over the Yunam valley — the way to Spiti. We sat in silence staring at the jagged peaks, millions of years of bared geology, and the graceful sweeps of the multi-coloured talus that

Ladakhi woman and children offer us baked barley grain.

As if from a fantasy, Potoksar village in Ladakh sprouts from the barren mountains.

stretched down into the Yunam valley. It was isolation personified, eerie and cold, forgotten. A place not made for man... nor life.

'There is truth there,' Tashi murmured pensively.

Graeme and Corrina arrived and we heaved our shoulder-fatiguing loads on to our backs. Together we walked down the switchbacks of the road into the Yunam valley... a depression amidst age-old crumbling rock.

For the next day and a half we marched down the broad valley following the narrow, dusty road; across vast flats of sparse, wind-burned grasses under the flak of squalls laden with dust that filled our eyes, hair and clothing. The mountainsides were like gigantic mosaics from an expressionist's palette; our world was restricted to two long strips, bright blue sky and peachy-hued earth.

Our destination for lunch was Sarchu, marked prominently on our map. To warrant such a mention it must surely be of some consequence... a teashop perhaps? Filled with dubious anticipation, I approached the stream upon which Sarchu was supposed to be. Peering around the bend in the road I looked upstream to a lone bridge surrounded by garish monuments and signs. On approaching them I discovered they listed the distances from Sarchu to towns around the state and the country. Presumably to illustrate the obvious: just how far we were from anywhere. Leh, for example, was 250 long, lonely and windswept kilometres to the north. The signs did not finish with distances, they went on to proclaim the Yunam valley as "Valley of the Gods"... and I thought of Tashi's words the previous evening. Yes, there was something special about the place, inhibiting perhaps, ideally suited for hermits and retreats. A place where abstention would be not a discipline, but a matter of course!

Beyond Sarchu a large river swept in from the south joining the Yunam river. We waded across its freezing waters, wishing we had an inflatable raft as the Yunam river flows into the Zaskar river, where we were heading, and eventually the Indus river and Ladakh. We continued along the road for the remainder of that day and half of the next before we met other people. There was a wild-looking Tibetan with a huge sheepskin cloak, long, black braids of hair and a fur-trimmed Tibetan hat perched upon his head. He wore turquoise and gold earrings and across his features the furrowed lines of many a high-plateau winter. He peered at us with his squinted, Mongolian eyes and proffered 'tashi dilli' (greetings). He and his two companions were shepherding their flock to lower country before winter. In Tibetan, Tashi quizzed them about the route ahead, where the best tracks were and where we could procure some food.

'They don't know much about the route,' said Tashi, visibly despondent. Not far beyond the flock we followed a track down the river from the elbow of the first switchback of the road as it climbed above and out of sight. We passed willows, an autumn gold, and scarlet thorn bushes that lined the perfect transparency of the turquoise-blue Yunam river.

Where the river entered a gorge, a track traced a line up above it and from a minor pass we surveyed the desolate, mountain wilderness that spread before us. We wondered if we would find water so far above the river. We followed our noses along the path to yet another pass where prayer flags fluttered in the breeze. From down in a gully below the pass rose a slender wisp of smoke. There were men and animals there. Overjoyed, we rushed down in the evening light towards them, like a horde of savages, to be met by two very tough Ladakhi men. Their horses and mules carried loads of tsampa (barley flour) in heavy wool sacks so we hastily purchased some.

We were famished. Stuffing the dry tsampa into our mouths, we consumed all we could before solja, hot Tibetan tea, appeared. We mixed our tsampa with the salt tea in traditional Tibetan style and swallowed the paste mixture produced with relish.

Across more small passes and dusty, brown hillsides we went with the river several thousand feet below. I scrutinized the geology, the contorted and twisted strata uncovered exposing the agonies of a young planet, an ever-changing world. On one pass at about 13,000 feet an unusual rock caught my eye, some regular patterns and shapes. Leaning down, I picked up a two-inch square stone, rust-brown in colour, imprinted with the fossilised coil of a large sea shell, an ammonite. To think that these great mountains once lay beneath the surface of the sea... I sauntered off along the track feeling insignificant. My entire life would be but a speck on a geological time scale. My own contributions to humanity were miniscule and man's impact on the solar system throughout time would be almost as fleeting. With my ego, my self-esteem somewhere around the level of my ankles, I followed Tashi around a bend in the track. Nestled before us in a cul de sac lay dwellings. It was mythological, transported from another time, incongruous, that humans should dwell in this environment. Although beside the blue Yunam river, the walls of rambling rock peaks rose all around and there was not a trace of vegetation anywhere. There was a compact cluster of flat-topped houses, whitewashed, with small dark windows arranged haphazardly along the walls. Bundles of grass and winter feed were stacked on the roofs. People were working, threshing grain by urging tethered yaks to walk around a central stake, trampling the barley heads beneath their hooves. Others worked in the empty fields, hoeing the soil for next season's crop. We descended into the village and stepped back in time.

The path led between two mud-plastered walls and at the far end stood a woman with a child tied to her back. She stared at us. Tashi smiled in his usual infectious way, and called 'Julay' (greetings in Ladakhi). A white toothy grin creased her pretty round face, but she turned and scurried away. Around the corner of the building we came across more people who appeared less bashful. The women remained shy, staying behind the less inhibited men. They had striking Mongolian features and rosy cheeks with long dark braids. All the women wore black bakus (cloaks) and yak-skin shawls, large, white seashell bracelets and on their heads an elaborate headpiece decked out with the family wealth — turquoise, red coral and precious prayer-boxes. On the sides of their heads hung decorative black woollen wings, like enlarged ears. They were a people of smiles, inquisitive and generous. We were invited inside for solja (salt tea). Bending low we filed beneath the low doorway and scrambled up the steep stairway in the

Lamayuru monastery in Ladakh.

darkness of the basement to the living area on the upper floor. It was only marginally better lit, a shaft of light beaming through a small window opening. Crosslegged on the earth floor we sat by the yak-dung fire while we were plied with solja, curd and tsampa. Tashi tried to talk with them but found that, although their nuance and accent was Tibetan their vocabulary was of a dialect he could not understand. The universal smile seemed sufficient.

We left their isolated world, continuing down the gorge till we reached another village where the valley broadened slightly. Yarsun was a thriving little community where the threshing of grain was very much in progress and yaks, goats and sheep browsed on the stubble of the harvested fields. Just beyond Yarsun we reached the compact, medieval village of Marsun. To conserve the limited level ground for agriculture the houses were built on a rock outcrop above the river. They perched upon it like a fortress. We crossed the bare fields to beneath the complex and Tashi and I went inside, leaving Graeme and Corrina to fend off two savage mastiffs that romped about barking and growling.

Two old women greeted us from the top of some steps. They guided us along a labyrinth of dimly lit passages to a room where a square hole in the wall looked out over the river. There was firewood and a fireplace in the middle of the floor and plenty of floor space for us to spread out our sleeping

Corrina looks around Lamayuru monastery.

bags. The two grinned at us benignly with their toothless gums as we gestured approval. We asked them for tsampa and for chung before returning outside to call the others.

The Ladakhis lead a tough and simple existence. There is a short two-month monsoon season to grow the barley crop and collect fodder for the animals. There are no shops or manufactured items. Everything is made by the villagers themselves out of the materials they possess: wood, straw, leather and stone. They have no money because they need none. They are self-sufficient. Their lives are hard, they have little knowledge of hygiene and the distractions of western society are unheard of; yet they are a happy and contented people. The stresses and problems of other societies just do not exist here.

It was the last day of September as we manoeuvred ourselves and our packs out of the rabbit-warren building into the fields. We descended to the river where a precarious rope bridge made of twisted vines spanned the crystal clear waters. A number of ropes bound together formed the footpath and a rope on either side the hand rails. It was a wobbly, unstable bridge so we crossed one at a time, clinging to the side ropes and moving gingerly. A spectacular track led down the right side of the river, winding through bluffs on narrow ledges with the cliff face spreading above for thousands of feet and below a sheer drop of 2000 feet to the river. For several hours we followed the cliff-face path till it descended to the river where we were able to reach water.

The track traced its way around the banks to where the river turned abruptly south. Here it was joined by another stream for its lengthy dogleg to the Zaskar valley; so we turned off, following the side stream above the lines of bluffs that flanked its gorge. We planned to cut across country by way of Tantar Gompa (a monastery) to the Thonda La pass and thus reach the Zaskar more quickly than by following the indirect route along the Yunam river. Tashi and I chatted as we walked along the track, agreeing that since we had had decent quantities of food we had felt much stronger. However, we decided that our drive was waning. We both looked forward to completing the traverse and to going home.

I moved on ahead leaving Tashi with Graeme and Corrina. The valley veered north-west and I descended to the riverbed, walking through thickets of willow until the track climbed on to an alluvial platform beside the river. As I reached level ground, a movement in front of me caught my eye. A small agile dog... no... a golden brown fox with a big bushy tail, a white tuft on its end. It looked quickly at me and sprung in a series of nimble bounds across the dry grass, disappearing into the willows. Another movement above brought my attention to another fox that slunk reproachfully further up the hillside and out of view... a silent rendezvous.

I approached Tantar Gompa with a degree of awe — a collection of desert-coloured mud buildings clustered together on a windy hilltop above the alluvial plain. There was an air of austerity and as the cold, shrill wind draughted past them I became apprehensive. What strange being in pursuit of philosophical enlightenment could live in such an inhospitable place?

Before too long we were all comfortably ensconced in the almost subterranean room of a house that was built down the side of the hill from the gompa. It was completely enclosed from the elements outside and was consequently pitch black within, due both to the soot that coated everything and the lack of light. The kindly man and woman of the house bestowed hospitality upon us which dispensed with all my initial apprehensions and returned a rosier glow to our cold and windswept complexions. We sat on woven wool mats by the flickering fire as we consumed our food and grinned at our host and hostess. They had weathered a few storms up here. Their faces were creased and smudged with soot from the fire — a complexion we were also acquiring — but their eyes were sharp, there was a sparkle there. Their rough clothing was of no significance to us as we had become quite used to the standard of living these hardy people must endure. The soiled woollen clothes and tangled plaited hair on both men and women is a matter of having nothing else to wear and no way of keeping clean. The water is too cold to wash in and fuel for the fire is so scarce that it cannot be wasted on heating water for washing.

Anyway, I have found the first week of not-washing is the most uncomfortable, the second is not too bad and by the third you have no desire to wash at all, as you feel quite comfortable. Everyone around you is the same, you are merely complying with what is the norm.

From Tantar Gompa we moved up valley towards the Thonda La following a vague track connecting isolated fields and grazing areas. Superb rock buttresses rose from the bare, rubble-strewn hillsides, a blended mosaic of brown, gold and red. Huge reptilian dorsal-fin ridges rose in serrated curves from the red talus slopes that flanked them, till they reached the ridge-tops, dusted with light snow and tormented by the cold, early-winter winds. Above our lunch spot, a sunny dell among willows by the river, the track was hemmed in on the river bed by the walls of the weatherbeaten mountains necessitating seventeen fords of the stream; a mighty chilling experience in the clear melt waters of the gorge which the sun had already left for the evening.

Where the stream bifurcated we halted in the dimming light to erect our tent fly over some walls that we built using large river stones. At 14,000 feet in the early winter the wind is very cold so we hastily retreated beneath the fly to the warmth of our sleeping bags. While Graeme, Corrina and Tashi slept at one end of the shelter, I slept by the fire, producing cups of piping hot black tea and our by now notorious dehydrated stews. Two packets of "dehy", salt, masala, soya bean protein tasting like unflavoured sausage meat and tsampa to thicken the deadly brew. Another cup of tea with salt and some tsampa to top it off and we shrunk into the warmer confines of our bags, nose only protruding through the tiny hole left by tightly-drawn draw-strings. Only the sounds of the night filled the darkness, a cold breeze, the flap of the tent fly, sleeping noises and the not-so-dormant noises of tummy rumbles and flatulence as the tsampa did its thing with our digestive juices.

It was damned cold at 6 am as I half-emerged from my sleeping bag, coaxed the fire to life and produced a cup of black sugarless tea from last night's tea leaves. With some tsampa to thicken the mix the breakfast ritual was soon over and we headed off up the right-hand branch of the stream towards the 16,000-foot Thonda La. For three and a half hours we plodded up the stony mule-track that ascended gradually through the desolate mountain landscape. Tashi and I reached the freezing, windswept pass; graced by a pile of stones and a wind-lashed pole adorned with prayer flags. Far below I could see the Thonde monastery, the Zaskar valley and the massive bends of the Zaskar river. Into our isolation filed a line of mules with a little girl bundled in wool cloaks riding astride the rear animal as they climbed slowly on to the pass. We exchanged smiles: 'Where are you going?' and 'Where are you coming from?' She disappeared down the way up which we had just come. We huddled behind our packs in the cold wind on that broad and barren pass to await the others.

After forty-five minutes there was no sign of them and we were frozen with the cold. Descending 500 feet to where the on-blast of the chilling wind was less, we sat with a group of young Ladakhis. They were going across the pass with mules to collect that very elusive commodity in these parts, firewood. They shared their lunch of spiced roti with us before they moved on up the hill. Two hours had passed when two figures appeared on the pass. We were very cold from our wait and Graeme's gruffness on his arrival upset us both.

Graeme crosses a vine bridge to the 'cat-walk'
ledge-track on the far side of the Yunam river.

Tashi and I stormed on, our cold bodies thawing in the warmer airs of the lower Zaskar valley. Thonde Gompa was perched on a rock outcrop above the immense plain of the Zaskar valley. A large and austere building, it was whitewashed and had red trimmings around windows and doors. The conglomeration of monks' cells and the large gompa had an air of exclusiveness and remoteness. Only a group of golden poplars nearby broke the lines of the monastery's walls that grew out of the rock on which it was constructed. We walked down the dusty path past groups of white chortens and mani walls as we descended towards the Zaskar valley floor. A patchwork quilt of brown fields with a scattering of houses over its vast expanse. In the distance jagged, snowcapped peaks shimmered like cellophane images beyond the clouds of windborne dust.

We spent the night at a house, sheltered from the incessant wind and warmed by the good food we consumed. The man of the house was a cheery, powerfully-built man with large calliper-like hands, a tattered woollen cloak, smooth brown complexion, and alert narrow eyes. He worked tirelessly to fulfil our requests and once we were satisfied turned his attentions to his family's dinner, working by the flickering light of the cow dung fire and a simple kerosene wick lamp. Every so often his pretty little daughter would peer through the narrow doorway into our room, her hair like a pampas bush and her eyes and expression that of awe and curiosity. Her tiny brother, barebottomed, would also look in as if to say: 'What are these strange beings that Daddy has allowed to stay here?'

The still of the morning was invigorating as we marched across the great plain, eyeing the bare rocky peaks that flanked the valley with their huge folds and faults, colourful striations and sweeps of talus. After two hours we reached a small village where people toiled in the wind that had increased as the day wore on, threshing grain, preparing for the long winter. Here we procured more tsampa and Tashi and I stuffed it into our packs.

We hiked up a side valley to the summer village of Sundo below the Chachan La pass and the next day succeeded in getting ourselves well and truly lost in a maze of barren canyons. We retraced our steps to Sundo and after taking stock of our supplies, the poor condition of Graeme's footwear and the slowness of the party, we descended to the Zaskar plain again and the large village of Zongla. A typically Tibetan village of sod-brick houses, whitewashed, with heavy wooden doorways and window frames and heaps of animal-fodder stacked on the roof for winter. We stayed with a family of entrepreneurs who succeeded in extracting a substiantial sum of money from our rapidly emptying pockets. We planned a new route that would take us to Lamayuru Gompa near the Indo-Pakistani ceasefire line and which would be the end of our traverse within India. We have to cross into Pakistan and continue from their side of the ceasefire line to K2. We estimated we could reach Lamayuru in five days and would then travel by road east to Leh, the capital of Ladakh, where we would rejoin the support team.

Down the broad, brown riverside plain we tramped for an hour in the morning heat before the winds rose, rushing furiously down the valley buffeting all before it. After an hour we turned east and climbed a steep gully flanked by towers of brittle stone which brought us into a desolate land of hills and vales, smooth and round and void of life, a wilderness of shingle. The track followed a miraculous stream that oozed mysteriously from the rubble until we climbed abruptly to a pass at 14,500 feet, the Namtse La. From there we descended into the barren wilderness, returning to an elevation at which a narrow strip of autumn-gold willows again flanked the stream. We marched past a guard of honour, alluvial tors capped with topknots of morainic boulders that lined the stream like wilting giant wax effigies, tilting as if melting in the evening light. The valley narrowed, flowing through a slot carved in solid rock, sculptured by the whims of time.

At a junction with another stream, we ascended, crossing a subsidiary pass then traversing long scree slopes till we reached the Nera La at 16,000 feet. Below was the Zaskar gorge — we had cut across country to avoid one of its lengthy meanders through rugged mountains. On the far side of the Zaskar gorge I could discern a trail climbing up the desolate mountainside to yet another 16,000-foot pass over which we would have to cross. Scattered across the face, seemingly so inhospitable to life, there were tiny villages, places where man and beast eked out an existence.

It was cold on the pass, so we began the 5000-foot descent to the Zaskar and Noerak village where we planned to have lunch. Tashi and I moved quickly along the dusty track past dry irrigation canals for diverting monsoon waters to the village far below. We descended wind-burned pastures to the snug little village, alive with noise — the shouts of children shepherding animals, that strange rather hysterical shriek that mules make and the deep grunt of yaks. We walked past mani walls and chortens and into the narrow alleys running through the village. Being diverted by a savage mastiff we found ourselves at the local school where ten Buddhist children learned Urdu, the language of the Moslems. It seemed paradoxical in this high, Tibetan mountain wilderness.

From Noerak we dropped down to the Zaskar river, a huge torrent of swirling blue, that passed swiftly beneath the wooden cantilever bridge that spanned a constriction in the gorge. We climbed steeply for two hours to Yulchung village at nearly 14,000 feet where we halted for the night in the house of the most wealthy and influential family there. We clambered into the large house via a meandering corridor that ducked and dived through low doorways until we climbed into the light of a central patio. There stood the father of the house with long greying plaits, a huge sheepskin cloak and dark steady eyes, well practised at picking out a lost sheep or goat amongst the vast mountain wastes of the area. He wore a small, padded top hat on his head, and a nonchalant air. A rosy-cheeked man, his son, appeared wearing a maroon woollen cloak and a pair of well-made European hiking boots that Graeme immediately observed and attempted to purchase. He was not interested and beamed even more thanks for the interest in his possessions.

Mother, also, was standing by to witness the influx of strange foreign beings into her house. She wore the traditional headpiece studded with turquoises, coral and gilded prayer boxes that reached from her forehead over to the nape of her neck, and with huge woollen lobes that hung at the sides of her head. The son's wife rushed across the patio with her baby in her arms to put on her equally impressive head-dress. She was a beautiful woman with fine Mongolian features, large, dark eyes and a pale gold complexion. Children, bright eyed and puffy cheeked looked on, scrutinizing our every move. When we produced a compact bag from our packs from which we hauled our sleeping bags there was a hush. When we wriggled into our warm bags the children giggled with delight. 'These people from a far-off villge are very funny.' They would ask us where we were from but the names of distant nations meant nothing to them. Even the concept seemed far fetched... we were from a distant village many days' walk away.

Just off the room in which we slept was the family's private gompa. I watched the young woman and a child go inside. They decanted water from the brass vessels lined in front of several gold images of Buddha and his followers. They beat drums and clashed cymbals as a sign of homage then closed the heavy wooden door leaving the room filled with the soft, gliding light of a butter lamp.

From Yulchung we climbed to the Singi La pass, 16,000 feet, that we had seen the previous day from the Nera La. We followed a path across a large slip and then on to a spur up which we climbed towards a rock outcrop. This we sidled around; then began to traverse towards the pass.

'Look, a mountain goat!' Tashi called to me. Silhouetted against the sky stood a very formidable-looking goat.

'That can't be a goat, can it? It's too big.' Two more animals joined it on the skyline. 'Do you think they could be ibex?'

The three animals descended around the base of the rock outcrop, coming quite close to where we stood. The buck was a huge animal with short fawn hair, pale underbelly, a short dark-coloured tail, large ears and impressive horns which were its most distinctive feature. The horns rose straight from the head curving gently backwards; they were nurled. The two nannies were considerably smaller. I was really excited as we had seen one of the world's rare animals and one of the most magnificent and nimble of mountain inhabitants.

We crossed the Singi La and without any delay marched down the far side. We had the "bit between our teeth" and with Lamayuru not too far ahead, there was no stopping us. Traversing dry pastures we passed mani walls and chortens until we crossed a ridge and looked down upon Potoksar. It was a scene taken from a fantasy; it was hard to believe that the cluster of whitestone buildings was real. The houses sprouted from the earth like a forest of mushrooms. They were crammed together above a bank littered with tors (fragile geological oddities); a few barren fields lay behind the village and above rose 5000 feet of rock; massive, convoluted, almost timeless.

Another high pass loomed ahead, the Sese La (16,400 feet). We crossed it in strong winds after a night at Potoksar and charged down the far side to Honupatta, a quiet little village engulfed by trees. We trekked through a gorge and out in to an open valley where small hamlets nestled in groves of apricots ablaze with autumn colour. The track crossed harvested fields and turned up an eroded gully that led to the Wan La, a pass of 14,000 feet.

The track followed a gully on the far side down to a large chorten where a river flowed peacefully by. I raised my eyes above the shingle slopes across the river to the sculptured rock forms from which protruded the white-washed stone of Lamayuru Gompa. It stood above us, imposing and solid. A cubist's artform, a haphazard group of rectangular forms, joined together and thrusting upward. Prayer flags flapped above the monastery and a deep blue sky spread in unmarred perfection overhead.

We climbed up to the monastery, my head spinning with the significance of the moment. This was as far as we could go in Indian teritory. We would not have to take a circuitous route to reach Skardu, the Pakistani town just 100 kilometres to the west. From there we could complete the final phase of our long journey. Our marathon adventure was nearly over. One last march into the mountains would see us through.

We wandered along narrow paths that ran between the sod buildings of the monastery — whitewashed with red ochre trims. There were spherical chortens with red wooden spires, nurled and sculptured, pointing to the sky, and tall Ladakhi monks wearing maroon cloaks, murmuring prayers as they went about their duties.

Above Lamayuru wound a tarseal road. It led east to Leh, Ladakh's capital and our rendezvous point with the support team, so we sauntered slowly up to it and waited for a vehicle. Eventually we got a ride in a truck and a jeep carrying liquor to the military cantonments in Leh.

'Do you mind travelling in the back of the truck?' asked the senior man.

'No,' intervened his subordinate, the driver. 'They will drink the rum!' No fool, that boy, thought I.

We squeezed into the front of the truck and the jeep and drove on until we reached the Indus river, a translucent, green ribbon cutting across the barren features of the valley. As darkness fell upon the desolate plateau of "little Tibet" we reached Leh. The palace of the Ladakh king and an ancient monastery lined the horizon, linked by lines of prayer flags that stretched across the northern sky. The palace was enormous: it dominated the city with its presence and its magnitude. The city is an overgrown village of flat-topped mud houses with a vibrant bazaar, thronged with Ladakhi people. We located Doug and Ann Louise, Shubash and S.P. and spent several celebratory days "on the town". We would continue as planned, through northern Pakistan, but this would not be possible for Indian citizens. However, the Indian members of the expedition had now received permission to continue 150 kilometres north of Leh to Karakoram pass where they would terminate their traverse. We agreed amongst ourselves that at least this way the expedition got the best of both worlds.

We reached Leh airport about half an hour late. We rushed to the check-in counter and discovered the plane had not yet arrived. Phew!

All too soon we were standing together before the security check, our departure imminent. Farewells were delayed to the last possible moment. We planned to meet again in New Delhi once we had both completed our final treks. We would not be together here in the mountains again, and the month that separated us from our reunion was going to be a long one. Graeme and I had spent so much time with Tashi and we had learned to love and respect him. I thought of the many hours of chatter I had enjoyed with S.P. as we had walked along during the expedition. I was sorry that it had to end when the traverse was still not complete but the "powers that be" had decreed it. I looked at S.P. and Tashi and Shubash as they stood there before me. We shook hands bashfully... then hugged each other.

The jet thundered down the runway and surged into the air, winging its way above the Ladakhi mountains; separating us.

*Tashi, Graeme and Peter in Leh, the capital of
Ladakh. The King of Ladakh's palace towers
above.*

K2 —Journey's End

THE OLD DELHI railway station was its usual clamour of colourful people and black steam trains: the stench of humanity and machinery, the high-pitched call of the platform vendors and the clank of steel on steel.

As we struggled along with our kitbags and packs we were propositioned by an Indian transvestite complete with sari, false boobs and a husky voice.

While the train rattled across the sleeping countryside we wondered whether this would be one of those trains ambushed by the well-organised gangs which had been terrorising travellers. The guard lying asleep on his back in the corridor inspired no confidence at all. His old .303 was chained to his belt, presumably so that he couldn't shoot himself when attacked by the fierce dacoits. At Amritsar we changed trains for the border. Getting out of India was relatively straightforward; getting into Pakistan a different matter.

'You look very thin,' said the first official to me.

'Unpack all your bags,' requested the second official. Then to Doug: 'How much money do you have?'

'Rupees 1100,' said Doug honestly.

'Too much for one man,' said the offical. Then to me: 'How much do you have?'

'1100 rupees,' I said. The official frowned and went to consult another man.

'Tell him you haven't got any money,' I whispered to Pete.

The offical returned and asked Pete, Ann Louise and Corrina in turn.

'No more Pakistani rupees.'

So the official added Doug's and mine together and divided it between the five of us. He looked pleased with himself as he told us to repack our stuff and get one more official signature on our customs declaration.

We had just discovered the crucial difference with Pakistan. Perhaps they had no axe to grind with the British but they appeared to possess a positive approach to problem solving. None of that all too familiar 'Oh my god no. You cannot go.' More an attempt to solve a problem rather than think of all the reasons why it couldn't be solved. We were going to like Pakistan. At Lahore we changed trains again and were soon rattling towards Rawalpindi and Mrs Davies' private hotel.

'Mrs Davies has passed on in 1957,' the kindly manager told us, but her memory lived on in the homely British atmosphere of her hotel. The butler's white coat and the tablecloths weren't as white as they used to be but the tea and the roast lamb and baked potatoes were just as Mrs Davies had always liked them.

After settling in we waited for the Ministry of Culture and Tourism to provide a liaison officer. One evening he arrived, Major Matlub Nuri, chief instructor for the school of mountain warfare. We immediately liked the warmth and sincerity of this amazing man. It was with a sense of deep personal loss that after our return to New Zealand we learned of his disappearance on the Diamir face of Nanga Parbat.

Nuri listened to our plan to finish our journey by moving quickly to K2.

'No porters?' he queried. 'Who will do your cooking? But how will you keep warm... it is already winter in the mountains.'

We tried to sound like sane and competent mountaineers but his reasoned questions made the escapade look like the plan of crazy people.

We all liked Nuri's spirit for, despite his horror and his conclusion that we were mad, he was prepared to go along with our madness. To carry his own gear — to eat little and to suffer with us. As we had to the incredulous Indians nine months before we now explained our concept of "alpine style" to the wide-eyed Major Nuri.

Over the next few weeks we were to learn slowly what a truly amazing man Nuri was. At thirty-one he was already very successful. He had completed a master's degree, majoring in English. He was one of the top men of the military courts, feared for his uncompromising honesty and sense of duty. He was born Muhammed Matlub-ul-Hasan Nuri, son of a well-to-do Pakistani and a princess of the Afghan royal family, who had fled Afghanistan after the 1920s coup. Like most Pakistanis, Nuri was very religious, belonging to a Moslem sect known as Amediat. The Amediats have been widely persecuted in Pakistan for their modern interpretation of Islam.

We left Rawalpindi on 24 October and flew to Skardu — a flight that surely must be one of the most spectacular in the world. The green foothills slowly gave way to craggy snow-spattered summits, then beyond rose the giants of the Himalaya — resplendently white with early winter snow. As we flew up the mighty Indus gorge Nanga Parbat towered 10,000 feet above our plane — her massive upper slopes glistening in sunlight, her lower buttresses and valleys deep in shadows.

From the Friendship's cockpit we had a great view. Away in the distance a blue pyramid rising above all the other Karakoram peaks was K2, our objective. The pilot pointed to a thin line across the brown countryside below and said: 'Along that trail, Marco Polo travelled 400 years ago.'

The Indus turned sharply right around the northern ranges of Nanga Parbat and we began our approach to Skardu. The countryside and buildings were much the same as we had become used to on the other side of the ceasefire line. Or, as they called it here, line of control.

Only the people were different. There weren't so many military people about but those we saw had an air of purpose about them. The locals were different, too. Not so many people of Tibetan stock but in their place similarly rugged-looking Baltis — Moslems of course and according to Nuri followers of the Ayatollah Khomeni for the last thirty years or so. Ann Louise and Doug had been lucky to meet Brigadier Aslam Khan who during the 1948 war led the local Balti fighting units to some amazing victories.

On 25 October we began the last section of our journey. We bounced in an old jeep up the Shigar river, which flows down a broad valley between the

Braldu valley villagers thresh their grain with yaks.

*Graeme, Doug and Peter bathe in a hot spring in
the Braldu valley.*

We hike up the loose morraines of the Baltoro
glacier. The Trango Towers lie ahead.

Ann Louise, Nuri, Peter and Doug cross the
freezing waters of a Karakoram river.

Haramosh and Masherbrum ranges. At Dassu the rough road ended and we began again on foot. The group atmosphere was now different from what we had become used to — no Tashi but instead an equally amazing Nuri. Ann and Doug seemed distant, Pete fairly relaxed — all of us longing for the end, and home.

We passed through Dassu like the proverbial dose of salts, keen to get on — perhaps too keen! After about two hours of dry but cool travel the track bifurcated and sod's law determined that we would take the wrong one. It led us to a flying fox across the Braldu river. Beyond this, bluffs dropped smoothly into the river so there were only two choices — to cross or go back. A couple of Baltis were all too aware of the options and immediately demanded twenty rupees each for the use of their cable. We assured them that we hadn't come down in the last shower and began back down valley while Nuri negotiated. Before long there was a triumphant call — the final price, twenty rupees the lot.

The flying-fox ride was the highlight of the day — suspended sixty feet above the river in a little flimsy cradle, clutching one's pack we sped across, the cold winter air whistling through our hair. Thirty minutes up river we camped beneath some boulders. The days were drawing in — it was dark by 5.30 pm.

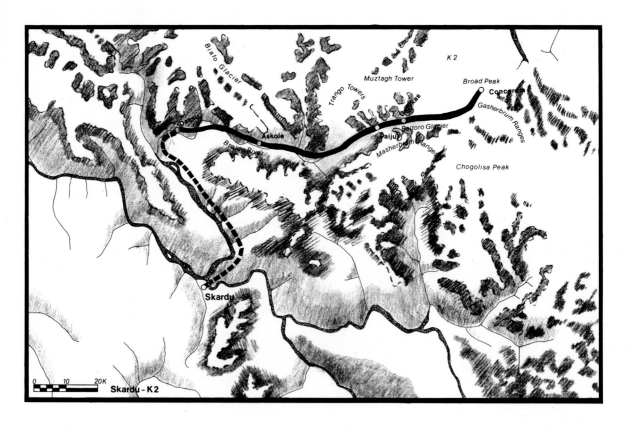

The next two days were similar to the previous 250. We lost the correct track at least six times and each time I vowed that we would hire a guide. Pete kept declaring that we should have an adventure. Doug always answered that an adventure was the last thing he needed and Nuri oscillated somewhere between — keen on one hand to succeed without local assistance but just as exasperated as everyone else when we got lost.

At about our fourth mistake we came across a trio of funny little dwarfs (common in this valley) and although Nuri couldn't communicate very well with them, he took the most intelligent-looking one by the arm and said 'Askole.' When I gave our little guide a sweet he was quick to respond 'bakshish' with a big dirty-toothed grin. A couple of hundred feet down the hill the little fellow balked so Nuri gave him a good-natured shove in the approximate direction of Askole. And singing 'hi-ho, hi-ho, it's off to work we go,' we followed the dwarf's funny little shuffling walk for a further 300 metres. There he pointed to a main path below and gave us another big grin. When we gave him some rupees for his trouble he shook each of us by hand, touching his forehead respectfully for each. What a happy simple world his seemed to be.

We moved on through a golden autumn paradise to the main track again. Here a road was being built with pick and shovel in defiance of the locals' wishes. A road to them meant one thing — it denied them the seasonal portering work for expeditions going up valley to the peaks of the Baltoro. Earlier that day we had met the contractors heavily armed in case the locals got stroppy!

For the most part the countryside was barren with scarcely any grass, let alone trees. Then we would reach a place where a stream tumbled down from the mountains and we would move into an oasis of golden-leaved trees, perhaps a few flat-roofed houses of mud and stone, some Balti people getting the last crops in before winter and a few shaggy-haired yaks. The people would often ask us where we were going, why we had no porters, did we know the winter snows were already on the way. When we told them we were going to Concordia they would stare in amazement and answer: 'But the snow up there will be up to here,' pointing to their waists.

We would part with smiles and salaams, them to their ancient toil and us to complete our modern pilgrimage — a product of a technological world where we must expend our energies in contrived toil known as adventurous pursuits. Their whole life was an adventurous pursuit.

Late in the afternoon of 26 October we were treated to two delights. First we found a hot spring — Pete and I quickly stripped off in the freezing air and sat happily in the pool, washing each other's backs while the others dangled their feet in the soothing water.

An hour later we watched four ibex cavorting about on a slope across the river, apparently oblivious of our presence. They were nuzzling the rocks of a grassless scree slope.

'God knows what they find to eat,' said Pete in amazement. Suddenly the buck danced down the slope and bounded over a thirty-foot vertical cliff. He touched the face once before landing nimbly on the scree below and continued his nuzzling.

*Graeme crosses a frozen stream with the Trango
Towers above.*

Paiju Peak.

Trango Towers.

On the third day we reached more hot springs. In the first a man was washing his coat so he directed us over a nearby hill. The next pool, to our astonishment, was absolutely full of stark naked women — naked that is except for their hats. Doug, Ann and Pete respected their "go-away-type waves" while Nuri, Corrina and I descended to a pool near them. In a country where the men scarcely allow their women's faces to be seen, let alone their bodies, we could be excused for searching the horizon for the telltale glint of sun off the barrel of a gun. Although the women were exceptionally shy to begin with they soon became quite brash and began to make weird signals to us by poking out their tongues and flicking them with their forefingers. Even Nuri didn't know the meaning of this.

We reached the last village, Askole, later that day and settled into a room owned by Haji Meedi, the headman — his title "Haji" indicating that he has made the Muslim pilgrimage to Mecca. The haji was a trader from way back and was soon serving us tea around an old expedition folding table and doing a fairly good marketing job on an old leg of ibex. Although keen conservationists, we were hungry conservationists and enthusiastically purchased the meat. 'It's dead anyway,' said Doug in excuse.

'Yeah, several weeks ago,' said Pete.

The haji was adamant that only women were allowed in the kitchen so the cooking fell to Corrina and Ann Louise. Two hours later the enormous stew was unceremoniously plonked on the table by Ann. A moment later the table folded up, plunging the stew and the kero lamp on to the floor and the room into darkness. By now we were all used to bitter disappointment. Not a sound was uttered as we all sat hungrily in the darkness. Eventually someone struck a match to reveal a miracle. The stew had landed upright without a drop being spilled and the kero lamp was unbroken. We ate the unfortunate animal with the greatest enjoyment.

Next morning, 28 October, we plodded on with full tummies. The first obstacle beyond Askole was the Biafo glacier, which rather unreasonably cut across the main valley forcing us to climb over its chaotic ice and moraines. The next problem was an icy bridgeless river — just the thing for the demented antipodeans but the despair of Pakistani liaison officers. Again despite his conclusion that we were quite mad Nuri went along with our madness without question.

'I have come to learn,' he would often say when we were faced with such obstacles.

Corrina and I linked arms and ploughed through the unbelievably cold water, then we watched with great amusement as the others followed. As the rushing water crept up his thighs, Nuri's face was a picture of utter misery. They emerged dripping while a scantily-clad Ann Louise squealed: 'You guys cold or something?'

The following afternoon, after pausing for lunch in the last glade, a paradise called Paiju, we climbed up on to the Baltoro glacier. For me, this was much more than the climax of ten months' effort. To see this glacier and its surrounding peaks had been my dream for nearly twenty years; ever since I got to know Carlo Mauri who had made the first ascent of Gasherbrum IV,

214

I had wanted to come to these mountains where "four worlds meet" — Russia, China, Pakistan and Afghanistan — the mountains that are the hingeing point for the great plate movement that has thrown up and indeed is still forming the Himalaya. It was a logical if perhaps unstable place for our journey to end. We had trekked and climbed 5000 kilometres, climbed and descended 1.5 million feet and traversed past, through or over almost every major mountain area in the Himalaya between Kanchenjunga and K2.

You could say we were jaded, although we called it something else, and after so much it would have been a pretty spectacular mountain area that would move us — but we were moved.

The Baltoro glacier itself is perhaps one of the most unattractive places in the world. The traveller is confronted with fifty kilometres of depressing grey rock-covered glacier that looks like a gigantic construction company's gravel yard. But the consolations are great. Probably nowhere else on earth will you discover such fortress-like mountains and towers — granite spires carved out by the huge glaciers.

At times there seem to be too many mountaineering wonders for one area. Here many peaks rise over 23,000 feet, several rise over 26,000 feet, climaxing in the remarkable pyramid of K2, whose horribly clinical survey name does not do justice to the bastion which to the world is the second highest and to us was the checkered flag.

As we crossed the rubble-strewn ice humps toward a camp spot called Liliwa, Paiju peak — a maze of exquisite buttresses and gullies — rose behind us. To our left the Trango towers and the Cathedral pointed with clean granitic splendour at the leaden sky.

Another day took us to the last vestiges of vegetation in the valley, Urdukas, where we crawled under some immense sheltering rocks. It was only 1 pm but everyone was keen to have a rest afternoon. It was a rare treat to be able to lie warm in our sleeping bags while it was still daylight.

> Diary — 31 October: Today travel on the glacier improved immensely as we made our way up the strips of white ice (much better than scrambling over loose blocks and scree). On our right the well-defended walls of Masherbrum slipped slowly by. Dead ahead were the Gasherbrums with Gasherbrum IV stealing the show with its giant flat-topped wedge and fantastic south-west face — a great prize for some future team. Immediately to its left was Broad Peak radiating the distinctive blue-black look of the very high peaks.
> On the left of the glacier the view was dominated by Mustagh Tower, a peak which had been one of the first of the more difficult medium-altitude peaks to be climbed by that legendary British trio: Joe Brown, Tom Patey, and Ian McNaught-Davis.

We camped beyond where the Younghusband glacier flowed into the Baltoro. Pete slept in the tent with Nuri so that he could catch up on his diary. The rest of us slept under the fly.

'More trouble with the bloody stove,' my diary records. 'I have to pull it to

*Corrina on the Baltoro glacier, with Gasherbrum
IV ahead.*

*Nearing Concordia, Gasherbrum IV looms more
impressive.*

Ann Louise Mitcalfe

Mustagh Tower.   Doug Wilson

Gasherbrum IV.   Doug Wilson

pieces each time before we use it. Everything that is damp freezes as soon as the sun goes down — I have my shot road-shoes in my sleeping bag — God help me if they fall completely to pieces before we get off the glacier. Yipee — Concordia tomorrow — then home!'

The first day of November dawned fine but a few wisps of high cloud worried us. At this altitude with our light equipment we could not withstand a storm. If the weather became bad we would have no choice but to flee to the relative safety of lower altitudes and even this would not be easy if heavy snow fell. We toiled forward in kneedeep snow but no matter how we tried Concordia never seemed to get any closer.

To our right rose the peaks Chogolisa (final resting place of the legendary Herman Buhl) and the Golden Throne, both pleasantly clothed in snow and ice in contrast to the other brown rocky giants. As the sun fell low behind us and camp-time approached again, the temperature plummeted well below zero and we began to worry that we would not see K2 after all. It was still out of sight somewhere to our left and the cirrus cloud now almost covered the sky giving promise of a storm.

Out in front Pete and I put on a concerted burst of speed, taking turns to plug steps in the dry, cold snow and sneaking glances to the left every few steps for some sign of the last giant.

As the sun disappeared Pete shouted: 'Spindrift coming off something big to the left.' Sure enough the sky high above was smudged with wisps of windblown snow. A few minutes later the dark outline of a high mountain ridge came into view, followed by the immaculately white south face of K2.

We plugged on just as quickly, hardly daring to believe that our mountain marathon was almost over.

A million emotions and memories — a cocktail of the last ten months — sped through my head. Tomorrow every step would bring us closer to that longed for paradise — home! Hot baths, furry kittens, bacon and eggs for breakfast. No more wiping bottoms with rocks or snow, no more squalor, no more intolerable cold, hunger or bone tiredness — no more sickening tension.

Home meant almost any food we desired whenever we wanted — at least the staple requirements — all the oxygen we could breathe — and we could be warm and dry almost all the time.

At least until the next time we went in search of reality, peace of mind, or a knowledge of what was necessary for a good life and then we would go to the hills again — but for the moment such thoughts were almost abhorrent.

As K2 filled our field of vision I let out a cry of joy to those behind, for Corrina, Nuri, Ann Louise and Doug. To Pete in front I wanted to shout: 'Stop you bugger — I want to hug ya!' But something stopped me and instead I called: 'Drop down to that flat on the left... I think we should camp.'

'Let's go on until we can see K2 better,' he called. For the moment it looked as if our mighty adventure would end in another disagreement but a moment later he seemed to notice how cold it had become with the sun gone. He threw off his pack and stoically began stamping out a place to lie down. This was it — the end — probably the longest alpine journey ever done...

A wave of emotion rushed tears to my eyes. I threw myself at Pete and gave him a hug — choking out a scarcely audible: 'Thanks mate.' Then for Corrina a special one. And one for Doug... with a slightly more composed 'Special thanks old mate.' Nuri reciprocated my thanks with 'Congratulations, it is a really great thing you have done.'

Ann Louise managed to sneak past but I ran after her and demanded: 'Come on... give us a decent hug.' A one-armed one and a little grin was the best she could do — she wasn't very happy with me.

Unfortunately it was now time to go about the business of surviving — six people in the middle of a white freezing desert with the temperature plummeting to minus 30.

We were still a long way from home but in our discomfort we were savouring that fabulous warm emotion — success!

Peter writes:
'What a mountain!'
'Is that it?'
'I'll stand over there and could you take two shots. Use the zoom lens.'
'Kanchenjunga to K2... at last.'

Triumph. Success. A feather in one's cap. I felt none of these things. I wanted to weep — the journey was over; we had done it — but the struggles, the refusal to surrender was deeply ingrained in me. I was in a state of awe or, perhaps, confusion. I gazed with disbelief at the fierce form, the crisp triangular silhouette of K2. This had been our ultimate goal for ten months as we traversed the Himalaya and suddenly it was before me, above me... it consumed me.

From that moment I knew that all our efforts would be retracing our steps towards our homes. In a way they became my Mecca, more than the great mountain that loomed before me. I felt a tremendous relief as we had completed what we had set out to do and I was satisfied because of it.

In the freezing temperatures of evening, I began trampling down the snow where we would spend the night. My head downturned, I watched my feet compress the powder snow beneath me. It wasn't over yet.

Seven months later, having undergone a rigorous programme of "de-Indianisation" in my homeland I've been able to dwell upon our trans-Himalayan adventure in a retrospective light. A pleasant flush of elation fills me when I remember our journey and our achievement. But what stands out is not the single accomplishment, it is the multi-faceted experience that comprised our high-altitude odyssey. The isolated villages of times gone by, the smiling faces of the mountain people, our trials and tribulations along the way, and those high, desolate passes hemmed in by sheer walls of rock and ice. A plethora of life and living.

Our cornucopia brims and overflows.

Broad Peak.

Ann Louise prepares a hot drink in the freezing winter temperatures at Concordia.

K2, the savage mountain.

And a postscript from Graeme:

Perhaps that's where the story should end but this was no fairytale romance... Back in New Zealand, the skies were bluer, the countryside greener and the people on the whole honest and sincere. A few days after we got home I went to the doctor. He looked at my still sprained hand, my dislocated shoulder and my hernia and concluded that I was a bit of a wreck! An orthopedic surgeon told me there was little that could be done for the dislocated clavicle and the torn tendon in my right hand, but on the bright side the dislocated humerus (upper arm) appeared to have mended well. Just before Christmas a rather messy and painful operation repaired the hernia. The surgeon also diagnosed my sickness in Ladakh as toxoplasmosis, a temporary but generally severe disease that attacks the red blood corpuscles.

The story does, however, have a happy ending. On 3 April 1982, in a beautiful ceremony at Turangi and Waihi marae, Corrina and I were married. We now live in Hamilton and are planning happier adventures together.

Appendix 1

Expedition Diary

Date	Event	Season	Distance on foot kms	Height gained and lost ft
24 January	Arrive in New Delhi, India			
15 February	Doug, S.P., Graeme, Tashi and Peter together in Darjeeling			
18 February	First day of traverse. Leave Yoksam and hike into Sikkimese mountains towards Mt Kanchenjunga	Winter		
24 February	Reach the Ratong La (17,500ft) on the Nepalese border. Tashi, Graeme and Peter begin descent of Singalila ridge			
6 March	Cross into Nepal		500	80,000

15 March	High point on Milke ridge in Eastern Nepal			
3 April	Cross Far East and West Cols at 20,500ft			
6 April	Reach Kunde village and rendezvous with support team in the Mt Everest area	Spring		
20 April	Cross Tashi Lapcha pass (19,000ft) to Rolwaling valley			
5 May	Cross Tilman's Col (17,500ft) to Langtang			
22 May	Cross Lakya Banyan pass on the Tibetan border to Manang			
26 May	Reach Jomoson in central Nepal	Spring		
9 June	Dolpa incident — our arrest			
15 June	Reach Rara lake in western Nepal			
24 June	Reach Indo-Nepalese border. We are half way across the Himalayas		2800	750,000
20 July	Attempt to cross Surgarhunga Khal into the Nanda Devi Sanctuary in dangerous monsson conditions. Garhwal Himalaya, India	Monsoon		
1 August	Graeme's accident in Joshimath			
16 August	Reach Uttar Kashi and visit Gangotri in the Garhwal Himalaya			
31 August	Cross into Tons valley from Jumnotri via 17,000ft-high pass			
7 September	Peter attacked by villagers at Kamba near Sutlej gorge			
10/11 September	Cross Pin-Parbati passes — our six-pass epic in Himachal Pradesh			
15 September	Reach Manali and meet the Dalai Lama			
26 September	Cross the Bara Lapcha pass (16,500ft) in Eastern Kashmir			
2 October	Reach the Zaskar valley and Thonde monastery	Autumn		
9 October	Reach Lamayuru monastery near the Indo-Pakistan ceasefire line. We travel to Leh, the capital of Ladakh, where we rendezvous with the support team			
12 October	Farewell Indian members of the expedition			
17 October	Cross into Pakistan		5000	1,400,000
25 October	Leave Skardu on the Pakistani side of the ceasefire line for Mt K2	Winter		
29 October	Reach the Baltoro glacier			
1 November	Our journey's end. We reach Concordia at 16,500ft with Mt K2 above	Winter	5150	1,480,000
16 November	Return to New Delhi			

Our Concordia bivouac with K2 and Broad Peak behind.

Appendix 2

Important Peaks and Ranges in Approximate Order of Contact

SIKKIM/NEPAL:

Kabru (24,002 ft) – North of the Ratong La on the Singalila range. First ascent C.R. Cooke party, 1935. The nearby *Kabru Donne* is considerably lower but still unclimbed. There are many other unclimbed peaks in this area including the 21,000-foot-high *Pabil*.

Kanchenjunga (28,146 ft) – North of Kabru on the Singalila range. First ascent George Band, Joe Brown followed the next day by Tony Streather and Norm Hardie (British expedition), 1955. The third highest mountain on earth and perhaps the most massive with several summits over 26,000 feet high.

Success! K2 towers behind the five New Zealanders at Concordia.

EASTERN NEPAL:

Jannu (25,296 ft) – A spectacular satellite of Kanchenjunga and just to the west. First ascent French party led by Lionel Terray, 1962.

Makalu (27,824 ft) – Near the source of the Barun river. Also known as Armchair Peak. Fifth highest on earth. First ascent Jean Franco and party (French), 1955. Difficult routes have been established on the west ridge (French) and the south face (Yugoslav).

Chamlang (24,183 ft) – South of West Col. A broad peak first climbed in 1962 by S. Anma and Pasang Phutar (Japanese Expedition).

Baruntse (23,688 ft) – North of West Col. A popular snow and ice climb today. First ascent Geoff Harrow, Colin Todd, George Lowe, Bill Beaven (New Zealand), 1954.

225

KHUMBU HIMAL:
Lhotse (27,890 ft) – North of the Imja glacier. Fourth highest peak on earth. First ascent Ernst Reiss and Fritz Luchsinger (Swiss), 1956. The massive south face is one of the current 'big problems' of Himalayan mountaineering.
Everest (29,028 ft) – At the head of the Khumbu glacier. First ascent Edmund Hillary and Tenzing Norgay, 1953 (British expedition). Now often climbed several times each year, sometimes without the assistance of artificial oxygen.
Nuptse (25,850 ft) – A satellite of Lhotse. First climbed by Dennis Davis and Tashi Sherpa, 1961 (British expedition).
Pumori (23,442 ft) – A graceful peak rising above Everest basecamp. First ascent G. Lenser, U. Hurlemann and H. Rutzel, 1962 (Swiss-German expedition).
Ama Dablam (22,494 ft) – The most impressive of the lower Khumbu area peaks. First climbed Mike Gill, Barry Bishop, Mike Ward, Wally Romanes, 1961 (New Zealand expedition).
Kangtega (22,340 ft) – First climbed Mike Gill, Jim Wilson, Tom Frost, Dave Dornan, 1963 (New Zealand expedition). The nearby *Thamserku* was also climbed by a New Zealand expedition during the 60's.
Cho Oyu (26,967 ft) – On the Tibetan border west of Everest. Sixth highest peak on earth. First climbed Dr Herbert Tichy, Joseph Joechler, Sherpa Pasang Dawa Lama, 1954 (Austrian expedition).
Kwangde (20,299 ft) – A broad range with several summits, south of Namche Bazar.
Tengi Raggi Tau (22,779 ft) – Unclimbed 1982. A spectacular peak immediately north of the Tesi Lapcha.

ROLWALING:
Menluntse (23,560 ft) – Northwest of the Tesi Lapcha, in Tibet. A beautiful ice peak with no recorded ascent to date.
Gauri Shankar (23,440 ft) – North of the Rolwaling valley on the Tibetan border. A massive peak often mistaken for Everest from Kathmandu. First climbed American/Nepali expedition, 1979.

LANGTANG:
Langtang Lirung (23,769 ft) – On the Tibetan border north of the Langtang. First climbed Japanese/Nepali expedition, 1978. This range also contains *Shisha Pangma* (26,398 ft). The only 8000-metre peak which is wholly in Tibet. At the head of the Langtang valley is *Dome Blanc* (22,408 ft).

JUGAL HIMAL:
A small but interesting range south-east of the Langtang. Access is up the Balephi valley from near Lamosangu or over Tilman's pass from the Langtang. Main peaks are *Lonpo Gang* (23,238 ft), *Dorje Lakpa I* (22,930 ft), *Dorje Lakpa II* (21,380 ft), *Gyaltzen Peak* (21,998 ft) and *Phurbi Chyachu* (21,844 ft).

GANESH HIMAL:
A small range between the Buri Gandaki to the west and Trisuli Ganga to the east. Main peaks include *Ganesh I* (24,298 ft), *Ganesh II* (Lapsang Karbo, 23,458 ft), *Ganesh III* (23,398 ft), *Ganesh IV* (Pabil, 23,300 ft], and *Ganesh V* (The Bat, 22,802 ft).

GURKHA HIMAL:
Manaslu (26,760 ft) – The highest peak of the Gurkha Himal. Usually approached from the upper Buri Gandaki. First ascent T. Imanishi and Gyalzen Norbu, 1956

(Japanese expedition). Has now had a ski descent.

Himal Chuli (25,896 ft) – A good-looking peak rising above the Buri Gandaki. First climbed M. Harade and H. Tanabe, 1960.

ANNAPURNA HIMAL:
A large range to the north of Pokhara and well south of the Tibetan border. Major peaks include *Annapurna I* (26,504 ft), *Annapurna II* (26,041 ft), *Annapurna III* (24,787 ft), *Annapurna South* (23,805 ft), *Gangapurna* (24,457 ft), *Machupuchare* (22,958 ft), and *Lamjung Himal* (22,910 ft). Also in this range are Roc Noir, The Fang, Tilicho and the Nilgiri group.

Annapurna I was the first of the 8000-metre peaks to be climbed, by Maurice Herzog, Louis Lachenal (French expedition), 1950.

DAULAGIRI HIMAL:
Another massive range to the west of the Annapurnas. *Daulagiri I* (26,810 ft) was first climbed in 1960 by a Swiss expedition: Kurt Diemburger, P. Diener, E. Forrer, A. Schelbert, Nyima Dorje and Nawang Dorje. (Perhaps a record number on the first ascent of a high peak even to this day.)

Other important peaks in this range are *Daulagiri II* (25,429 ft), *Daulagiri IV* (25,135 ft), *Churen Himal* (24,184 ft), *Putha Hiunchuli* (23,774 ft), *Gurja Himal* (23,600 ft) and *Tukucha* (22,703 ft).

KANJIROBA HIMAL:
This small range situated north-west of Daulagiri has several attractive peaks of moderate height. *Kanjiroba I* (22,580 ft) was first climbed in 1970 by a Japanese expedition.

INDO/NEPAL BORDER AREA:
In the north-west corner of Nepal rise three attractive peaks which were all first climbed by Japanese expeditions: *Api* (23,399 ft) 1960, *Saipal* (23,100 ft) 1963, and *Nampa* (22,162 ft) 1972.

GARHWAL/KUMAON HIMALAYA:
A large area of mountains stretching nearly 300 kilometres from the Bhagirathi, in the west, to the Indo-Nepal border in the east.

Nanda Devi (25,645 ft) – A twin-summited peak at the head of the Rishi Ganga — first climbed by Noel Odell and Bill Tilman, 1936.

Trisul (23,360 ft) – An easy but high peak on the southern edge of the Nanda Devi sanctuary. The first 7000-metre peak to be climbed, in 1907 by Tom Longstaff, the Brocherel brothers, and Karbir Burathoki.

Changabang (22,520 ft) – A beautiful rock and ice thumb within thz Nanda Devi sanctuary. First climbed by our own Chewang Tashi with Chris Bonington, Balwant Sandhu, Martin Boysen, Dougal Haston and Doug Scott, 1974.

Kedarnath (23,100 ft) – An attractive peak normally climbed from the Gangotri glacier but with an attractive south face rising above the Kedarnath temple.

Shivling (21,467 ft) – A difficult peak rising above the lower Gangotri glacier. First climbed in 1974 by an Indo-Tibetan border police expedition. Other important peaks rising from approximately 22,000 ft to 25,447 ft are Kamet, Hardeol, Dunagiri, Nilkanta, Ghori Parbat, Hathi Parbat, Chaukahamba, Mukut Parbat, Bhagirathi I, II and III, and Mana Parbat.

SPITI/KULU/LAHUL & ZASKAR:
Although there are no peaks here of outstanding height, there is much good climbing to be done on both difficult rock peaks as well as mixed rock and ice. Access by road to Kulu, Manali and beyond is easy. To the east of Kulu the Pin/Parbati area offers a mecca for both rock and ice climbers. Access is by a short walk from Mani Karan. Main peaks of these areas are: *Leo Pargial* (22,210 ft), *Kulu Pumori* (21,500 ft), *Mulkila* (21,380 ft), *Papsura* (21,165 ft) *White Sail* (21,148 ft), *Menthosa* (21,140 ft), *Deo Tibba* (20,410 ft) and *Indrasan* (20,410 ft).

The country to the north of Lahul is desolate and apart from some good-looking peaks above the middle Zaskar river, near Padam, we saw few really attractive mountains.

PAKISTAN:
Nanga Parbat (26,658 ft) – A huge mountain to the south and east of the Indus, considered by some to be the western extremity of the actual Himalaya. Many German attempts to climb it culminated in Herman Buhl reacing the summit in 1953. To the north of the Indus the mountains are generally known as the Karakorams.
Haramosh (24,299 ft) – A sprawling mountain west of Dasso. First ascent H. Roiss, F. Mandl, S. Pauer (Austrian expedition), 1958.
Masherbrum (25,660 ft) – A difficult ice peak rising on the eastern side of the Baltoro glacier. First ascent George Bell and Willi Unsoeld (American/Pakistan expedition), 1960.
Mustagh Tower (23,860 ft) – A spectacular rock and ice peak on the western side of the Baltoro. First ascent John Hartog, Joe Brown, Ian McNaught-Davis, and Tom Patey (British expedition), 1956.
Gasherbrum IV (26,000 ft) – Spectacular eastern neighbour of Broad Peak. First ascent Walter Bonatti and Carlo Mauri (Italian), 1958.
Broad Peak (26,400 ft) – A relatively easy peak popular for alpine-style ascents. First ascent M. Schmuch, Kurt Diemberger, Herman Buhl and F. Wintersteller (Austrian expedition), 1957.
K2 (28,253 ft) – Also known at Mt Godwin-Austen. Second highest in the world and perhaps the most difficult of the 8000-metre peaks. First ascent A. Compagnoni and L. Lacedelli (Italian expedition), 1954.
Other important peaks rising around the Baltoro glacier are: *Hidden Peak* (Gasherbrum I 26,470 ft), *Gasherbrum II* (26,360 ft), *Gasherbrum III* (26,090 ft), *Paiju Peak* (21,700 ft), *Trango Towers* (20,500 ft), *Chogolisa* (25,110 ft), and *Golden Throne* (Baltoro Kangri).

Appendix 3

Equipment, Food, Travel and Permissions

As with any major expedition, we had large quantities of equipment, clothing and food — all of which were specially selected for the rigours of our 5000km trans-Himalayan journey. We received tremendous assistance from Air India who transported the mountain of baggage and boxes that represented the expedition's equipment and supplies, along with five New Zealanders, all the way to India. I'll never forget their faces when they viewed the quantity of baggage we flippantly referred to as 'a little over weight'. However, they bundled us and the expedition's equipment aboard the 747 shuttle to our adventure and the Himalayas. In India, the Indian Mountaineering Foundation liaised with the Indian Government for the various permissions we required, and arranged the Indian members of the Indo-New Zealand Expedition. In Nepal, Mountain Travel Nepal advised and assisted us with route planning and Government permissions.

All photographs were taken by members of the expedition using Olympus cameras. OM2 and OM1 reflex cameras with 28mm, 50mm Macro, and 75-150 zoom, and 300mm lenses were used. Convenient and lightweight XA and XA2 pocket cameras with 35mm lens were also used extensively. Other than a small amount of black and white photography, and a few rolls of Kodak Ektachrome 200 ASA film, all our film (300 rolls) was Kodak Kodachrome 25 ASA and Kodachrome 64 ASA. This relatively slow speed film was ideal for the generally bright conditions we encountered during the expedition.

We received our equipment from expedition sponsors whose support was invaluable, and to whom we are very thankful.

Equipment	Sponsor
Packs, tents, one piece suits	Hallmark International (N.Z.)
Fairy-down sleeping bags	Arthur Ellis & Co. (N.Z.)
Fibrepile suits	Wilderness Products (N.Z.)
Polypropylene underwear	Damart-Thermawear (U.K.)
Woollen jerseys and socks	Norsewear (N.Z.)
Klimate fabric used for tents	Howe & Bainbridge (U.S.A.)
Adidas running shoes	M. O'Brien Ltd. (N.Z.)
San Marco climbing boots	Red Wing International (U.S.A.)
Wrist watches	Montres Rolex (Switzerland)
Cameras	Olympus Cameras (Japan)
Photographic film	Kodak
M.S.R. stoves	Mountain Safety Research (U.S.A.)
Ice axes	La Prade (France)
Elite climbing ropes	Roy Turner (N.Z.)
Sustalyte (electrolyte powder)	Bristol-Myers (N.Z.)
Sustagen milk drink	Bristol-Myers (N.Z.)
Freeze dried foods	Alliance Freezing Co. (N.Z.)

Traverse Kit:
(a) For general use (including passes up to 17,500 ft) per Traverse member:

Running Shoes	1 pr
Socks (wool and synthetic)	2 pr
Fibre pile saloupettes	1 pr
Fibre pile jacket	1
Damart long johns	1 pr
Damart skivvy	1
Underpants	1 pr
Damart gloves	1 pr
Damart balaclava	1
Shorts	1
Snow glasses	1 pr
Down sleeping bag	1
Insulite mattress	1
Lightweight pack	1
Two-man tent or tentfly	1
1 piece Klimate overalls	1
Diary and pen	1
Olympus XA camera	1
Olympus OM2 camera and 75-150mm zoom lens	1
Plastic bowl	1
Spoon	1
Toothbrush	1
Comb	1
Ice axe or umbrella	1
Water bottle plus team food	1
Medical kit	1
Billies and lids	2
MSR stove	1
Maps and compass	1
Penknife	1

(b) For specialised mountain use (addition gear):

San Marco plastic boots and gaiters		
Crampons and straps		
Rope 100 ft x 7mm	1	
Ice screws	2	
Pitons	1	
Laprade nut	1	tótal technical
Slings	3	gear
Carabiners	6	
Prussics	2	
Additional Damart skivvy	1	
Fibre pile mits	1 pr	

Appendix 4

A Layman's Guide to Physiological Survival in the Himalayas

When you are living simply, perhaps like nomads or cavemen, you need to be that much more careful about your health and your physical wellbeing. On a trip like ours, the whole adventure hinged upon it.

I put a great deal of emphasis on food and lots of it. When you are extending yourself, not just physically but mentally as well, you expend a great deal of energy so you need to increase your food intake. You can monitor the quality and the food types both by a vague knowledge of what types of foodstuffs the body requires and by the way you feel. The rule of thumb in the mountains is: eat the maximum whenever you can, and you will be O.K. Tashi and I operated on this principle and both of us retained our weights at reasonably constant levels throughout the journey. Graeme lost a lot of weight during the first two months and this probably contributed to his becoming run down at times.

We took multi-vitamin pills and vitamin C every day and sometimes increased the dosage after particularly long and difficult days. Fluid intake was very important and could be gauged most easily by thirst and urine colour. Pale-coloured urine indicates proper hydration. At medium altitudes, during periods of high exertion, I consider four to six litres a day of fluid intake desirable. At very high altitudes, you require six to eight litres a day due to the dehydrating effects of the air at those elevations. The rule of thumb is drink the maximum!

Acclimatisation to high altitudes is very important as without it you will suffer from altitude sickness. This is unpleasant when the symptoms are minor, such as headaches, nausea, loss of appetite, sleeplessness and tiredness. In the unfortunate few who develop severe altitude sickness, fluid leaks into brain and lungs, giving rise to breathlessness, exhaustion, severe headaches, disorientation and eventually collapse and death. However, if you ascend at a steady rate, your body adapts to the altitude partly by producing more red blood corpuscles to absorb the lower content of oxygen in the lower than normal pressure environment. Well acclimatised, you can live happily up to altitudes of 18 or even 20 thousand feet. Above this level, man can remain for only limited periods (days, weeks or months — individuals vary) before high-altitude deterioration sets in.

One of the problems with the build-up of red blood corpuscles in your blood due to high-altitude acclimatisation is that it thickens your blood and impairs circulation. This, combined with the reduced availability of oxygen, makes extremities such as hands and feet more susceptible to cooling and frostbite. Warm, dry socks and gloves are essential.

A rule of thumb for high-altitude acclimatisation is ascend at an averaged out rate of 1000 feet per day between about 10,000 feet and 15,000 feet. After a rest day, ascend at a rate of about 500 feet per day to about 18,000 feet. From there, acclimatisation is even slower as you ascend. Five to six weeks is considered necessary for acclimatisation to the altitudes of the highest peaks. Should you experience a headache or other altitude sickness symptoms during your ascent, then stop and rest a day. If it persists, descend a couple of thousand feet or until you feel well again and recuperate at that lower elevation before attempting to ascend again.

Pushing on, regardless of symptoms, can lead to disaster — sudden collapse and eventually death. Climbing high during the day but descending to your camp to sleep at night, is a well-proven system for acclimatisation and the prevention of altitude sickness.

Keeping yourself warm in the mountains is important as insufficient insulation can lead to an excessive use of energy to maintain body temperatures or even hypothermia, a dangerous condition where a person becomes very cold and can die. By keeping yourself well clad when it is cold, including head, neck, arms and legs, you can prevent excessive heat loss. Extremities such as hands and feet should be well insulated too so that they don't work as heat radiators and cool the body. The rule of thumb is: Be prepared for cold and windy conditions and tog up when it is.

During our trans-Himalaya marathon, it became quite clear to me that real fitness for mountaineering and trekking was more than just physical fitness. You need to be acclimatised and fit. You need to be resilient in the face of insufficient food and fluid intake and one needs to develop a tolerance for temperature change. These are things you get used to by exposure to them, coupled with the determination to persevere regardless.

A layman's guide to a physiological survival in the Himalayas?

* Eat the maximum whenever you can.
* Drink the maximum whenever you can.
* Ascend to high altitudes at a rate of 1000 feet per day to 15,000 feet and 500 feet per day thereafter. Acknowledge altitude sickness symptoms and descend.
* Be prepared for cold conditions and keep yourself warm.

Peter Hillary

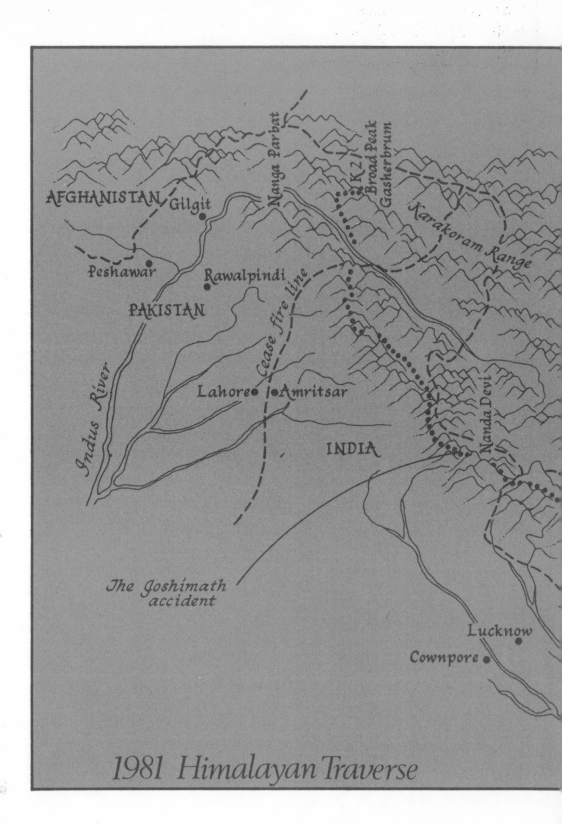

1981 Himalayan Traverse